THERE ARE TWO SIDES TO EVERY STORY . . .

Personal Space

HIS . . . Suddenly your wife is everywhere you want to be. She's in your chair. She's hogging the kitchen. You spend all day at the office trying to get from point A to point B, and when you come home, you can't walk down the hall without running into your wife.

HERS . . . Husbands sprawl. Their personal space has no defined boundaries, and so, amoebalike, they expand to fill a bedroom, leaving little area in which you can breathe. Oh—you want to be in there, too? Hmm, *that's* something he didn't anticipate.

Cleaning

HIS . . . Your wife did not marry you for the joy of picking up your dirty socks. Sheet changing, toilet scrubbing—it's all so degrading for a man who should be sitting on the couch watching *Nick at Nite*. But it's the dawn of a new millennium, so welcome to a place we call "division of labor."

HERS . . . Since nine out of ten men will not be bothered by dirt as quickly as nine out of ten women will, the simplest thing is to assign your husband nonurgent household tasks that you can't stand doing: taking out the trash, squashing bugs, and cleaning up the mess produced by a cat who likes to eat rubber bands.

Holidays

HIS . . . Remember when you used to enjoy Thanksgiving? Well, forget it. You've got three families now—the one you had, the one you married into, and the one that consists of you and your wife—and that means every fourth Thursday in November will be Eating and Driving Day.

HERS . . . Holidays throw reproductive issues into stark relief. Be prepared for a barrage of innuendo and oh-so-subtle hints, like "Look at those little devils tear into their gifts. I expect you'll be getting more presents than usual this time next year!"

HOW CAN YOU GET IT TOGETHER? FIND OUT IN . . .

THE HIS & HERS GUIDE TO SURVIVING
YOUR FIRST YEAR OF MARRIAGE

THE HIS & HERS GUIDE TO SURVIVING YOUR FIRST YEAR OF MARRIAGE

David and Wendy Hubbert

A DELL TRADE PAPERBACK

A DELL TRADE PAPERBACK

Published by
Dell Publishing
a division of
Bantam Doubleday Dell Publishing Group, Inc.
1540 Broadway
New York, New York 10036

Library of Congress Cataloging in Publication Data
Hubbert, David.
    The his & hers guide to surviving your first year of marriage / David Hubbert, Wendy Hubbert.
        p.   cm.
    ISBN 0-440-50811-8 (pbk.)
    1. Married people—United States—Psychology.   2. Man-woman relationships—United States.   3. Communication in marriage—United States.   I. Hubbert, Wendy.   II. Title.
HQ734.H9164   1998
646.7′0086′55—dc21   97-27166
                                                                                        CIP

Printed in the United States of America

Published simultaneously in Canada

February 1998

10 9 8 7 6 5 4 3 2 1

BVG

Acknowledgments

First and foremost, we owe an enormous thank you to the couples who answered our surveys, gave us advice, and provided the stories that made this book come alive. To our literary agent, Angela Miller, and Selene Ahn: our deepest gratitude. This book wouldn't exist without you.

Special thanks go to Maureen O'Neal, Laura Cifelli, and Leslie Schnur for their initial input and support, and to Cherise Davis Grant, our intrepid editor at Dell, who threw into the mix a few strange-but-true newlywed tales of her own. We extend our appreciation as well to Dr. Peter Fraenkel for his expert contributions.

And finally, to our families and friends who spilled their guts about every marital problem they've ever experienced; rest assured, it was all for a good cause. Thanks, Mom and Dad, for your support and guidance. We love you very much.

Contents

Money 183

Recreation 223

Foreword

As a couples therapist, behavioral researcher, and director of PREP® workshops that teach couples communication and problem-solving skills, I've counseled literally hundreds of newlyweds. And I've heard literally thousands of arguments. Arguments about money, household responsibilities, jealousy, sex, drugs, and rock 'n' roll (one husband liked music hard, fast, and loud, his wife preferred it soft and wafting). Arguments about in-laws—keep them or kill them; or who should talk to whom about which insult over what at last year's Thanksgiving dinner.

Arguments about children—whether and when to have them, what to name them, how to raise them. Arguments about time—how much to spend with each other alone, with each other and friends, with each other and family, at work versus with each other, and apart from each other. Arguments about where the newlyweds are now as a couple, where they've been, and where they're going.

And arguments about . . . chicken. Yes, after years as a therapist and scholar, I have found one of the best predictors of relationship success is the number and intensity of chicken arguments. One couple I met in their first year of marriage once had a knockdown-drag-out fight in a supermarket over whether to buy chicken breasts with the bone left in (his preference—let's save money, he said) or the more convenient but more expensive boneless breasts (her preference—she did the cooking, after all). Bone in, deboned, bone in, deboned, back and forth it went, each partner repeatedly stating his or her point of view, their voices getting louder and angrier until the wife slammed the chicken breasts down in the meat case and stormed out.

Her husband bought boneless.

Now, there are many lessons to be learned from this example. First, arguments about seemingly innocuous topics—chicken, toilet seats left up or down, time spent in the bathroom, TV remote controls—are often surface manifestations of deeper, more pervasive issues such as struggles over power and control, concerns about closeness and caring, issues of respect and recognition, and, ultimately, the wish to be accepted by one's partner.

In the case of the couple arguing about chicken, the husband thought his wife was unhappy with the amount of money he was making, and so, in an attempt to be fiscally responsible, he tried to spend as little as possible. But he felt unrecognized for his efforts to conserve cash. She, on the other hand, believed his insistence on buying breasts with the bones in signaled disrespect and lack of caring, since she'd told him it was easier for her to cook boneless breasts. Each felt pushed around by the other.

These deeper, "hidden" issues acted as fuel for other arguments and mutual dissatisfactions, such as his annoyance that she left her pantyhose drying in the shower for days and her frustration that he would fall asleep while she was telling him a tale from work. So for this couple it was important to recognize that the deeper issues needed to be addressed directly.

The second useful "chicken lesson" is that this couple's fight—like the unproductive arguments of most couples—quickly became more about *how* each person was talking (or not talking) to the other than about the topic itself. In other words, the process of the argument quickly obliterated the content. During their fight, this couple engaged in the "big four" destructive patterns of communication. Research has shown—and my clinical experience has more than borne it out—that these communication patterns often distinguish distress from happy couples, and can be strong predictors of trouble down the road:

❶ *Escalation:* Each partner answers the other with increasingly negative comments and emotions, usually critical, contemptuous, or blaming.

❷ *Withdrawal and defensiveness:* One or both partners give verbal or nonverbal signs that he or she will not further engage in the discussion, and will not listen to the partner's point of view.

❸ *Invalidation:* One partner puts down the other's ideas or character, or points out problems and mistakes without acknowledging the other's positive efforts.

❹ *Negative interpretations:* One partner persistently believes that the other's behavior is negatively intended, when this might not be the case.

Locked into these destructive habits, my couple's chicken fight escalated into something predictable and essentially indistinguishable from their previous fights—or from the fights of other couples, for that matter. After all, once you start calling your partner a "stupid, inconsiderate idiot" or a "lazy princess" (and those were just the polite names they used!), does it really matter whether you're arguing about chicken, investments, housework, or sex?

A colleague recently told me he and his wife were celebrating their one hundred and twenty-third wedding anniversary. When I raised an eyebrow, he explained: "Well, our wedding was twenty-three years ago, but in the first year of marriage we gained a hundred years of experience!"

There's no doubt that the first year is a crucial period for getting a marriage off to a good start. I compare it to the first year of a baby's life, in which an uncoordinated, inarticulate little being becomes one who develops perceptual abilities, who gains the ability to coordinate eyes and limbs, and who expresses him or herself.

In the same way, during the first year of married life, newlywed couples develop joint rhythms of time together versus time apart, of work and play, of sleep and wakefulness (not to mention snooze-button usage). The partners coordinate their efforts to get things done: making money, paying bills, doing household chores, planning trips. They bring together their individual perceptions of events and situations—often quite different at the start—and learn to combine their points of view. They learn to talk together; they even learn to walk together. My wife and I struggled mightily over this one—I'd always run half a block ahead, and then she'd yell, "Pete, it's not a race!"

So what skills and ideas will help lay the foundation in your first year of marriage for a long and healthy relationship? Here are my Ten Best Distress-Prevention/Relationship-Strengthening Techniques (adapted from the Prevention and Relationship Enhancement Program, or PREP® course and *Fighting for Your Marriage* by Howard Markman, Scott Stanley, and Susan L. Blumberg.):

❶ *Listen Without Defensiveness to Your Partner's Concerns.* When your partner has a gripe, a concern, or a complaint, really try to listen to his or her point of view, and try to understand it even if you don't agree with it. Paraphrase your partner to make sure you've heard him or her correctly ("So what I hear you saying is, you're kinda peeved that I took all our money and spent it in Atlantic City—am I hearing you correctly, dear?").

❷ *Make Your Complaints Specific.* When you have a gripe to air, do so without insulting your partner's character, criticizing or calling names, or speaking in a contemptuous tone. Anger is fine, nastiness is not. Tell your partner what it is you're specifically unhappy about ("When you leave your dirty underwear in the living room, I get irritated") rather than generalizing ("You always make a mess, you're just a slob, you come from a long line of slobs, slobbery is in your genes . . .").

❸ *Avoid Mind Reading.* Nobody likes to be told "You did that on purpose," "You don't really love me," or "You're just trying to piss me off, right?" Don't try to get inside your partner's head—stick to what you see and hear, and invite your partner to tell you what his or her real intentions were. Chances are, your partner was thoughtless at worst, not malevolent.

❹ *Stay on One Topic.* In one discussion, don't move from problems with housework to problems with sex to problems with money to problems with in-laws—you'll just create a feast of pain, a smorgasbord of disaster. Stick to one topic so that each of you can express your points of view on it.

❺ *Separate Problem Discussion from Action Planning.* Make sure each of you has a chance to air your perceptions, feelings, and beliefs about a problem before you try to solve it. Premature problem solving can lead to frustration, and can result in planning a course of action that doesn't address the real issue.

❻ *Schedule a Regular Time to Talk About Problems.* Of course, you can never plan when problems will arise, but if you've got a regular weekly appointment with each other to talk about such things, you'll feel less pressure at other times to launch into a full diatribe.

❼ *Make Time for Fun.* Couples in our time-pressed, work-oriented world sometimes put off fun so long that they forget how to have it when they finally get around to it. If you decide to have kids, your time for each other will get swallowed up even more, so enjoy yourselves now! And remember to separate problem-solving discussions from fun time. Nothing ruins a great meal or a night of lovemaking more quickly than mixing issues with pleasure.

❽ *View Problems as Third Parties.* Rather than getting caught up in who's right or who's wrong, try to view problems as third parties in your relationship. Join together as a *team* to defeat the intruder!

❾ *Two Heads Are Better Than One.* For every issue you and your partner face, there are at least two perspectives (never mind the contributions of in-laws, friends, and TV talk show hosts). In the courses I run for couples, and when I see couples in therapy, I note that these two perspectives can be a couple's greatest asset, providing a deeper appreciation of the issues at hand and leading to more creative and resourceful solutions.

❿ *Make the Health of the Relationship a Priority.* To paraphrase a late, great United States president, "Ask not what your relationship can do for you, ask what you can do for your relationship." Rather than thinking about what you can get out of your partner, or what you can get for yourself, look for opportunities to add value to your marriage. Pay attention to your relationship. Take the time to nurture it and help it grow.

Keep these skills and ideas handy as you read the following pages. From interior design to bathroom habits, from laundry to finances, from sex and romance to religion and recreation, this book is a friendly guide through the joyful, sometimes challenging roller-coaster ride that is your first year of marriage.

While it's not meant to take the place of a communications course or serious relationship counseling, The His & Hers Guide offers wit and wisdom that will help you surmount everyday rough spots and appreciate both the complexities and the triumphs of marriage—in your first year, and in every year to follow.

Peter Fraenkel, Ph.D.
Clinical Assistant Professor and Director, PREP® at New York University Medical Center
Director of Research, Ackerman Institute for the Family

Introduction

In the months before our wedding, our married relatives and friends offered a lot of free advice. Even though we had dated for nearly eight years, everybody, including our minister, insisted our lives would change once we actually tied the knot. "It happens to everyone." "It's just different, you'll see." "The first year's the toughest," they told us. But no one could explain why.

Now we know, because we learned the only possible way a couple can. We experienced our first year of marriage, and we survived.

Being married feels undeniably different from being single or even engaged. Part of it is the contrast between wanting to spend the rest of your life with someone and having a contract that legally commits you to doing just that. But mostly it's the little things, the subtleties of sharing the same space, the same money, the same life. Suddenly you're thinking for two, whether you're considering a job offer across the country or planning to roll over in bed. Since most people spend their first twenty or so years desperately trying to be independent, the feelings of trust and reliance that are essential for any successful marriage may take some getting used to. And many of these feelings come to the fore the minute the afterglow of your wedding day dies down. The first year really *is* the toughest.

The numbers seem to back this up. Today, almost half of all marriages fail in the United States—about 1.2 million each year—and of those, nearly one-third last less than four years. That life expectancy would probably be even shorter, except for the fact that many states have laws that prohibit divorce within the first year of marriage.

Our role models certainly aren't helping matters. Of all Americans born after 1960, 50 percent grew up with divorced parents. We've reached a point of such cynicism toward marriage that we're actually surprised when Hollywood couples and rock star/model weddings last the week! As Katharine Hepburn put it, "Sometimes I wonder if men and women really suit each other. Perhaps they should live next door and just visit now and then."

Not only do marital problems reflect society's ills, they can literally make you sick. Recent medical studies show a clear relationship between marital stress and illness—especially in women. In one study, newlywed couples who had a "highly negative" arguing style (sarcasm and insults flying) showed a decline in immune system function after arguments—leaving them more vulnerable to illnesses like colds and the flu. Sickness. Fights. Disappointment. Divorce. These are just a few of the evils that await those who enter marriage unprepared.

Okay. Now that we've scared you to death, here's the good news. Not only can you make it through your first year of marriage, we guarantee you can make it one of the best years of your life. All you need is a strong desire for it to work, a bit of guidance, and a resilient sense of humor. By reading this book, you're already taking the first step. In it you'll find stories and advice gathered from successful married couples, renowned experts, and our own personal experience. You'll read about the female shopping instinct, the male inability to see dirt, and dreaded in-law visitations before you actually witness these horrors in the field.

Because every marriage is made up of two unique individuals, you'll see every issue from two very separate and biased points of view: male and female. This format isn't meant to start arguments between you and your spouse; nor are we trying to provide you with ammunition to use against each other. On the contrary, our intention is to show you how a husband and wife can think completely differently about an issue and still work through it as a team.

Most women's magazines contain a section that tries to explain how men think. Men's magazines aren't much different in reverse, although the debate there seems to rage over whether women are capable of rational thought at all. But instead of throwing gasoline on the fire and taking an Us Against Them approach, we've tried to give you insight into both worlds, to show you how to think as a couple. So no matter whether you're the bride or the groom, we encourage you both to read on, and to read both sides of every issue. Then talk about it. Nine times out of ten, you'll find that calmly discussing the topics in this book before they come up will prevent them from ever becoming real problems.

Even if problems occur, though, there's still hope. Many newlyweds discover after a few months of living together that they have fundamental disagreements about some very important issues. But while you and your spouse may never see eye to eye on abortion rights or politics or the color of your mother's drapes, you can discuss these things without throwing frying pans at each other or kicking the cat. Of course, it's not always easy to act reasonably when you feel your partner is being unreasonable. But we are working from the point of view that you *are* partners, and that you're both committed to seeing your partnership succeed. In the end, that's the most important thing, the lifelong goal about which you both should be in total agreement: the success of your marriage.

Two quick notes before you read on. First, we are assuming that you are past your wedding itself and are currently embroiled in the first year of marriage. But if you're still engaged or are even just considering marriage, you'll also get a lot out of this book. Think of it as essential preparation for the year to come. Second, we make a lot of jokes, sometimes about very serious issues. It's not that we're trying to make light of problems; we simply believe that a strong sense of humor is a very powerful tool for overcoming conflict. If you can both develop the ability to laugh at yourselves, even in the darkest of times, then you have what it takes to make a committed relationship survive.

Best of luck to you and your marriage. May all your years together be as memorable as the first.

LIVING TOGETHER

Relocating—His

Perhaps you and your wife lived together before your wedding but are now ready to move to a bigger place. Maybe you had separate apartments and you need to decide which one will be your home. Or maybe you're ready to purchase a house. But no matter what your prewedding housing situation, chances are you'll need to make a move of some kind after the wedding. For those of you about to embark on this wondrous journey of mysteriously missing underwear, doors that are too small, and couches that are too big, there is very little I can offer in the way of solace. Welcome to hell.

If you're one of those lucky couples who've started their marriage with two apartments, deciding which one to jettison is your first problem. This is an area where a man's normally logical brain tends to go haywire. You rationalize keeping your bachelor-days apartment any way you can, citing reasons like:

- It's already broken in.
- It smells like you.
- If you move, you have to clean it.
- You have great memories of wild nights over here, over there, up there, in the corner . . .
- The set of 36DDs frequently on display in the apartment across the street.

Let it go. Your bachelor days are over, and believe it or not, most men discover that's a really good thing.

If, however, you do decide to live in your apartment after the wedding, make sure it's a mutual decision, and do it for logical reasons: economics, space, location, and room to expand. Better yet, ditch both of your original apartments. Find a brand-new one that fits both of your needs and sets the tone for your new life together.

When moving day comes, do yourself a favor: Splurge and hire someone else to move your stuff for you. Picture yourself staring up three flights of stairs. Your giant sofabed is sitting next to you on end. Well, actually the sofa part is sitting; the bed part has sprung out sideways, and now it's making groaning sounds as the metal strains against gravity. The ceiling is too low to proceed, but you've just spent an hour muscling this uphol- stered behemoth through the front door, so you don't want to turn back. Your wife is making all sorts of bright suggestions that defy physics and common sense.

Here's a suggestion: Call a mover. It's *so* worth the money. Our friends Stacy and John once moved, literally, around the corner. They spent an en- tire day walking their belongings from the old apartment to the new one, only a block away. By six P.M., the couple—active people, both of them— reported being more exhausted than ever before in their lives. If you hire movers, the couches, bookcases, tables, and chairs become their problem, and you can focus on all the little stuff.

Speaking of stuff, you suddenly have twice as much of it. Somebody has to give some things up, and undoubtedly, it's going to be you. Unless you can somehow wrangle a room, garage, or shed of your own, all that great junk you've accumulated over the years is going to have to go. To your wife, the beer cans of the world, the fifteen-year-old Atari cartridges, and the assorted "entertainment" magazines you've never had the heart to part with are useless space hogs.

Deep-six them, or see if your parents can keep your things until you find a bigger place. Marcie and Tim moved into a new house together but kept Tim's original apartment just for his stuff. This worked out well, un- til retaining the apartment began to seem emblematic of a general reluc- tance on his part to ditch his single-guy past. It was clearly a more effective solution in theory than in practice. Wherever possible, try to consolidate and compromise on your stuff—but no matter what, don't let your wife convince you to chuck the baseball card collection. Someday it'll put your kids through college.

Moving is stressful for everyone. It's one long day of labor, during which you can never find anything you need. There are a million things to worry about—parking, pets, rearranging, hooking up the phone, cable, the heat. And on top of all that, because it may be the first time you and your wife work together as a team, there are bound to be rough spots. Watch your temper, especially when she asks you for the fifth time to "see what the sofa looks like . . . over there."

In the questionnaires we sent out for this book, some couples offered us a few *do's* and *don'ts* on moving day. One guy waited until his wife went to the deli for some midmove sandwiches, then he picked some flowers from their new lawn, grabbed a vase, and set up a bouquet on the one real piece of furniture they owned—the dining-room table. Something that small can score big points with the wife: always a *do*. Another unfortunate fellow loaded up the new fridge with beer, invited a bunch of buddies over to help move furniture, then passed out in front of the TV surrounded by empty bottles and drunk friends while his wife finished unpacking. That's right: a big *don't*. His wife didn't speak to him for a week.

And finally, one gentleman decided to create a little romance. He thanked the guys who helped him move in, gave them each a beer, and sent them home. Then he dug out a candle, turned on some soft music, and ordered in take-out Chinese. He and his wife ate dinner together in the candlelight, on the bare floor, drinking wine while surrounded by their worldly possessions. See if you can make the first night in your new home equally special.

Relocating—Hers

*U*nless you're an unusually lucky or overly prepared couple, at some point during your first year of marriage you'll be singing the moving blues. If you've planned ahead, all you need to do when you return from your honeymoon is get used to the lock on your new front door and figure out where to put all the treasures you picked up in Mexico. But more likely, your posthoneymoon will be a period of physical as well as emotional adjustment.

You'll be making decisions including (a) the geographic location of your physical space, (b) the architectural structure of your physical space, and (c) how you'll decorate it and who gets the bigger closet (no contest). Let's assume that you've wisely chosen not to move into his place (who knows what's behind the fridge and what memories the living-room floor holds for him) or to have him move into your place (where you know all too well what the walls would say if they could talk). So you'll be looking for a new place altogether.

This is a chance for the two of you to truly meld your lives, mix your respective cultures, realize your collective values, and learn the meaning of the words *formal dining room*. Moving into a new place together is not just a symbolic gesture, it's your first meaningful opportunity to define the rest of your lives as a couple. It doesn't really matter what type of place you live in, as long as you both agree you can make it a home.

But before you can begin to do that, you have to move in. Moving into your new home tends to bring out a lot of old clichés. Try as you may to avoid it, you'll probably find yourself asking your husband to "try the bureau over there, just one more time." He will be absolutely unable to comprehend your need to arrange visually rather than mentally, mainly because he's trying to avoid a hernia. So the best idea is to create on paper, in advance of the move, a furniture floor plan.

When moving day comes, try to stick to the plan. And rather than assigning your husband duties that he'll never be able to live down if his friends walk in, hang on to the dust mop yourself and make him the king of heavy lifting. Give him regular praise and treats (beer, doughnuts, kisses), and let him know how impressed you are by his upper-body strength. Soon enough, he'll start to see rearranging furniture as a chance to show off.

Which brings us to another cliché, usually spoken by a man who has just dropped a hundred-pound chair on his big toe while "trying it over there": *"Why did you ask for my opinion if you're just going to tell me what to do anyway?"* It's usually followed by your response: *"Because I didn't know this is what I wanted until a few minutes ago, when I decided that what I wanted before wasn't what I really wanted."*

Also, his opinion on where a piece of furniture would look best is invariably delineated in his mind as the place that's dead easiest to get to. Your indecision puts your husband at a crossroads. His brain is spinning, his toe is throbbing, and all he wants is an end to the pain. In the best of all possible worlds, he will use the phrase "Yes, dear" here (see the "Yes, Dear" chapter for proper usage) and do whatever you tell him to do. The worst-case scenario is that he'll leave the chair in the hall and tell you to move it yourself. You never know how your husband will react in the Battle of the Clichés.

Here's one more: the "his stuff/her stuff" old bone. Remember the fight over the wagon-wheel coffee table between Carrie Fisher and Bruno Kirby in *When Harry Met Sally?* Most men are very attached to their stuff, hideous though it may be. While we instinctively know that our childhood teddy bear collection belongs somewhere in storage, your husband's comfort zone is created in part by the presence of those very things you hate and he loves—the framed poster of Heather Locklear from the pre–T. J. Hooker era and the three-crate record collection, even though neither of you owns a record player.

When you fight over what to do with these things, you're really fighting over what they mean to each of you. To you, his stuff means unattractive clutter; to him, it holds fond memories of—well, the pre–T. J. Hooker era.

The solution is for each of you to somehow create space of your own. Even the tiniest apartment can have a "his" drawer and a "her" drawer. Keep your old love letters (hidden), and let him have his coin collection. Just remember to monitor and maintain the spaces so they don't overflow. His will expand like a marshmallow in the microwave if you don't keep an eye on it.

One final tip: From day one of living in your new home, try not to keep anything in boxes. They have a disturbing sense of impermanence. Instead, unpack your belongings as soon as possible, even if it means stacking things on the floor. Moving in after marriage is hardly a trial run, so do everything you can right away to make your home feel permanent.

Decorating—His

*P*icasso. Da Vinci. Rembrandt. Monet. Many of the greatest artists in history were men. And you can bet these guys knew their way around interior decoration as well—just look at what Michelangelo did with the Sistine Chapel. Yet here we are in the nineties, with centuries of human progress behind us, and suddenly Johnny can't color-coordinate.

Where is the masculine desire to make things beautiful? Have we forgotten an age-old ability, or have women always possessed superior skills? Neither. The fact is, while many men could easily find their way around Bed, Bath & Beyond, for the most part we choose to leave soap-dish and toothbrush-holder decisions to our partners.

Why? No good reason, except that most modern males feel silly deciding what color curtain valances should be. Rummaging through swatches of cloth just doesn't feel like a manly activity. (Yet for some reason, it's okay for us to *hang* the very same curtains, probably because we get to haul out our power tools and show our wives a thing or two about using 'em.)

When called upon to shop for housewares and furniture, though, some men do rise to the occasion, only to be rebuffed for their efforts. I've been known to march into a store with my wife and point decisively at a three-thousand-dollar crushed-velvet recliner with remote-controlled Magic Fingers—only to be told that my input, while appreciated, will not be considered in the final decision.

You see, the problem is not that men aren't given a chance to contribute. It's that when we step up to the plate, we strike out far too often. If you want to be in the game when it comes time to decorate the walls, the living room, or the kitchen, you have to demonstrate consistently good taste over a number of at bats.

So, where does this good taste come from? Easy. Some men are born with it, some men have it thrust upon them, and some men get it by subscription. *Architectural Digest* and *House and Garden* may seem like the world's most boring magazines, but you only have to look at the pretty pictures once a month to learn the ropes. Encourage your wife to subscribe to these publications, then sneak peeks at them in the bathroom when no one's around. *Details, GQ,* and *Men's Journal* will not only help you mature stylistically, they'll show you how to dress yourself. Most of us could use a little help there anyway.

Over time, if you stick with it, you'll start to develop a sense of taste and style, which your wife already has in spades. As an amateur, your opinion is of no use to her. But once you graduate from the Mail Order House of Style, you can give your wife a run for her money. Imagine how delighted she'd be if you picked out an amazing piece in an antique store that she, with her practiced eye, had overlooked.

Of course, you may not be the slightest bit interested in what your home looks like. Your feeling may be that a room is about sleeping, eating, sex, and TV, and decor is only an issue insofar as it promotes those functions. Or your approach may be "Whatever makes my wife happy is all right with me." And that works for her, as long as you're supportive of her choices. In other words, unless you can do better, don't go around saying, "Honey, did someone barf on our new couch at the factory, or is it supposed to look like that?"

Now, if you were living on your own for some time before you got married, you may be faced with a classic problem. You want to keep your stuff, and she wants to keep hers. Before you get defensive, take a moment to consider the choices you've made on your own. Eighty percent of your things are black. The rest are chrome. This is what men buy when alone in

SEVEN SURVIVAL TIPS FOR DECORATING YOUR HOME

1 The statute of limitations for changing the position of the couch is two moves. Here or there, tell your wife to take her pick.
2 When it comes to hanging, plastering, or refinishing, her job is what, where, why, and when. Yours is how.
3 Give all prospective furniture the comfort test. Ask yourself, can you lie on this for four hours with a tray of snacks on your chest while watching football?
4 When your wife presents you with a choice of colors, choose the darkest one. No matter what the item, the darker it is, the less you have to clean it. (Unless you have a white dog.)
5 Always get your wife's approval on the wall position of art. You and the wall will both suffer if you have to move it once it's been hung.
6 Convince your wife that at least one chair has to directly face the television, or you'll set yourself up for a highly painful case of TV Neck.
7 Do what you're told. You are but a pawn in the decorating game, and your movements will always be dictated by the omnipotent queen.

department stores: Black and silver are safe spots in the untamed wilds of the color spectrum.

The thing is, your wife knows that blue, green, off-white, and even salmon have their place in a properly color-coordinated home. So you're probably going to give up a few prized possessions that don't go with the general decor, though there are a few points on which you can negotiate. Allow your wife to do whatever she wants with the rest of the house as long as you can have a cave of your own. Even if it's the garage, it's a place where you can let your creativity run wild: a place with a door your wife can lock when guests come over. In that den goes your favorite chair, your autographed sports memorabilia, your skull-and-crossbones ashtray, and all the other things she can't stand.

Unfortunately, if you're an apartment dweller like me, you tend to be a little short of storage space. But the stuff my wife hates still has to go somewhere. I take it to the office, where I've created a shrine to the things I hold dear—a sanctuary of frighteningly bad taste. It has the added advantage of keeping those annoying guys in the accounting department from bothering me; they're scared of the sexually ambiguous mannequin and the pencil sharpener shaped like a gorilla.

We all know that if you wanted to, you *could* fight for the right to display your stuff proudly and prominently at home. But sooner or later you'd discover your wife has shipped it off to the dump like so much leftover spaghetti. So save yourself some aggravation. Keep your prized possessions out of sight and away from the (female) hands of those who would do them harm.

Decorating—Hers

*I*n high school, you probably inherited your older sister's junker car. You dumped it when you bought a used car from an ad in the paper. Then you moved up to car payments on a brand-new Saturn.

Decorating your home works the same way. No matter how expensive your tastes, it's likely that you'll start with a hand-me-down bureau left over from your parents' early days of marriage. You'll replace all that old stuff with one good shopping spree at Ikea. Then, in a year or so, you'll realize that furniture of this ilk lasts about as long as cardboard in the rain, and you'll start replacing items one by one with solid Ethan Allen. Eventually, you'll tire of having a dining-room table that looks exactly like Fran's and Amy's and Carol's, and you'll progress to "the real stuff": one-of-a-kind furniture and accessories that are either quintessentially modern, antique, or pseudoantique (less than one hundred years old but classy, original, and valuable nonetheless).

Unless you come into fast money, decorating is excruciatingly slow and unsatisfying. Here are some been-there-done-that tips for coping on a budget:

1 Skip the futon, and buy a real foldout sofa. It will "anchor" your living room, and you won't feel like a fraud as a hostess if you offer overnight guests a place to sleep that has the look and feel of a real mattress. (Imagine how it'll be when you have a guest room that contains an actual guest bed!)

2 McFurniture from Ikea gets real old real fast. Sure, you can spend three hundred bucks and furnish your entire home—but you'll start to hate it almost immediately. This is a universal truth: How else to account for all that used low-budget furniture you see waiting forlornly by the curb for the garbageman? If you must buy supercheap, buy only those items you absolutely can't live without—like a kitchen table—and then start saving money for a real dining-room table and chairs.

3 Scam old, good furniture. Poke around your parents' basement and be shameless about asking for hand-me-downs. You mother might be on the verge of needing to redecorate. With a little skillful prompting—*"Gosh, the living room looks just the way it did when I was little. It's so wonderful that you've never gotten tired of the way you furnished it, what, two, three decades ago?"*—you may come into a windfall of really decent furniture. You could find something great in the attic that just needs a little paint, some finish, or a new cushion. Don't be shy about begging: You don't receive if you don't ask.

❹ You don't have to furnish the big places first. Remember, you're in charge, so don't let an empty room taunt you. Cut out ideas from magazines, and put them in a futures album of what your place will look like when you get the money to finish it.

❺ Use throw rugs and pillows. These can exude style, particularly if you've picked them up from somewhere exotic and interesting. That trip to Mexico may have sucked up the money you were saving for a sofa, but the Ethnic Bohemian look it furnished can disguise the nakedness of your living room. While you'll never regret having ripped up the grotty pink wall-to-wall carpeting "donated" by your home's previous tenant, you'll have to put something on the floor to keep the Kitty Litter from spreading. A kilim, berber, or sisal rug will do the job inexpensively.

❻ While curtains may be the last thing you'd normally think of, they really make a big difference. Order them cheap from a catalog, or if you have rudimentary sewing skills, you can fashion perfectly serviceable curtains from sheets. Eventually you'll be able to step up to something called "window treatments," which are curtains with attitude.

❼ Buy plants. You know how some people are able to make a room look like something out of *Southern Living,* using salvaged gimcracks and gewgaws plus the deep red velvet sofa they picked up at a garage sale? It's a special gift, and not everyone has it. Plants, however, are universally cool. They're cheap; they grow; they add oxygen to the air; and there are some indestructible species that will thrive in any light. Best of all, if you keep your home devoid of all other decoration, plants can bespeak a sort of Calvin Klein-meets-Bill-McKibben enviro-minimalist chic. No one will know you're decor-impaired (not to mention broke).

❽ Martha Stewart. How could this chapter be complete without a mention of the Queen of Household Minutiae? If you're a fan, you know what to do. But even if you can't stand her ubiquity, you can garner some good tips on decorating with style on a budget. For example, use unexpected objects in everyday roles. I know, I know, Martha Stewart was the one who created a line of house paints in the colors of the eggs her chickens laid, but she also popularized the idea that nothing has to match. Some friends of ours were obsessively "doing" their entire kitchen in Mediterranean yellow and blue. They bagged the whole project when they caught themselves getting upset about not finding the exact right sugar and flour canisters. Now they keep such things in mismatched antique tobacco jars.

You may be wondering about your husband's role in all of this. To you, the desire to include him in the details of feathering your nest is a loving gesture. But he may be bewildered by your attempts to involve him in decorating issues. It doesn't mean he doesn't care; he may genuinely not know what kind of wallpaper he likes or wants or why you even need wallpaper in the first place. And he may be frustrated by your attempts to pull this information out of him.

Test the waters. Ask your husband if he wants to accompany you to the mall to choose a bath mat and a shower curtain. If he says no, he really means "*no!*" Take it at face value, and don't be put out. Rather than taking your partner's lack of interest personally, enjoy this period as one of the few times in marriage when you'll be unquestioningly encouraged to spend money. Someday you'll look back with envy on the times he dropped you off at the mall with a credit card and said, "Remember, honey, only the best for our house." When you mentioned the phrase *home furnishings department* and he chucked his wallet at you and ran screaming in the other direction. When he stared blankly at the American Express bill and asked you where that seven hundred dollars went, and you told him gleefully, "You're sitting on it, dear."

Some men have definite decorating tastes and will want to share their ideas with you. But typically, you'll end up decorating according to your taste. Decorating is one of the few scenarios where you're the huntress and your husband is the gatherer. Once you've found that great bargain or perfect thingamabob, you're done. It's your spouse's job to gather up what you acquire and somehow get it home. Just keep in mind that he has to live in your home, too. He may never be entirely comfortable approaching a toilet covered in big happy sunflowers, so be careful not to make your entire residence too feminine. Your husband should feel at home, not like some alien visitor to the planet of ladies-who-lunch.

Remember that your home is yours, and it should be comfortable and functional. Enjoy making it gradually reflect both your personalities, and keep in mind that even if you do nothing at all, your space will eventually decorate itself. Go slowly, and let your furnishings evolve. If you can't find a table you both like, make eating on cushions on the living-room floor your personal trademark until the right table comes to you.

Personal Space—His

*H*ere's something you never notice until you live with someone for a while: For some reason, your wife is everywhere you want to be. She's in your chair. She's in the bathroom. She's on the phone. She's hogging the kitchen. You spend all day at the office trying to get from point A to point B, and when you come home, you can't walk down the hall without running into the woman you love.

It's especially difficult if you have a small apartment. When you're living in two rooms, there are only so many places to sit, so you have to accept the fact that another body will always be a matter of inches away. Since it's a body you're extremely fond of, unlike any male roommates you may have had, you're less likely to entertain thoughts of bodily harm when your wife plops her exercise bike right in front of the TV.

Even if you have a bigger place, you'll probably experience some womanly crowding. The more time you spend in a room designated as your den, office, or Don Mattingly memorial shrine, the more your wife will want to be near you. She'll come all the way across the room, ignoring an empty recliner and a love seat in order to jam her way onto the sofa with you. Why does she need to be in your space? Certainly not because it's amazingly comfortable. The simple answer is that she doesn't really see the space around you as yours. When you married her, your space became half hers. You gave up all usage rights to the phrase "I need my space" when you said, "I do."

Of course, your wife is not necessarily staking her claim to your bodily property every time she nudges closer to you. She's probably just letting you know that she likes to be near you, that your body next to hers makes her feel warm and safe and loved. She's telling you that there are times she wants to be close to you other than when you're going to have sex. In fact, many times throughout your life together she'll want to snuggle up to you with absolutely no sexual intentions whatsoever.

Women call it intimacy. If you're not familiar with it, you're not alone. Hey, you're a guy. We're not taught intimacy in Woodworking 101, so most of us learn it from our wives. If you're uncomfortable with it, ask your wife for a lesson in intimacy skills pronto, because her need for it is only going to increase in the years between your first anniversary and your fiftieth.

You can start now by recognizing that the time has come to jettison a few of your more single-guy urges. For example, the yen to lie spread-eagle on the couch with your pants unbuttoned. The need to nap unencumbered by the weight of your wife on your arm. The need to flail your arms about and scream in a desperate attempt to change the course of events in a Yankee game.

Once you realize you have no constitutional right to do these things, you may begin to enjoy the fact that your wife is sitting in your lap. Let's face it, there are worse things in the world than a woman lying all over you, even if it is the bottom of the ninth with two men on.

Personal Space—Hers

Why do men take up so much space? In terms of simple skin surface, they're not that much bigger than we are. But when you put one husband in one living room, he'll somehow manage to fill up every inch of it.

When your husband sits on the sofa, he sits on the *whole* sofa. His snacks overwhelm the coffee table; his collection of strength-building squeeze toys overflows from the end table to the floor. The newspaper is spread in a trail of sections from the coffee table to the kitchen door. His shoes are smack in the middle of the rug—each one about a foot long, separated by exactly a foot of space (which you'd think would take more effort on his part than if he took his shoes off and placed them together and out of the way).

In short, husbands sprawl. Their personal space—the amount of room they physically occupy at any given time—has no defined boundaries. Amoebalike, they expand to fill a room, leaving little area in which you can breathe. Oh—you want to be in there, too? Hmm, *that's* something he didn't anticipate.

The biggest spatial difference between the two of you is that your husband sees your need to be near him as a problem, while you think of closeness as a really super thing. After all, one of the reasons you got married to begin with was to share personal space. We women love being a little crowded on the same sofa. We enjoy rubbing shoulders in bed before falling asleep. Many of us even thrill at the thought of wearing his & hers aprons as we chop vegetables together—yes, in the very same kitchen.

For women, physical space is closely linked with emotional space, and part of the emotional space you and your husband share lies in his closet. A woman's magazine recently found that 92 percent of the women it surveyed liked to wear their mates' sweaters, and 39 percent borrowed their boxer shorts. Sure, our husbands may have great stuff, but physically wearing it also helps us feel emotionally connected.

Sometimes we need our own space, too, which is why we take long baths and shut the bedroom door when we talk to our best friend from junior high school. When we're in the middle of *doing* things, we need room.

If we are cooking something difficult or working on the computer, there are mental boundaries surrounding us that must be respected. Your husband should learn that when you're sitting still in one place for a prolonged period of time, it's not an open invitation to start kissing your neck, just as you learned that his urban sprawl on the sofa is not always an invitation to snuggle in.

The real challenge is to get our husbands to soften their personal space boundaries as they simultaneously learn to respect our mental space. Start with sofa sharing. To worm your way onto an already-occupied couch, one new wife suggests a technique that large dogs have down to a science. First, casually work your way into snuggling position on your husband's right side. From there, bring various body parts one by one into his lap until you are in a bona fide cuddling position that he's helpless to undo. Practice moving like a sloth. Act as though you're not really there. The more subtle you are, the less likely it is he'll (a) notice or (b) confuse your attentions and think you want sex.

Eventually, he'll learn to let you in when you want to be in, and to stay out when you want him out. When it comes to physical intimacy and personal space, you'll learn to find both your husband's comfort level and your own.

Cooking—His

During your first year of marriage, you and your wife will gravitate toward one of two roles: the one who cooks really well, and the one who does the dishes. Once these roles are decided, they will remain forever constant, the chef and the dishwasher working in blissful wedded tandem.

If your wife is a talented cook, that's probably one big reason you love her. Men naturally have great affection for women who feed them well. Since your wife enjoys knowing that her cooking pleases you, it's a good idea to compliment her often on the food she prepares. But try not to do it while she's actually making it. In fact, maintain a safe distance whenever she picks up a frying pan. As a newly married man, you will quickly learn the six rules of any cooking wife's kitchen:

❶ Stay out.

❷ If you have to ask if it's ready yet, it's not.

❸ No, she doesn't need your kind of help.

❹ If she's out of something, go get it. Now.

❺ If she needs something chopped, chop it. Now.

❻ Whatever it is, it smells great.

If, on the other hand, you're the cook in the family, then your wife is a lucky woman. A man with the talent to prepare meals should do it as often as possible, and be confident that his wife is grateful even if she doesn't always say it. One husband we heard from found himself standing in the kitchen shaking an oven mitt at his unappreciative wife and saying the equivalent of "I slave all day over a hot stove, and this is the thanks I get?"

If neither of you can cook, you may end up with a budget problem. Few people can afford to go out to dinner every night, and that "food" you ate as a bachelor hardly seems appropriate now that you're respectably married. Although I did enjoy the occasional bowl of SpaghettiOs during my first year of marriage, I eventually grew tired of my wife taking the can out of the trash, reading the ingredients out loud, and staring at me in horror.

The solution can be as simple as investing in a cookbook, a spice rack, and some basic utensils. Cooking is a natural talent, but as with golf, with a little practice anyone can become okay at it. Take it from me, though, start with simple stuff like boneless chicken breasts or chili. Rice Krispie treats are not as easy as you think.

A lot of newly married couples have told us that when they get home from work, neither one feels like cooking. Either that, or they arrive home at different times and so never sit down to eat dinner together. This may not seem like too much of a problem at first, but over time it may contribute to a feeling of distance between couples.

One solution is to start planning "family nights" for just the two of you. Set aside one night each week to come home early, cook a great meal together, then sit at the table and enjoy dinner by candlelight. Spend part of the weekend planning and agreeing on your menu, then shop for the food and wine the night before. When family night comes around, do everything you can to avoid having to reschedule it. If your job gets in the way, try to explain to your boss why it's important that you make it home on time. If your boss doesn't seem like the type who will understand, schedule dinner for later in the evening when you know you'll both be home.

No matter how busy you are, eating dinner together regularly, at a table with no television on and no reading materials present, is one of the most important things you can do to maintain the long-term health of your marriage. It's a powerful touchpoint between you and your wife, a time to talk, not just about your day but about your lives, your feelings, and your futures. Over dinner you can solve problems you didn't even know you had, and stay in tune with the slow and steady changes that occur in your lives.

Too many couples wake up after ten years of marriage and find that they know almost nothing about each other anymore, from little things like which foods you hate to bigger things like the reasons you're still in love. These feelings change over time, sometimes making 180-degree turns, whether you notice it or not. Regular dinner conversations can keep changes from turning into surprises, putting your marriage on much steadier ground for the long haul.

Cooking–Hers

*H*ere's how newlyweds Barbara and Mitch prepare dinner: One pint Ben and Jerry's Chocolate Fudge Brownie Frozen Yogurt; two spoons. Barbara eats the chunks of brownie; Mitch gets whatever's left.

This Chunking Principle, we've found, is universal among women, though it is executed in a variety of ways. When Jamie extracts the chunks of good stuff from the ice cream, she hides the evidence by smoothing out the pockmarked surface with the back of a spoon. Melissa uses the sod-removal technique, dumping out the top of the ice cream onto a plate, chunking the lower regions, then replacing the top layer over the well-mined innards. Dave and I tested all this subterfuge in our first year of marriage, but now that we've been around the married block a few times together, I shamelessly leave frozen yogurt containers full of giant Swiss-cheese holes. The Chunking Principle is your wifely prerogative. We all do it, and we do it well.

But no matter how many pints of ice cream you have in the freezer, sooner or later you're going to have to eat something with substance. This means one of you might actually have to cook. The old cliché is that most men are inept in this area, and that if you come across one who can cook, you should "land" him with alacrity. Well, the truth is that men come with varying degrees of cooking capabilities, from gourmet chef to my friend Meg's husband who, when she's not home, feeds himself by removing the label from a can of soup and warming the contents by sticking the open can right on the stove burner.

Given the fact that many couples either eat at restaurants or enjoy home-made cooking courtesy of Mom before their marriage, the cooking style of the man you've ended up with might not become clear until you're well into your first year. That's when you encounter the question that will dog you for the rest of your married life: "So, whaddya want to do about dinner?"

After just a few months of marriage, you should see your husband fitting into one of the following most common categories. He may be:

- Capable of cooking a meal that consists of more than charred meat;
- Comfortable cooking anything in one pot: spaghetti, chili, hot dogs, soup;

- Able to pour a mean bowl of cereal; or
- Gifted with an unerring eye for the best items on a take-out menu.

No matter who cooks during your first year of marriage—your husband, you, or Domino's—dinner inevitably becomes a big deal. Other than weekends and vacations, it's the biggest chunk of quality time the two of you get to spend together. But if you thought that contemporary married life consisted of experimenting with gourmet recipes and eating tranquilly by candlelight on your new wedding china, you're in for a dose of reality. Sure, we spoke with plenty of couples who do actually sit and eat lovely dinners together on a regular basis. But more often, newlyweds can't even afford a real table.

We discovered six basic ways that couples eat dinner: (1) eat out, (2) order in, (3) you cook, (4) he cooks, (5) every man/woman for him/herself, (6) you cook together. Options 1 and 2 are easy and great—if you're made of money. Option 3 is fine as long as you maintain two sacrosanct rules— she who cooks the meal chooses the menu, and he who doesn't cook washes the dishes. Option 4 seems like a peach until you realize you're either going to be getting Option 2 in disguise, or hot dogs.

Option 5 is by far the most common, since getting married doesn't change the way you both like to eat. When Todd wed his health-nut wife April, he quickly surmised that she wouldn't be sharing his Swanson frozen deep-fried chicken nuggets. On the other hand, mysterious bite marks never appeared in the blocks of tofu she kept marinating in the fridge. Today, three years later, they still come home and make very separate meals—and often eat them at separate times, as well.

This is actually a big regret of many couples we spoke with. One of the best solutions they came up with was Option 6. Todd and April eventually came to the realization that they were very efficient at dietary coexistence, but they weren't seeing very much of each other. So now, once every two or three weeks, they pore through cookbooks and devise a meal which they shop for, cook, and eat together. Todd has discovered a knack for pasta, and April makes amazing desserts with whole-wheat flour.

Since April bought Todd a cookbook with large print and no more than four ingredients per recipe, he will occasionally surprise her with a home-cooked meal. They still fight over the cleanup, but they've developed a tradition that brings them together—at the same time creating a bit of weekly emotional maintenance that helps their marriage flourish.

Cleaning—His

Unless you're in a small male minority, cleaning is an alien concept to you. If you drop half a hamburger on the floor, the dog will eat it. Using paper plates means you'll never have to clean the real dishes that are fermenting in the sink. A mopped floor may look pretty, but it'll just get dirty again in a day or two, and if you instead leave the grime alone, it will eventually turn an attractive shade of green.

When you live by yourself, it's easy to tolerate filth. When you live with other guys, you usually end up fighting about whose turn it is to clean, and *then* you tolerate the filth. But now you live with your wife, and there are certain things no self-respecting woman will tolerate. Such as filth.

Chances are, when you were growing up, your mother cleaned the house. Common wisdom and Freudian gobbledygook aside, this may be a good time to point out that you did not marry your mother. And I may be going out on a limb here, but your wife probably didn't marry you for the joy of picking up your dirty socks.

In short, you must now clean up after yourself. Yes, it's horrifying. The sheet changing, the dishwashing, the toilet scrubbing. It's all so degrading for a man who should be sitting on the couch watching *Nick at Nite* reruns. But we live in the dawn of a new millennium, where there is no longer any such thing as "women's work."

The new lingo is "division of labor." This means you and your wife can either switch off doing the laundry, or if you don't mind washing clothes, you can choose to do it every time while she has to vacuum every time. Most couples end up choosing complementary chores. If she cooks, he washes the dishes. If she does the toilet and the sink, he scrubs the bathtub. If he does all the outside work, she does all the inside work, and so on.

Typically, I pick the jobs that I think I do better than Wendy and vice versa. For instance, when permitted near the kitchen sink, she'll commit the crime of putting dishes in the dishwasher when they're still dirty. Some malfunctioning part of my brain says that you must clean dishes thoroughly in the sink, then run them through the dishwasher to—I don't know—*cauterize* them or something. Instead of insisting that she do it my way, I simply do the dishes all the time. So far I haven't heard any complaints.

Once you decide who does what, you still have to deal with when. After your wedding, the male instinct to default to "never" is quickly replaced with a typical once-a-week routine. Not that everything gets cleaned every week. It's just that part of one day, usually Sunday, becomes cleaning day. Laundry gets done, and the lawn gets mowed. If you and your spouse each do one sizable chore every week, the specter of cleaning doesn't grow quite so large. Cleaning is one of those things in life that everybody hates to begin, realizes in the middle it's not so bad, and gets a certain amount of satisfaction from once it's finished.

Want an even more satisfying solution? Sacrifice some other expense in life, and get a maid. Your home will be more clean more often, and you'll eliminate unpleasant domestic nitpicking about whose turn it is to do what. But once you bring such a person into your lives, be prepared for your wife to display the paradoxical behavior of cleaning the house before the cleaning service comes so the maid won't think she keeps a slovenly home. Like black holes and Fabio, this phenomenon is inexplicable.

Now that I've made every man seem like a dirty pig and every woman sound like Snow White, allow me to introduce you to a special type of female with whom you may be intimately familiar: the shlob. This is a female slob who leaves stockings hanging on the shower curtain rod for weeks, sheds Snackwell's crumbs on the sofa cushions, and substitutes wall-to-wall clothing for normal carpeting.

If you're a guy who likes to clean, getting along with a shlob should be no problem. But if the two of you make up the dreaded slob/shlob combo, you have no choice. When your house gets dirty, it's time to move out.

Cleaning—Hers

"Men tend to overlook everyday chores because they think that if they don't do them, others will. Maybe elves."
—Cosmopolitan (April 1997)

You thought you knew all about your husband's hygiene before you committed to a lifetime together. He smelled good. His shirts were stain-free (if sometimes wrinkled). His teeth looked flossed on a regular basis.

Then you became his wife and found out the awful truth: His physical appearance masks a multitude of domestic sins. He can't clean to save his life.

Oh, maybe he thinks he can. He'll push the Dustbuster around and run the dishes under a trickle of cold water. But there are a million and one little things that have to get done to keep your home from feeling grimy, like dusting, mopping the floors, and taking a sponge to the top of the stove. Not only does your husband not know that you do these chores regularly, he's completely unaware that they exist.

With today's abundance of dual-career marriages, chances are good that you and your husband have similarly hectic lifestyles. This means the days are long over when all a husband had to do was mow the lawn and you would take care of the rest. Frankly, most women I know would rather get exercise and fresh air from yard work than hunch over a bathtub inhaling Tilex. So unless you can afford to hire a housecleaning service, keeping your home clean in your first year of marriage is going to be one long exercise in negotiation and self-discovery.

You'll learn all kinds of things you didn't really want to know about your husband. For example, he doesn't mind seeing the garbage or dishes pile up half as much as you do. He has an amazingly high tolerance for dirt: If you can't see it, it's clean! If you don't look inside the oven, you'll never have to worry about that black sticky sculpture at the bottom. (If it smells like it's burning every time you cook something, just order in for the rest of your lives.)

The bathroom doesn't need servicing more than once a month. Sheets and towels change themselves. Mopping? What's that? Beard shavings biodegrade when left long enough on a Formica counter. The toilet is really only a manufacturer's suggested target for urination—the important thing is to just hit *something*. Yes, dirty dishes left in the sink can attract roaches. So why not shut them in the refrigerator and wash them only as needed? Everything has its place, and the place for everything from dirty socks to last February's sports section is under the bed.

I'd really like some scientist to do a study on the male eye versus the female eye. A husband and wife can look at the exact same mess and see completely different things. For example, Dave once dropped a giant bowl of chili on our kitchen floor. The place looked like a bloodbath: chili everywhere, on the walls, the fridge, bits on the ceiling. There was chili all the way out onto the white hallway rug. I handed Dave a bottle of carpet cleaner and a sponge.

When I came back, after half an hour of sincere, diligent labor, my beloved made a sweeping gesture with the sponge and said proudly, "It's like nothing happened, huh?" But just from where I was standing, I could see about fifty spots of chili he'd missed. The hallway rug was dotted with the same blobs of red I'd noticed on the way out. He hadn't touched them—simply because he didn't *see* them, any more than the male eye is capable of noticing food around the stove burners or the stuff spattered on the wall behind the sink.

Here's one male cleaning accident that's almost guaranteed to happen at some point in your first year of marriage. Your husband, thinking a trip to the supermarket is way too much trouble, will substitute hand-washing liquid dish soap for the detergent that's supposed to go in the dishwasher. This will probably take place while you're out of town. If you're lucky, it will only happen once. Your husband will learn his lesson when he goes to get a beer and finds the refrigerator engulfed in bubbles. Looking on the positive side, he may actually mop the kitchen floor after he discovers his mistake. Or he may just grab all his beer, put it in a cooler, and avoid the kitchen until you get home.

At any rate, even though cleanliness is next to ignorance for your husband, your task is to ferret out your spouse's strengths and exploit them. When he does clean, what kind of worker is he? How often does he notice dirt, and how long after noticing it does he take action? Men are truly better at doing certain tasks—clear-cut, goal-oriented jobs like laundry and vacuuming. Exploit his physiological strengths and his socialized role expectations by having him lift heavy things and take care of all car maintenance issues.

Furthermore, since most men will not be bothered by dirt as quickly as most women, the simplest thing to do is assign your husband nonurgent tasks, performed on a regular basis, that you can't stand doing. The division of labor between Dave and myself couldn't be more straightforward: He does disgusting things, and I do everything else. I highly recommend this arrangement. This way, your husband will handle regular chores like taking out the garbage, as well as anything that arises extemporaneously, such as the mess produced by a cat who likes to eat rubber bands.

This extends to jobs any woman is physically capable of doing but would be crazy to do voluntarily: squashing and/or transport of any sort of bug (dead or alive), bat removal, and disposal of anything in the fridge that stinks. Learn to appreciate your husband's predilection for tinkering with broken things, taking apart and assembling electronics, or changing any sort of fluid, and you'll be much more forgiving of his inability to replace used-up toilet paper rolls.

Bediquette—His

*I*t's a scientific fact that the coldest region on earth is the female foot. And you may not have known this before your wedding, but a husband's primary purpose is to warm those feet each night. As the only sex blessed with real circulation, this is a cross we guys must bear.

There are four major types of female footjammers, each with their own insidious modus operandi: the Heat Sucker, the Sneak Attacker, the Opportunist, and the Faker. My wife usually jams her frostbitten feet under my thighs two seconds after I get into bed. Then she shifts them up and down, constantly searching for warm areas, until she has completely transferred all the heat from my body into hers. Wendy is a classic Heat Sucker. I've tried sleeping in sweatpants and long underwear, but somehow she always manages to find flesh. My only effective defense is to offer her a good foot rub before bed, which has the dual advantage of saving my skin and making me seem like an awfully nice guy.

The Sneak Attacker usually has her feet on you before you even know it. She'll think nothing of distracting you with a story about work, or a nice kiss, or even a back rub, while she quietly inserts her icy appendages into your pajamas. The best defense here, as in most games, is a strong offense. Let her know you know what she's up to. Grab a pair of socks, and make her wear them until she thaws out. Keep one eye on her feet at all times.

The Opportunist piles whatever's nearby on top of her feet. The covers, a pillow, a sweatshirt, the cat, the dog, and finally, your butt. The key is to make sure there are plenty of pileable items available before she gets to you. If it means tying the cat to the bed, so be it. Better Whiskers than you.

Then there's the Faker, an expert at feigning sleep. She lures you into complacency, waits until you're snoring, and then leaps into action. Suddenly her feet are glued to the warmest area of your body, and you're having dreams about crossing the frozen tundra. Frankly, if you've got a Faker, you're outmatched. She's too patient and you're too sleepy. I suggest you wear a ski cap to bed and call it a draw.

You and your wife won't have to sleep in the same bed long to discover other little annoyances. One of you hogs the entire bed. One of you steals the covers. One of you is a midnight snacker. And one of you snores.

Snoring is a tough one, because whoever is doing it can't help it. And even when faced with evidence on tape, very few women will admit that they snore. "It's the dog," they'll say. Or "That's coming from next door." Anything to avoid the unladylike proposition that they sound like a busted muffler when they sleep.

Holding your wife's nose, flipping her over, and waking her up are effective, if only temporary, solutions. But there is help for the snoring and the sleepless. Get a box of Breathe Right Nasal Strips. They're those things you see football players wearing on their noses during a game or runners wearing during a race. The strips open up your sinuses, allowing you to breathe better and thus preventing snoring. If one of you sounds like a buzz saw—making it impossible for the other to saw wood—Breathe Rights might be the solution.

When it comes right down to it, bediquette is a matter of common courtesy. The majority of any couple's time in bed is spent sleeping (sorry guys), and although we call it "sleeping together," it's really one of the few things a couple can't share. It's a solitary act performed on common ground, requiring a certain amount of personal turf. The best solution for space-challenged, sleep-deprived couples is to ditch your full-size mattress and upgrade to a queen- or king-size bed. And buy the biggest comforter you can find so that you're still covered whenever your blanket-stealing spouse performs her nightly yanking act.

Learning to gauge your sleeping comfort zone against your partner's isn't an easy process, no matter how big your bed is. But with time, patience, and practice, you can learn to sleep with the one you love.

Bediquette—Hers

Did you like to watch sappy movies before you got married? If so, you probably envision one of the joys of marriage to be snuggling close every night as you and your husband fall asleep, and waking up every morning in each other's arms.

Here's the truth. Your husband is probably going to go his own way shortly before he heads into REM sleep. Over time, you can train him to cuddle as he drifts off (spooning is tolerable for most men), but you're going to have to adjust to the fact that before long, he'll throw off your arms like rotten banana peels and roll to the far side of the bed. Don't take it personally. Men feel the need for more space than we do as they sleep. Your husband has erotic dreams of owning a king-size bed.

There's also the myth that the two of you will be retiring to the boudoir at the same time. Sometimes you will reach mutual sleepiness, but more often one of you will want to read one more chapter and the other will be catching the end of David Letterman. You can keep from feeling too far apart by making a point of being in the same room—and in the same bed—right before lights out, even if you are doing separate things. You may not get up at the same time, either. So make sure you each have separate alarm clocks, one on each side of the bed. You shouldn't have to rely on your partner to wake you, and you sure as heck don't want to be climbing over each other to hit the off button at six A.M.

Above all, exercise good snooze-button etiquette. What's more annoying than sleeping with someone who hits snooze every nine minutes for a solid hour, jarring you repeatedly from slumber *when you don't have to get up?* The snooze function is a privilege: don't abuse it. Using the button once or twice in a given morning is okay, but remember that the alarm wakes your husband up every time it goes off—and he might not be able to drift back off as easily as you can.

Men have two functions in bed, aside from the obvious. They are footwarmers, and they are cover-stealers. Your husband will eventually accept that warming your feet is one of his marital responsibilities, and you'll have to accept that you're destined to wake up every morning sheetless and shivering. When this happens, just yank the covers back to your side. It's all right if he wakes up. He'll feel terrible about being a bed-hog and may even spoon for a while before reclaiming his sleeping space.

It's also inevitable that in bed, one of you will be hot and one of you will be cold—at the exact same time. After David eats a big meal, he's like an anaconda who's ingested a deer. His brain shuts down as the blood rushes to his digestive system, and his metabolism zooms to Red Alert. You could toast bread on his skin. It's ten degrees outside, and he's hot sleeping under just a cotton sheet.

The solution? Work out a balance between weight of bedcovers and number of inches the window is open. He'll be able to tolerate slightly heavier bedcovers if the window is cracked, and you can pile an extra blanket on your side of the bed.

Finally, it's good to establish exactly what the bed is for. If you both agree it's not just an intimate resting place, you won't ever have conflicts over cookie crumbs, a ThighMaster, or the odd *Rolling Stone* finding its way under the covers. But one of you may have been brought up thinking of the bed as a combination study/recreation room. If this is the case, get one lamp for either side of the bed (so you can have separate lights-out) and agree that cookies in bed are fine, in theory, as long as everybody cleans up their own crumbs.

The Bathroom—His

*T*o men, the bathroom is a place of business. You go in, you do what you have to do, and then you get out. Your wife, as you've probably noticed, doesn't see things that way. To her, the bathroom is a place to spend leisure time, a sort of mini–health spa complete with exotic facial creams and rejuvenating bath salts. Once she goes in, you may need an emergency rescue team to pry her out.

Women simply have more they want to do to themselves before they face the world. You wash your face, she deep-cleans hers. You shave about ten square inches of chin, she shaves one hundred square inches of legs and armpits. You comb your hair; she mousses, blow-drys, teases, and shellacks hers with hairspray.

Then there's the makeup. It takes forever to put on every single morning, and it costs a fortune for the privilege. And how scary is the application process? Make a point to watch your wife some morning as she puts on mascara. There she is in a bra and the bottom half of a suit, wearing a towel turban, two inches from the mirror, squinting at her reflection. No one has yet been able to explain why a woman's jaw drops open while she's working on her eyes. My advice is to thank God every day that you don't have to deal with any of this stuff yourself.

Though many women realize they look terrific with little or no makeup at all, that doesn't mean they'll leave the bathroom free for your use. It just gives your wife more time to call her mother in there and read "27 Ways to Create the Natural Look" while your bladder is ready to blow.

The easiest solution to the busy-bathroom problem is to get another bathroom, or at least a bigger one. If your housing situation prevents either of those options, however, you'll have to find more imaginative solutions. First, you can establish a morning rush-hour schedule. Figure out how much time you both need, and plan accordingly. One of you may get the bathroom from 7:00 to 7:30 A.M. every day, while the other gets it from 7:30 to 8:00 A.M.

Alternatively, lay down this law: If you don't absolutely need to do it in the bathroom, do it somewhere else. This applies to reading (while not otherwise occupied), shaving with an electric shaver, hairdrying, toenail clipping, and ham radio operating. Maintain an open-door policy. Practice sharing limited bathroom space by moving station to station—shower to sink to mirror—without getting in each other's way. In a few months you and your wife will be functioning as a finely tuned bathroom-using machine.

We can't leave the topic of bathrooms without talking about, well . . . going to the bathroom. Typically, this is something every human being does in private, meaning alone with the door closed. But to some newly married couples, even this personal domain is open to interpretation. One couple we spoke with insists that marriage is the ultimate state of intimacy, and if you know and love nearly everything about your spouse, you should have no problem with him or her using the bathroom with the door open.

For many people, the reaction to this idea is, "Yeah, intimacy is one thing, and I love my husband/wife, but I have absolutely no interest in watching him/her pee. And I don't want him/her barging in on me in the bathtub, either." That's fine, too. To date, there have been no studies that link going to the bathroom privately with failed marriages.

We think it's safe to say you should make your own decision on this matter, as with every bathroom problem. Although it's not exactly dinner conversation, you should discuss it before you come right on in and start brushing your teeth. Privacy is a two-way street.

The Bathroom—Hers

Consider the case of Melinda and James. Married just over a year, they recently gave up a skylit, rent-controlled, one-bedroom apartment in the middle of Manhattan. They packed up their things and moved out to a two-bedroom town house in New Jersey, adding hours to their daily commute.

Why? Was it for the joy of seeing trees on their way to work? The privilege of free parking? That second bedroom perfect for visiting in-laws? Well, yeah. But most of all, it was the extra bathroom. In Manhattan, Melinda and James could afford only one lavatory. Moving to New Jersey allowed them two: his and hers. After they moved, James was able to use his bathroom the moment he needed it, and Melinda was empowered to stay in her bathroom for as long as she wanted. They applied basic math to their living situation: Add a bathroom, subtract several arguments per week.

One year of marriage is just about the length of time it takes a couple to realize that husbands and wives are meant to each have their own bathroom. Aside from the fact that everyone seems to need it at the same time, the bathroom invites countless minute negotiations that take up entirely too much energy. For example:

Toothpaste: One of you will inevitably squeeze the tube from the middle; one will squeeze from the end. And nobody's happy with the pump.

Counter space: You need it. All of it. Period.

This isn't a library: Your husband leaves his car magazines everywhere, water-stained and curling at the edges.

Toilet paper: How many rolls have to sit on the back of the toilet before someone installs one in the holder where it belongs? Tip: Hide the spare toilet paper so one day your husband gets caught without it. He'll learn to change over the roll, fast.

Toilet seat: He's up, you're down. Train him now; it's only going to get worse.

Toilet bowl: Does he really just forget to flush? Or is he doing it to annoy you?

Soap: What's the smallest sliver of soap that still produces a lather? Personally, we're going for a record.

Shavings: He drops his all over the sink as if he's seeding it for new growth. You don't have to clean them up too many times before you realize that this shouldn't be your problem.

Time: His need for the bathroom is urgent, yours is relaxed. This is the primary cause of bathroom-related unrest in the American household.

> **SEVEN SURVIVAL TIPS FOR GETTING HIM TO PUT THE TOILET SEAT DOWN**
>
> 1 Write "Please put me down" on the underside of the seat.
> 2 Put a spring on the seat so it slams down after use.
> 3 Let the dog pee on his favorite chair. He'll get the idea.
> 4 Make him feel your pain. Squirt his butt with a water gun.
> 5 Hang a sign at eye level: "Seat Down or You Die."
> 6 Simple rule: He leaves it up, he cleans it.
> 7 Declare war. He gets no bathroom privileges for a month.

Cleanliness: He's gross, you're not. And worse still, you recognize the problem, and he doesn't. Hair on the soap. Toothpaste in the sink. Who-knows-what all over the toilet.

Sometimes these little differences cause us to forget what the bathroom is actually for. But if you don't work them out, one thing's for sure: Your bathroom will be a war zone in the battle of the sexes.

The Telephone—His

Most houses or apartments have more than one chair, more than one closet, more than one lamp, and more than one clock. But the vast majority of newly married couples have only one phone line. The law of supply and demand tells us that this means trouble.

Why is your wife always on the phone when you're expecting an important call? Why does grass grow? It's just fate, a fate all married men must accept. She might ask why you insist on snatching up the receiver and shouting "Yell-O!" Other phone fetishes: One of you lets the phone ring and ring, despite being the closest person to it. One of you uses Call Waiting as if it were a percussion instrument. One of you leaves the cordless on the couch so the charge runs out. And one of you pulls the phone onto the bed and leaves it there so your spouse trips over the cord at three in the morning en route to the bathroom.

If you happen to be the one who does the majority of these things, then I have to tell you something your wife won't, because she loves you. I'll try to put it as delicately as I can. You're a phone jerk.

I'm explaining this now for your own good, because someday you're going to shout "Yell-O" one time too many and your wife is going to start beating you with throw pillows. I think you'll agree that some arguments are best avoided, so here's a guide to averting the phone-jerk fight and achieving household telephone harmony in an hour or less.

Sit down with your wife and take sixty minutes to figure out how you want to deal with every aspect of the telephone. Compose and record your answering machine message together. Come up with a monthly budget for long-distance spending. Decide on a long-distance company. Determine what kind of phone answerers you are: Let it ring three times? Pick it up immediately? Screen your calls? She always answers? You always answer? Whatever you decide is fine as long as you agree on it. Create a permanent, visible place to write messages for each other. Decide if you want phone services like Call Waiting and Call Messaging.

Now, if only you could have that one-hour meeting with the rest of the world. You would be able to explain to telemarketers that, although 6:00

to 7:00 P.M. is the time they are most likely to reach you, it's also the time you're most likely to be eating dinner and therefore the time you're least interested in purchasing a seven-hundred-dollar set of encyclopedias.

Fortunately, somewhere in your manhood training you learned how to cut off these unfortunate salespeople in midsentence by saying "No, thanks," and hanging up. It's possible your wife missed that rudeness seminar, so you may very well come home and find her embroiled in a pointless conversation with an AT&T customer service representative. Suddenly, she drags you into the pitch: "Honey, do we know how much we're saving each month on long distance, in actual dollars?" "Are we *truly* receiving crystal-clear connections?"

Ask her if you can speak to the nice person on the phone, then proceed with the appropriate "No, thanks," and hang up. I'm not saying most wives end up buying whatever these marketers are offering; they're just more likely to talk to them for longer periods of time, which blocks incoming calls that might actually be important.

Telecommunications technology has always been a mixed blessing. The more ways we invent to keep in touch, the more phone jerks our society creates. They rear-end you with their cars while talking on their cellular phones. They have secretaries call you and then put you on hold. They give you their beeper numbers, assuming that you absolutely cannot wait to speak to them. The best you can do is plant the seed of common phone courtesy in your own home by neutralizing the phone-jerk virus right at its source.

Telephone–Hers

Does your husband turn into a disk jockey the second he picks up the phone? All of a sudden, every other word out of his mouth is "man" or "cool," or a ridiculous phrase like "okeydokey." For some reason, your spouse may have developed a persona for his voice that's completely separate from the one you experience every day, and it's particularly obvious, and bizarre, when you observe him talking to someone on the phone.

Well, at least husbands like this say *something*. Many men are so uncomfortable on the phone that they become virtually silent. If one of your husband's friends or family members calls and you pick up the receiver, you'll make small talk for a bit, right? Not so when the shoe is on the other foot. If you're in the shower and your mother calls, your husband will appear to be on the verge of panic as he shoves the handset into your soapy hand. God forbid he should take a message or chat with your folks until you towel off.

For some reason, your husband would take facing his in-laws in person any day over speaking with them on the telephone. A 1990 survey reported that men would rather work in the yard than talk on the phone. Sixty-three percent of the women in the survey listed making phone calls as their favorite leisure activity. (The men preferred watching television.) Clearly, women see the telephone as a social device while men see it as an instrument of torture. It's possible they think of telephone chitchat as "a woman thing," something that, like foreplay, is a time-waster standing in the way of the real objective.

Perhaps something reminiscent of our caveman ancestry—when everything was communicated with a series of grunts—turns an ordinarily talkative guy into a telephone mashed potato. Otherwise, it's hard to explain why your normally gregarious spouse may become so businesslike on the phone, giving nothing but the facts and trying to hang up as soon as possible.

These are just two examples of the male Jekyll-and-Hyde phone personae, with which, now that you're married and presumably sharing the phone, you're going to have to deal. A tip: It's probably best if you don't make fun of your husband when he says "I gotcha, man," for the third time in five minutes. Using the phone can make a man feel awfully vulnerable. It's a love/hate paradox. On the one hand, talking to people is scary. On the other, the phone is a sort of technological playground, which a man may see as kissing cousin to the television remote control.

Of course, there are all different kinds of men, and therefore all different kinds of husbands. You can't get some men *off* the phone, especially if it's one of those cool pocket cellular jobs. No matter who you married, you can probably find in your husband a bit of one the following types:

• *The Obsessive.* Displays and uses his cell phone like a badge of honor. Constantly checking messages—voice mail at work, the machine at home. Fully equipped with the latest in digital technology. A menace to drive with, around or behind, an embarrassment to dine with in public.

• *The Hog.* Is always on the line when you want to place an order with J. Crew. Constantly switches long-distance companies to get the maximum combination of rate and bonus offer. Never mastered the art of getting to good-bye.

• *The Snoop.* Gets antsy the minute you pick up the phone. Doesn't understand why you may want the door shut when you talk to a friend. Insists on being on the extension during all personal conversations. Asks who you're talking to while you're talking to them. Interjects opinions about whatever you're discussing—especially if it's about him: *"I never said that!"* Uses you as a conduit to the person you're talking to with: *"Does Bob want to go see the new Schwarzenegger movie tomorrow night? Just ask Mary to ask him. Oh, what time? Tell him eight-thirty. No—tell him ten o'clock. No—I'm wrong. Tell him nine-fifteen. Why are you throwing the phone at me?"*

On the other hand, your husband may have had a traumatic childhood experience with the phone: victimized by his mother's PTA telephone tree. You may see vestiges of this youthful scarring in:

• *The Selectively Deaf Avoider.* Phone's ringing. You're covered in bread dough, the answering machine's not on. He lies on the couch. He's happy to let *you* know it's ringing, but the thought of actually picking up the receiver is terrifying. Or, alternatively, when you finally lunge across the room for the receiver, he may play coy: "What, was it ringing?" He knows you're more interested in who's on the other line, and he uses this to his advantage. This type is often a big fan of e-mail.

• *The Bungler.* Can't take a message to save his life. Call Waiting equals Instant Disconnect. Confuses "play all" with "erase all" on the answering machine. Says helpful things like "Oh yeah, your mother called . . . last Tuesday."

• *The Interferer.* "Are you done yet? When are you going to be done? Aren't you off the phone yet? Will you be off soon? When? Why aren't you done yet?" Just writing that is annoying.

No matter what type of phone personality your husband has, it will take some getting used to. The real trick is to get him to drop the act and speak like a human when you're the one on the other end of the line. Especially if one of you is calling in from a business trip. No matter how much the two of you say "I love you" in person, you probably won't hear it on the telephone if he's in a position to be overheard. What you'll get instead is the all-too-common "Me too," "Yeah," or "Uh-huh."

And he'll never admit to picking up the phone because he misses the sound of your voice. Instead, he'll call to say something like "*Seinfeld* was really funny tonight. I just wanted to let you know that I recorded it in case you were wondering."

These are all annoying but manageable phone quirks—except the Hyperdrive Sign-Off. The old joke goes, "How can you tell when a man is finished talking on the phone? You hear a dial tone." Men hate dealing with endings, and that's why you're likely to find yourself in midsentence addressing empty airwaves. This is easily correctable behavior: just ask that your husband give you a two-minute warning when his telephone tolerance is running low. You might even squeeze an "I love you" out of him before he hangs up.

The Clicker—His

Clicker. Zapper. Remote control. No matter what you call it, it's the one piece of property in the house that is truly yours. Since the dawn of time, man has labored to invent devices that afford him the leisure he so richly deserves. Rather than trudging all the way across the ice sheet to bonk a woolly mammoth over the head with a stick, cavemen invented the spear so they could kill from a safe distance behind the cover of a favorite rock. Then they invented the wheel and the cart, so they wouldn't have to drag the hairy carcass home to dinner by its trunk.

Time marched on, and man's inventions further increased his comfort: the saddle; bed pillows; elastic waistbands; the twenty-four-hour convenience store; the recliner. Finally came the penultimate example of his mastery over the world: the clicker.

Men everywhere rejoiced with its creation, which eliminated for all time the need to get up. Together with a cooler of beer by the couch, a bag of chips on the coffee table, and a full lineup of NFL games, here was everything necessary to create the Sunday of our dreams. *Click*—there's the Cincinnati game. Uh-oh, a commercial. *Click*—there's Green Bay. A blowout? How boring. *Click*—it's "The Making of the *Sports Illustrated* Swimsuit Issue" on VH-1.

Over time, clickers grew more sophisticated, allowing us to perform more functions than we ever thought possible. Too loud? *Click*. Not loud enough? *Click*. More contrast? *Click*. Tracking's off? *Click*. Will that dog ever stop barking? *Click*. Oops—the dog's in the kitchen, not on TV. Well, it's only a matter of time before we invent the clicker that takes care of real life, too.

With a clicker in your hand, you are truly master of the house. Until you get married. One dark day, you'll come home to find your wife will be watching *Oprah* on videotape. *"No problem,"* you say as you head for your favorite spot on the couch. You reach for the trusty clicker, which should be exactly where you left it last night and—oh no! *It's not there!*

You choke back the panic. There must be an explanation. Surely your faithful clicker, though packed with powerful and miraculous features, has not developed the ability to stand up and walk away. Sofa cushions go flying, carpets are lifted, drawers are thrown open—until, with a gut-wrenching pang of fear, you spot it. In the hand of the woman you love.

You hunker down and begin your approach low, so as not to spook her. Beads of sweat emerge on your forehead. You lock your eyes on the object of your desire. *"Okay, honey,"* you say, as if coddling a rabid bear, "nothing to worry about. Just hand me the clicker, and everything will be A-okay."

"No," she replies.

You burst into mad laughter, certain your ears are deceiving you. "Really, honey. Give me the clicker. I mean—*Oprah*? It's killing me."

Now you've gone around the bend. Your eyes are rolling, your tongue is lolling, and steam is starting to shoot from your ears. But your wife, like Oprah, is ignoring you. Martha Stewart is on the screen, turning prunes into cookies. Says your beloved, "For one night out of the week, you can live without the clicker. I'm watching this. Watch it, or go do something else."

Life as you know it has ended. She's stolen your power as surely as Delilah cut Samson's hair. You have no recourse. You might as well go in the bedroom and—gasp—read a book!

Of course, all this pain and betrayal can be avoided before you get married. You could get two TVs, but I suggest drafting a simple prenuptial agreement that lays down the following ten clicker commandments:

❶ Thou shalt honor the clicker's name and keep away from it.

❷ Thou shalt not covet my clicker when I have it.

❸ Thou shalt not complain when I channel surf.

❹ Thou shalt return the clicker to its proper place beside me.

❺ Thou shalt not spill liquids on the clicker.

❻ Thou shalt not scratch graven images on the clicker.

❼ Thou shalt never push the mysterious little red button.

❽ Thou shalt not hide the clicker in an attempt to punish me.

❾ Thou shalt sacrifice thy Walkman batteries for the clicker.

❿ Remember NFL Sunday, and keep it holy.

The Clicker—Hers

Amid stacks of junk at an antiques market, my friend Laura was once delighted to find a wooden shelf, elaborately carved, about four inches wide by eight inches long. "It's nice," I said, trying to understand her enthusiasm. "But what can you possibly do with a shelf that tiny? Isn't it kind of, well, useless?"

"Oh no!" she exclaimed. "It's perfect!"

"For what?" A thimble collection?

"This," Laura said in a reverential tone, "is going to be The Place of the Clicker. For months Carter's been misplacing the remote control, and he drives me crazy. He's always accusing me of hiding it. And it's as though he's lost all ability to work the television without it. He acts like the world's coming to an end."

If you visited Laura and Carter's home, you'd probably understand Carter's point of view, melodramatic as it sounds. He *has* lost the ability to work the television without the remote control—because he's got not one, not two, but *three* clickers all hooked up to form some maddeningly complicated electronic central nervous system. He, of course, is the "brain" into which the whole system feeds. This explains why he doesn't want Laura putting her paws on his gear. It also explains why, even if she wanted to handle his precious remotes, she'd have absolutely no idea how they worked.

If the remote control had been designed by women for women to own and operate, it would have three

SEVEN SURVIVAL TIPS FOR PREVENTING CHANNEL SURFING OVER THE SPEED LIMIT

1 Write him a ticket. $50 for reckless TV endangerment.
2 Act dizzy and fall down.
3 Tape the *TV Guide* to the clicker.
4 Say "That's good. That's good. That's good." Every time he changes a channel.
5 Keep a crate of tennis balls nearby. He gets one channel change per half hour—anything more and he gets a forehand to the head.
6 Rig an electric grid under the couch, and zap him (using your own remote control, of course).
7 Coat the clicker in Vaseline. He'll spend so many hours cleaning it, he won't have time to change the channels.

switches: on/off; volume control; and channels up/down. But this is clearly not the case. Pick up a remote and study the buttons. In addition to those that make sense, you'll find a bunch that are inscrutable. Something labeled "AB." Something called "Code." Another marked "Sleep." And two buttons that simply read "+ ↑" and "– ↓." Then there are the redundant buttons. In my home there is one clicker with a button marked "TV," another marked "TV/Video," and a third marked "TV/Cable." It's also got one button labeled "Jump" and another labeled "Return." Wouldn't common sense tell you these perform the same functions?

Well, if you want answers, the last place you should turn is the Master of the Remote: your husband. Clueless as you feel about the bells and whistles attached to what should be a simple invention, he's in even worse shape. Having total control of the remote is of life-or-death importance to your husband, but he has only a little more understanding than you do about how it works. It must be a power thing.

When our husbands fight so hard for something we have so little interest in, we're inclined to give in and let 'em have it. But on the downside, this means we have to suffer through endless bouts of channel surfing—a manifestation of commitment-phobia, and a throwback to the days when having "an itchy trigger finger" and being "quick on the draw" were sure signs of machismo. Lightning-quick clicker manipulation does not, however, extend to volume control. Either the man of the house genuinely doesn't hear that the volume went up ten decibels when *The X-Files* went to commercial, or he's noticed it, but feeling as he does about change (see the "Change" chapter), he's sticking with that original volume setting come hell or high water.

Unfortunately, there is no good advice for dealing with a man who is deaf to TV volume and uses the clicker like a paintbrush, creating an artistic mélange of split-second visual images and sounds as he flashes from channel to channel. (See "Minor Irritations" if this is really a problem for you.) So make it as easy on yourself as possible. Create a special storage place for the thing, so he won't misplace it and frantically uproot the cushions of the sofa you're sitting on.

On the upside, as a married woman, nothing could be easier than recording a television program. Instead of programming the remote control to set the VCR, program your husband to do it. He'll be torn between annoyance at your failure to understand how to work the remote, and fear that someday you'll figure out how to do it without him. Perhaps, he worries, any effort on your part to record your own shows is really an evil plot to take the clicker away from him.

That means, if there's a program you want to watch, you'll either have to ask his permission or leave work early and take the batteries out of the remote. Let's face it, a powerless clicker shell is as close as we'll ever get to having control of the television in our own homes.

Laundry—His

Why does "Laundry" get its own chapter, separate from "Cleaning"? Why do you separate lights from darks? (Okay, you're a guy, so maybe you don't separate lights from darks. But you should.) Different colors of clothing require different laundering treatment. And doing laundry is different from any other household chore. Every load of wash carries a load of unique problems.

Believe it or not, among the newly married couples we surveyed, one of the most frequent causes of arguments between them was laundry. No matter where these couples found access to a washer and dryer—in their homes, in the shared laundry room of an apartment building, or in a Laundromat—they had problems. Here's an example of each.

Case #9: You have a washer and dryer at home, and your wife has provided a laundry basket, but you don't think it makes sense to use the basket when you can stick your dirty clothes right in the washer. That way, when the machine is full, you just add soap and push start.

The Problem: Your idea of "full" is, shall we say, liberal. Somewhere down the line, your father instilled in you the idea that washing machines use up a great deal of expensive electricity. So you try to use the washer only when you really need to, that is, when you're wearing your last pair of clean underwear. If left to your own devices, it could be weeks before you'd start a load of laundry. By then there'd be such a backlog of dirty clothes that you'd try to do one mammoth load, jamming *all* the clothes in with a broomstick, thus clogging the machine and causing it to need repairs that cost more than you saved on electricity.

Your wife, meanwhile, is itching to do laundry almost every day. She needs the shirt on the bottom of the heap because it's the only thing that goes with what she's planning to wear tomorrow. So she ends up doing the laundry now because she can't wait for your underwear drawer to empty out. She eventually learns to toss all of your clothes on top of the dryer so she only has to wash the things she needs; that is, her clothes. Then you

50

get mad. How much effort does it take for her to wash some of your clothes if she's doing a load anyway? Can't she mix your clothes with hers? Do they fight during the spin cycle?

The Solution: First of all, use the hamper or the laundry basket. You're not saving time by storing your dirty clothes in the washer because, when you finally get around to doing the laundry, you'll have to take them out anyway and separate the colors. Discuss with your wife how often you can afford to do laundry. Once a week is a usual compromise, but if she really needs to do a miniload midweek, ask her to throw in some of your stuff from the same color group. Or take a lesson from the movie *Reality Bites* and hide your dirty underwear inside her dirty clothes. You may be able to get her to unwittingly wash your whole wardrobe.

Case #23:   Your wife brings the laundry down to the basement of your building, puts it in the washer, comes back up to the apartment, and expects you to go change the wet clothes over to the dryer.

The Problem: You're a man, and men have a simple rule: If you start a job, finish it. We don't leave tools strewn about after we've fixed the car, we don't leave the lawn mower sitting out in the lawn, and we don't leave our clothes in the building's laundry room long enough for our neighbors to pull them out and dump them, sopping wet, on top of a grungy communal washing machine.

Your wife has a different rule: The two of you should share jobs as evidence of loving solidarity. Not only does she want you to go down and do your part for the greater laundering good of the family, she wants you to *want* to go down and do it.

The Solution: As usual, try to reach a compromise. You may be willing to bend your rule if your wife is willing to bend hers. Yes, you can do this particular job together as long as you know which part of the job you'll be responsible for each time. Will she always put the laundry in and you'll always switch it over? Or will you switch jobs each time so neither of you gets stuck with the most annoying part? Soon your wife will understand that men are perfectly willing to do the jobs they've agreed to do. It's the surprise factor that bothers us. And one more thing: If you're going to share the chore of doing laundry, agree on when to start. She can't begin the laundry and expect you to run down and switch it when she never consulted you about starting it in the first place.

Case #45: You haul fifty pounds of dirty clothes to the Laundromat because nobody wants to go there more than once every two weeks. You bring crisp, new one-dollar bills in case the change machine is working, and a pocketful of quarters because it's probably still broken. Then you prowl the aisles looking for open machines.

The Problem: It's a deadly combination. Personal property, absolute boredom, shady characters, and myriad common courtesy violations. The questions run through your brain: "Why isn't my wife here to share this misery?" "Why am I the only one who can complete the laundry without losing a sock?" "Why is this giant hairy guy standing next to the same dryer I am when he knows I'm jumping in as soon as that old lady is through with it?"

Ask anyone who has ever done time in a Laundromat, and he'll tell you he's seen a fight. Maybe not an actual fistfight, but at least a screaming hissy fit. It starts when somebody takes someone else's wet clothes and dumps them on the floor, or somebody touches someone's else's wife's underwear. Boom! Conflict. Since you and your wife hate the Laundromat equally, the two of you constantly argue about whose turn it is to go there.

The Solution: There is nothing that will make the Laundromat jungle easy to navigate. So work it as a team. Agree on a specific laundry day; once a week for the brave, twice a month for the sensible. Use the fact that there are two of you to make the process go faster. While you're getting change, your wife should put detergent in the washers. While you're taking the wet clothes out of the washers, she can lay claim to dryers as they become available.

If a conflict arises with another one of the inhabitants of Dante's fabric-softener level of hell, you and your wife can fight on the same side, two against one. Nobody likes to get double-teamed at the Laundromat. Not even giant hairy guys.

Laundry–Hers

While there are exceptions, many men seem to feel no one else does laundry as well as they do. Other than their mothers, of course—you know, the ones who put spandex and Lycra in the dryer. Laundry is a precise, goal-oriented job, and it may be one your husband would rather do himself—not because he wants to pull his share of domestic duties, but because he feels you're incapable of getting his whites properly white. In the best of all possible worlds, though, he'd really prefer to watch TV and have his mother come over to do the wash.

Barring that, his goal is to train you—by hook or by crook—to do laundry his way. And what is "his" way? Well, it's not entirely rational. You can learn it by watching your husband's mother, or you can pick it up by having him nag you whenever you do something that bucks the rules, like adding detergent on top of the clothes, rather than clothes on top of the detergent and water. The best action is to throw up your hands and say, "Have it your way, fussy. Laundry duty is all yours."

Hah! Fat chance. That kind of thinking is a direct violation of Laundry Tenet #1: Accept Responsibility. Laundry is a fact of life, and you and your husband each have to do at least part of it. You must overcome evil thoughts like: "Hey, the laundry is mostly full of his smelly socks. Why am I cleaning up after him?" It always looks like your partner creates more dirty clothes than you do, but in fact, he's thinking the exact same thing. He has no desire to prance around the laundry room with your dirty bras or stockings. But even though we know an absurdly large number of couples who won't allow "boy" dirty clothes to mix in the washer with "girl" dirty clothes, you *have* to work it out between the two of you. Period.

That leads us to Laundry Tenet #2: Make Decisions. Who will do the laundry this time? Will we pay someone else to do it? When will it get done? Will we include the sheets? The towels? The comforter? The bath mat? Are socks folded together or rolled into a ball? If each of you isn't preassigned specific laundry tasks, such as folding, you'll have to make a decision each time about who is going to do what. The words "Well, I did it last week" are a guaranteed precursor to a fight on the level of Ali versus Foreman.

To prevent this strife, sit down and have a serious discussion. Make all the decisions at once. You do the washing, he does the folding, sheets are done once every two weeks, and the detergent will be Tide. Put it in writing, allowing for the occasional change: If your husband doesn't feel like folding one week, then he'll wash instead. It may sound ridiculous, but knowing each other's roles can really reduce stress. And it's great practice for when you and your husband encounter a truly serious problem.

Here's a short list of your husband's probable laundry quirks. Keep notes on these laundry regulations, and quiz yourself often.

❶ All clothing must be turned inside out before it hits the washing machine.

❷ Remove Kleenex from all pockets before washing anything.

❸ Drier sheets. Know them, love them, forget them at your peril. We don't really know what they do, but they smell good.

❹ If a single sock goes missing, the odd remaining article must be sequestered in Stray Sock Storage for one year or until its partner has been found, whichever comes first.

❺ Everything must be neatly folded. Underwear, jockstraps, you name it. Right-side out is a must.

Now it's your turn. Here's what he must learn about laundry to avoid making *you* nuts:

❶ No jamming the clothes in to make them fit. Just because everything is physically in the washing machine does not guarantee it will get clean.

❷ Loose bras *will* wrap themselves around the rotor in the washing machine, and loose stockings *will* run. Lingerie bags were created to prevent this from happening. Use them.

❸ Loose bras and stockings *will* melt in the dryer. Unless your husband wants them to fuse with his shorts, such items must be removed and line-dried.

❹ Separate, separate, separate. There's a reason washing and drying instructions are sewn into clothes. Launder clothing according to color and type of fabric, and recommended water temperature. Do not put anything in the dryer that does not belong there: wool, shrinkable cotton, spandex.

❺ If your husband insists on putting his sneakers in the dryer, at least two towels must be added to muffle that god-awful thumping noise.

❻ Dry cleaning: Fair's fair. You agree not to use the dry cleaners as a second closet, and he agrees to drop off and pick up both your and his clothes once in a while.

Which brings us to Laundry Tenet #3: Make the Most of It. Laundry is a chore that's as satisfying as they come once you've finished it, but in the interim, it's a miserable process during which people complain and tempers flare. So what do you do? Make laundry into Happy Fun Time! If you go to a Laundromat, bring a deck of cards or a Scrabble board. Do *something* inventive and crazy to turn this hideously mundane chore into something to look forward to (or at least tolerate).

It's your choice. You can stand in the basement and fight over dirty underwear, or you can dump it in the washer, get naked, and have fun.

Pets—His

Sometime during your first year of marriage, you're probably going to add a pet to your family. I'm not talking about a fish or a lizard or Sea Monkeys; those are strictly low-commitment animals, best left behind with the other trappings of bachelorhood. I mean a good old-fashioned dog or cat that brings with it a real personality and definite responsibilities.

Before getting a pet, you must be sure that your lifestyle can adequately support it. It should be properly fed, watered, inoculated, cleaned, and played with. Although you'll have fewer long-term responsibilities with a dog or cat than you would with a baby, you'll have every bit as much of a responsibility to treat the creature with love and respect.

The first potentially problematic decision for you and your wife is whether to go canine or feline. If you're both cat people, no problem. If you both like dogs, great. But if you're a dog guy and she's a cat lady, or vice versa, someone's going to have to compromise. In the former scenario, unless you absolutely hate cats, this might be a good time for you to give in. Although cats are more aloof, less likely to fetch things, and have a tendency to wave their tails in your face, they are much more self-sufficient than the average dog. You'll never have to get up and walk Mittens at six A.M. when it's ten degrees outside, and you don't have to make special arrangements when you go away for the weekend. Leave the cat with plenty of water, lots of food, litter in the pan, a few mousy toys, and he's set for a few days.

The second scenario might also be a good time to give in. (When isn't?) Dogs can be very rewarding. You can forgive Frisco's occasional accident on the kitchen floor when he finally learns to catch a Frisbee in midair. Walking your dog is good exercise, a great time for you and your wife to talk, and a fun way to meet people. The trick is to keep this task from becoming a "You do it this time; I did it last time" chore. Yes, the dog is an essential part of your family, but it's not *your* dog; it's not *her* dog; it's the couple's dog. So the majority of the responsibility for its maintenance should never fall on one pair of shoulders.

While where you live wouldn't necessarily affect what kind of cat you get, it should certainly play a part in your selection of a dog. A big animal requires a great deal of space, and typically a yard to run in. If you live in a small apartment, a large dog may not be your best choice. They say you can tell if a dog is going to get big by the size of his paws. Giant paws on a puppy mean he's going to become more than a handful very quickly, and if you don't have the room he needs to be happy, you're probably better off looking at the little guys. To find your new best friend, check out the local ASPCA—where the animals are more needy, less likely to have medical problems due to inbreeding, and often have better personalities than the ones you'd pay dearly for in pet stores.

Whether you get a dog or a cat, you and your wife are both going to have to deal with the most unpleasant aspect of pet ownership: poop. This is a major source of pet-owning couples' arguments, and the reason it causes stress is simple. It's gross. Neither of you wants to clean it up, but someone has to. The dog's certainly not going to do it.

Since this isn't a job two people can reasonably share, it's a good idea to agree on which one of you is the pooper scooper and when he or she should scoop. You can alternate days, or one of you can take the morning and the other can have the night shift. If you don't really mind it and your wife absolutely hates it, you might even volunteer to take permanent scoop duty. It's important that the two of you enjoy the dog or cat's company while you're together, but it's not worth it to try to exert your will over your wife. Nothing looks stupider than two adults arguing over animal poop.

If your wife already had a pet before your marriage, you'll have to get along now that you're "related." No matter how much your stepdog drools, no matter how much of a hairy eyeball you get when you touch the stepcat's food dish, you have to make nice to the beast when your wife is home. Never underestimate how she feels about her pet; if you put her in the position of choosing between you and the animal, you could easily find yourself sleeping in the doghouse (that is, if Fido will let you near the place). How strongly do women feel about their animals? A recent *Glamour* magazine survey revealed that 92 percent of the women questioned had bought a holiday or birthday present for their pet; 85 percent had decorated their home or office with its picture; 55 percent had hung a Christmas stocking for their pet; and 33 percent had left a message for Fluffy on the answering machine.

It may not matter how much either one of you loves pets if your spouse is allergic to them. However, if this is the case in your house, you don't necessarily have to give up altogether on the idea of a wet-nosed companion. Many people are allergic to only one kind of pet dander, so a woman who puffs up at the first whiff of cat hair may not react at all when a dog saunters by.

If you or your wife is only slightly allergic, but you love animals so much that you just have to get one, scout out a nonallergenic dog like a poodle, or a small hairless cat like a sphinx. They're not the prettiest little putty-tats in the world, but as we sagely quoted in this book's "Physical Appearance" chapter, love is blind.

Pets—Hers

*T*here are a lot of great reasons to get a pet: affection, companionship, and entertainment. But beneath it all, pets are a trial run for children. The parallels are endless. Want to know what kind of father your husband is going to be? Watch him play with the dog. Who's going to end up changing more diapers? The one who most often scoops the catbox.

As with having a baby, many difficult choices await the newlyweds who decide to add a pet to their family. First and foremost, it's important to make sure you're prepared to never be alone again. Pets don't go anywhere. When you're home, they're always there, and when they need love, attention must be paid. If your husband grew up with lots of pets, he's probably ready to make this commitment, but if you didn't have many animals as a child, you may initially want some pet-free time to settle into your marriage.

When you do get a new pet, I'd advise against the surprise-your-husband approach, unless you enjoy it when he acts out lengthy and painful scenes like "What are we going to do with a [fill in the pet]? The last thing we need is a [fill in the pet]! They're [negative adjective], [negative adjective], and [negative adjective]!" After an hour of this, you finally get to "They're [long pause] . . . so darn *cute!*"

Like babies, which come in his and hers flavors, there are two basic varieties of household pets: dogs and cats. Unlike babies (unless you adopt), you get to choose your poison, and you get the added bonus of picking the personality and physical appearance of your pet.

Once you pick a species, you have to agree upon a breed. Let's face it, when it comes to men and pets, as with houses, cars, breasts, and cuts of beef, the general rule is, the bigger the better. Have you ever known a man to voluntarily adopt a shih tzu or Pomeranian? Show him a rottweiler or retriever, though, or any other breed that looks good with a bandanna around its neck, and you tap into that deep-seated male desire that was so eloquently played out on *Gilligan's Island*: the need to have a little buddy all one's own.

It's the same dynamic that causes men to have special feelings for their sons. Why? Balls! (The kind you throw.) Your husband can't play catch with a miniature dachshund because no ball he'd care to be seen throwing would fit in the dog's mouth. A Persian-loving man? Not likely. He'll have none of that pansy, fluffy fur: he wants a hunter, the bigger the better. He'll clamor for a big old Maine coon or some giant mangy tomcat.

Once you bring home a pet, you have to name it. If it were a baby boy, your husband would want it to have a solid manly name, something you couldn't make fun of, something that would stand the creature in good stead as it grows up in a tough world. Something like Butch. Unfortunately, even if it's just a nickname, your husband is liable to call your pet this all the time, no matter what you've really named it.

So let's say you've now got a delicate female Abyssinian named Butch. Watch your husband handle Butch on a day-to-day basis. Does he drop what he's doing to feed her? Does he change her litter without whining about the smell? Does he spoil her rotten with wind-up mice and birds-on-a-wire? Or does he wake poor Butch out of a sound sleep by poking her repeatedly in the tummy? Does he approach with a running tackle and roughly rumple her fur?

Even if your husband is a minor-league pet aggravator, take heart. Chances are he'll love your pet to his dying breath. Sure, he may obsess about the logistics of pet ownership: "How big a bag of cat food can I physically carry out of the store?" And yes, he may experience the occasional twinge of jealousy over the attention you're lavishing on someone other than him, or resent the fact that you're more forgiving of the dog's bad habits than those of your husband. Even so, you know your husband stops off at the pet store every Sunday to surprise Butch with a fresh catnip refill for her toy mouse. Every man, deep down, is a pussycat when it comes to pets.

Finally, if you're merging the pets you both had when you were single, you have to consider their probable reactions to each other. When it comes time to bring together your husband's dog and your cat, you'll likely have to deal with all sorts of behavioral problems, from spiteful peeing in the corner to aggressiveness or avoidance of one spouse or the other. The cold shoulder is an animal's ultimate revenge. Both reactions occur when an animal feels its boundaries have been invaded, and that doesn't just mean Fluffy's place in the yard or living room; it includes her place in your affections.

Here are a few ways to ease the pain of pet combining. Don't give everybody the run of the house all at once; use gates and doors to give each animal a separate place. Exchange toys so pets become familiar with each other's smells. Don't scold them—your pet may associate the unpleasantness of your disapproval with the interloping new animal. The best thing to do is pamper both pets with extra catnip, toys, and affection. Most animals will eventually work out a truce with their furry new housemates. Before you know it, you'll have an episode of *The Housepet Brady Bunch* on your hands.

Minor Irritations—His

No matter how strong your love, no matter how much you adore your wife's every word, every gesture, every breath, there's that one little thing about her that just bugs the hell out of you.

Well, hopefully it's only one thing. You've got plenty of time ahead of you to nurture each other's pet peeves. For right now, though, in the happy blush of your first year of marriage, it's easy to forget about the little irritations—until a particular situation causes them to pop up again. "Oh, yeah," you say to yourself in a darkened movie theater. "This reminds me just how much I hate it when we're watching a movie and she asks me what Tom Cruise just said, even though if she couldn't hear it, chances are I couldn't hear it either, and now I've missed what the other guy said."

"Holy cow!" the voice inside your head exclaims. "Isn't it odd how she's very ladylike at a restaurant or when we're visiting my parents, but when the two of us eat at home, alone, she belches like she's got the fire of God in her belly?"

For two people who live in close proximity day after day, the list of potential irritations is endless. Many of them stem from body cavities better left unmentioned. Coughing, snorting, sniffing, sneezing, throat clearing, tuneless humming, and loud yawning are just a few entries in the annoying noises category. Then there's the pointless perpetual motion group, which encompasses nervous leg shaking and swinging, teeth clicking, fingernail chewing, knuckle cracking, steering wheel tapping, and pencil biting. Not to be outdone are the class of irritations in the "I'm being rude but I don't realize it" school, such as movie talking, gum popping, double-dipping chips in the salsa, and not looking where you're going.

No doubt, whatever bothers you about your wife is unique to her, a product of her upbringing and life experience. One new husband told us that his wife would make dinner but serve herself very little. Then, when she finished her portion, she would start to take food off of his plate bit by bit, all the while continuing the conversation as if nothing were happening.

It wasn't the reaching over and taking his food that annoyed him, but the lack of logic. He wondered why she didn't just serve herself more food in the first place. Finally, he confronted her, and she was stunned. She had no idea she had been doing it. She was concerned about her weight, so she always gave herself less food than she wanted. Then, while she was busy talking, her body must have told her unconsciously that it needed more food, and the most obvious place to get it was across the table on her husband's plate.

Like most minor problems, this one was solved by a simple conversation between husband and wife. The sooner you discuss what's bothering you, the less likely it is to turn into a major source of animosity. Try not to avoid an initial confrontation the first few times you're irritated by some little thing your wife does. The last thing you want to do is wait until you're genuinely angry about it, so that you end up embroiled in a full-out argument. Chances are, your wife is unaware of whatever she's doing, or she may not know it bothers you. If you say something nicely, she'll probably try not to do it again.

Or, even more likely, you'll realize that what's bothering you is such a stupid little thing, it wasn't even worth getting annoyed about in the first place. Talking about your wife's habit of leaving the cap off the toothpaste tube will soon lead to joking about it. And anything the two of you can laugh about can't be that big of a problem.

Minor Irritations—Hers

*I*f you look at divorce records, they're likely to reflect such legal grounds as infidelity, abandonment, or cruel and unusual behavior. Girlfriend to girlfriend, though, we know the real reasons were probably more like: "My husband left his stinky socks on the bed." "He watched TV with the volume set on 'stun.' " "He couldn't shut a door, a drawer, a cabinet, a refrigerator." "He chewed with his mouth agape." "He peed with the bathroom door open."

Sure, some marriages founder because of irreconcilable differences. But I guarantee just as many crash and burn on the rocky shoals of irritating behavior.

One of the things you were probably told ad nauseam when you got engaged was, "A good marriage takes effort. You have to work hard to make it succeed." Like most newlyweds-to-be, you shrugged this advice off (along with the meat loaf recipe Aunt Fritzie swore kept Uncle Harvey a happy man for five decades). But unfortunately, this is one cliché that holds water, because it can take serious self-control and unconditional love to overlook your husband's little bad habits.

What may have seemed like a charming quirk to you, premarriage, will deepen and ripen with time. It will mature into a full-fledged annoyance that makes the hair on the back of your neck stand up. For example, it happens when you find a used Kleenex sitting on a table or countertop two feet from a trashcan. Premarriage, you may have thought, "How cute. It's as though my husband has grown too attached to that piece of facial tissue to bid it a permanent good-bye." Postmarriage, you think "Where did this boy learn his manners?"

And bear in mind that both spouses were on their best behavior premarriage. Once you get comfortable, manners are one of the first things to go. This means that curly little hairs will start showing up embedded in the soap within a few months of tying the knot, and daily leg-and-armpit shaving may slide to every other day or even once a week. You must remind yourself that content does not equal lazy, and your husband doesn't like razor burn any more than you do. Premarriage, you took pleasure in anticipating his little bodily tics—the squeaky sound his eyes make when he rubs them, the remarkable speed with which his toenails grow. But when his feet have drawn blood from your shins for the third time in a week—and then he clips his nails sitting on the edge of the bed and lets the trimmings fall on the rug—that's when the hard work necessitated by marriage starts to manifest itself.

To handle his habit of saying "God bless you" when you cough as well as when you sneeze (making a common cold a symphonic experience of blessings), what you have to remember is the First Law of Cohabitation: For every irritating husbandly habit, there is an equal and opposite wifely habit.

I know, I know, we women are the souls of consideration in comparison to the oafs we've hitched ourselves to. But it's true. I found this out the hard way when I started making polite requests of Dave during our first year of marriage to turn lights off when he left a room and not leave undissolved toothpaste blobs in the bathroom sink basin. Imagine my chagrin when he came back with "Stop leaving wet towels on the bed in the morning" and a surprisingly impassioned plea to neatly roll the inner plastic bag in the cereal box.

I had no idea he felt that strongly about stale cereal—or that I harbored such tumorous irritating behaviors. Which is, of course, just the point. There's all too much truth in the proverb, "Judge not lest ye be judged."

Maybe your husband has ten irritating behaviors to each one of yours. Even so, you'll never get him to stop doing any of those ten things unless you use the Barter System. Monday: "Okay, honey, I'll stop leaving the cap off the shampoo bottle if you promise not to leave Kleenex in your pants pockets when you put them in the laundry hamper." Wednesday: "Here's a thought: How 'bout I try to always put the cap on the shampoo bottle if you stop slamming the car door when you get in and out?" Friday: "I've got the perfect compromise; I'll make sure the cap on the shampoo is replaced tightly every morning, and you'll remember to flush the toilet after you scoop out Fluffy's litterbox."

As long as he feels he's getting something in exchange for changing his behavior, your husband will never notice he's getting *the same thing* in exchange every time. But all joking aside, minor irritations may bug the living daylights out of you. In the broad scheme of things, though, they're just that: *minor* irritations. If you counterbalance them with the many small ways your husband makes you happy, the scale of your marriage will likely tip on the positive side.

Yes, Dear—His

"I have mastered at least one important marital concept. Know what the two most important words are? 'Yes, dear.' "

—actor Gary Busey, in *People* magazine

When you're looking to quickly end a conversation involving big important issues, "Yes, dear" can be the two most effective words in a husband's vocabulary. They can also get you killed.

"Yes, dear" is tricky. You have to know *when* to say it and *how* to say it. Conserve "Yes, dears" and use them wisely because, like antibiotics, they lose their effectiveness through overuse. "Yes, dear" can spell instant death to your personal manhood or utter triumph in the eternal battle against nagging. Here are a few pointers to guide you through the uses and misuses of this valuable marital tool:

1. "Yes, dears" are a wonderful way to cut phone conversations short. Your wife gets what she wants, and she can't see the look on your face.

2. Nothing stops her from telling you to take out the trash faster than a well-placed "Yes, dear."

3. Try not to "Yes, dear" your wife when you're with a group. While that may seem funny to your friends, you'll pay for your comedy later.

4. When she's trying to make a point or win an argument, the two words "Yes, dear" perfectly convey to your wife, "Okay, you win. Can I watch baseball now?"

5. Don't ever "Yes, dear" her mother. You'll regret your error for the rest of your life. Besides, that's another guy's job.

6. Never answer a "Do I look fat?" with a "Yes, dear." This shows you're clearly not concentrating.

❼ Randomly sprinkled "Yes, dears" are effective ways to make a back-seat driver think you're listening.

❽ "Yes, dear" is the answer to any question that begins with "Did you remember to . . ."

❾ In the history of mankind, the words "Yes, dear" have never been directly followed by sex. If you want it, you'd better think of something else.

❿ If your wife says you're using "Yes, dear" too often, try listening for a change. It's easy to fall into a lazy rut, taking her for granted without giving her ideas the respect they're due. The next time your wife sounds like she's launching into a speech about life and the universe as she knows it, turn off the TV, stop what you're doing, and talk to her. Your long future together holds unlimited opportunities to use "Yes, dear" some other time.

Yes, Dear—Hers

When you're looking to quickly end a conversation involving big important issues, "Yes, dear" can be the two most effective words in a wife's vocabulary. They can also put you in hell.

"What do you mean, 'Yes, dear?'" he says. *"You say that like I'm not actually right—like you're just saying that so I think I'm right while you still think you're right! Well, I'm right! And we can't go to sleep until you admit that I'm right and you're wrong!"*

"What do you mean, 'Yes, dear' again?!"

See what I mean? Use "Yes, dear" judiciously, and you'll save a lot of futile discussion. But if your husband gets wind that you're just shutting him up—well, look out.

The secret is in the tone. While it's deeply satisfying to sigh as you say the words, doing so is El Grande Mistake #1. If he asks, "Do you think your father is warming up to me?" you can't let even a hint of exasperation slip into your voice—even if he's asked the same question weekly since the day you met. Instead, add an enthusiastic "Oh." As in "Oh, yes, dear!"

"Definitely" adds authenticity as well, and is a good modifier to include in matters of insecurity. For example, "This new haircut hides my bald spot pretty well, don't you think?" can be answered with a "Yes, dear. Definitely!" but not with a simple "Yes, dear." Your husband needs to believe that his bald spot is inconspicuous, and it's okay to let him think so as long as he's not committing a major comb-over crime.

When you're not in the mood to hide your disdain, a good substitution for "Yes, dear" is "Sure." There's a world of difference between "Yes" and "Sure." "Sure" allows you to convey what you're really thinking while superficially going with the program. "So, Chuck's having everybody over to watch the Super Bowl. He didn't think you'd want to go, but I told him you're a really good sport and you'd be happy to hang out with all the other girls. Is that all right?" What's the only possible answer in this situation?

Pause. "Sure."

The TEAM Quiz

The married couples who tackle the challenges of living together most successfully are those who understand each other's differences and who work well together as a team. So we invite you and your matrimonial partner to take the TEAM, the Test that Evaluates your Aptitude for Marriage. The two of you should take the TEAM individually without sharing or discussing the questions. Then compare answers.

1 When you moved into your current house or apartment, who did most of the relocating and decorating work?
   a. He did.
   b. She did.
   c. We both did an equal amount.

2 Of the two of you, who has the better eye for decorating and furnishing?
   a. He does.
   b. She does.
   c. We're equal.

3 Think about personal space, blankets, and other things you share. Which of you is the giver and which is the taker?
   a. He's the giver, she's the taker.
   b. She's the giver, he's the taker.
   c. There is no give and take.

4 Who spends more time in the bathroom?
   a. He does.
   b. She does.
   c. It's equal.

5 Who does more cleaning?
   a. He does.
   b. She does.
   c. It's a completely cooperative venture.

6 Read this one carefully. Who uses the TV remote control most *responsibly*?
  a. He does.
  b. She does.
  c. There's no clicker abuse in this house.

7 Which of you is the better cook?
  a. He is.
  b. She is.
  c. We order in.

8 If you decided to get a pet (regardless of allergies), it would be a:
  a. dog
  b. cat
  c. other

9 When the phone rings:
  a. He picks it up.
  b. She picks it up.
  c. The machine picks it up.

10 Who gets stuck with the worst part of laundry duty?
  a. He does.
  b. She does.
  c. We share each other's pain.

The TEAM is scored sort of like *The Newlywed Game*—you get the most points when the two of you mark the same answer. For each question, if you both marked C, give yourselves one point. If you both marked A or you both marked B, give yourselves two points. If you marked different answers, you get zero points. Your TEAM score is evaluated as follows:

0–4   You're having trouble agreeing on your respective household roles. This may cause aggravation as you struggle to get things done. Take some time to discuss each question you answered differently, and ask questions to find out how you feel about the stupid things: bathrooms, laundry, TV. Then try to establish day-to-day roles that satisfy you both.

5–8   Sometimes you work together like a finely tuned machine, other times you clank and rattle like a busted air conditioner. This test should help you locate your problem areas so you can talk about them reasonably before you both overheat and combust.

9–16   You're pretty well in sync. Of course, occasional disagreements arise over the odd household chore, but overall, you have a fair understanding of each other's roles.

17–20   Nice going. Not only do you understand each other's roles, you accept them as fact, which indicates that you're exceedingly happy with the environment you've created together.

Incidentally, if you got a perfect 10 by agreeing on every C question, you're probably just sucking up to each other. That's okay for the first year of marriage, but sooner or later you're going to have to admit that one of you cleans the toilet all the time and isn't happy about it.

FAMILY AND FRIENDS

Your Family—His

*I*n their first year of marriage, many newlyweds go through a period of postwedding stress. A major contribution to this phenomenon is the difficulty couples can have assimilating themselves into each other's immediate families. For your wife, that stress can be significantly reduced if she gains a basic understanding of how your family relates to her and to the two of you as a couple.

Dad is usually just happy you found a woman who can tolerate you. If she floats your boat, she's okay with him. Your brothers and sisters have their own lives to lead, and while you would prefer that they love your wife as much as you do, the world isn't going to end if they don't. Either your siblings will be good friends with your wife, or they'll become "event friends," hanging out at family get-togethers and not really speaking in between. While every family is different, your wife will usually find it relatively easy to please your brother, sister, and father in most social situations.

Mom is another matter altogether. She could probably count on one hand the women who are good enough for you: the Virgin Mary, Joan of Arc, June Cleaver—that's about it. Unfortunately, all your life, you've been thinking more along the lines of Drew Barrymore, Courtney Cox, and Madonna. In time, your mother will come to love your spouse. But for now, your new wife is the enemy.

Let's look at some of the ways in which this phenomenon manifests itself. Your mother's strategy upon meeting your wife will be to kill her with kindness, then aim the brunt of her motherly angst at you. You probably sensed this before the wedding when Mom complained to you about your wife-to-be's choice of caterer or floral arrangements, mistaking you for someone who cared about such things. And of course, with each comment came the suffix, "Not that it's any of my business."

Well, that's just the point. For many years, caring for you *was* your mother's main business. When you scraped your knee, you went to her. When you were hungry, you went to her. And when Tracy and Tina and Amy and Jenny jerked you around in high school, Mom was always there to support your belief that girls are, in fact, jerks. Now you've married one of them, and your mother realizes she's been replaced as primo female in your life. That's a big demotion. The fact that you're not depending on her to worry about you anymore doesn't mean she's stopped worrying.

That's why she'll make a big show of cooking your favorite meal whenever you visit. It's as if she's saying, "I can't be there to make sure you're eating well, but at least I can show your wife how to feed you." All those clothes she'll give you for Christmas? Not so much a dig at your wife—as if she were incapable of dressing you—but more likely your mother's way of saying, "I'll do what I can to show him I still care about keeping him warm, dry, and safe."

Your mother's motives are really quite noble. When she appears to be picking at your wife, she may just be trying to instruct her. After all, most mothers have years of invaluable experience as wives themselves. When you and your wife have a disagreement, your mother will likely take your side. Not necessarily because she thinks your wife is wrong, but because she wants her son to be right. And when she points out your wife's shortcomings, she's probably just trying to say that she wants nothing but the best for you.

Understandably, this kind of treatment can be hard on your wife, but the last thing you want to do is completely avoid parental interaction. Family visits are an essential and rewarding part of a healthy adult life. They reinforce your sense of home, history, and worth, and like a light snowfall that accumulates over time, visits build essential memories and contribute to an overall feeling of happiness. So it's to your benefit as a couple if you work on ways to manage the stress when mother and spouse come together.

One couple we spoke with uses a simple Change the Subject approach. Whenever Joe's mother wonders out loud how his wife could let him out of the house with holes in his socks, he simply turns the conversation toward the weather—a topic no self-respecting, Weather Channel–watching parent can refuse to discuss.

Another couple employs the classic Butt-Kisser, a hybrid of the approach detailed in the "Yes, Dear" chapter. In this mode, a typical response to a motherly put-down might be "You know, you're absolutely right. I must remember to work on that. Can you give me some pointers?" Effective, though personally unsatisfying.

If all you want to do is get away from the wilting gamma rays of criticism, and you have a younger brother, try Redirection. Just mention something he did wrong, and watch Mom lay into him. You won't gain any friends in the sibling department, but hey, this is a battle zone. Many couples simply put up with the pain until the younger brother gets married himself. This is called *Natural* Redirection, and it's a beautiful thing.

More and more wives are using the Independent Young Woman approach. Here, your wife gets Mom to identify with her by simply being her normal headstrong and opinionated self. This often results in a sort of grudging mutual respect between mother and daughter-in-law, eliciting comments from Mom like "She's not doing it the way I would, but you know how these independent young women are." If your mother can't tell you how to take care of yourself, at least you've got a strong woman who can. God forbid you actually think for yourself. That's how men end up with nasty head colds.

It's difficult to imagine it now, while your wife is just beginning to mess up the physics of your nuclear family, but in ten years nobody, not even your mother, will remember what the family was like before your wife was a part of it. As time goes by, any petty differences and jealousies that naturally occur during any major change will smooth themselves out, and your mother will come to see your wife as a true daughter. (Hint: The process is quicker if you start popping out grandkids.)

Your Family—Hers

In choosing our life-mates, it is said, we look for our fathers and marry our mothers. No wonder your mother likes your husband so much—he's just like her! Your father, on the other hand . . . well, how much does he love having a male version of his wife competing for the remote?

Let's examine the couple's relationship with both your mother and your father, starting with Mom. Many women truly feel that their mothers prefer their husband's company to that of their own flesh-and-blood. Your mother has waited a good long time to see you married off, and she'll go to great lengths to ensure that you stay that way. She may take your husband's side in arguments, lavish birthday presents upon him, and try to force-feed him until he explodes. She'll spend half your phone conversations making sure you're taking care of him properly, which is particularly annoying since you're getting the same treatment from your mother-in-law.

So how do you keep your own mom on your side where she belongs? Reverse psychology is the key. Make sure she knows how well you're treating her new son-in-law. Call her for advice on something ridiculous that you'd never do in a million years, like starching his socks. You can regain some maternal sympathy by telling her how well you cared for your husband the last time he was sick. Throw in the part about how he sat on the couch whining for three straight days about his sore throat while you selflessly served him soup, warmed him with hot chocolate, and pumped him full of Sucrets. But be warned: When you characterize your husband as a big baby, your mother is likely to say something like "All men are babies, dear. That's why we love them." Not the most satisfying comment when you're seeking a little empathy.

Want someone real to talk to about your husband *and* your mother? Try Dad. He'll tell you exactly what he thinks about both of them. After all, your father may not be a psychological wizard, but he does know two things: the mind of a young man and the mind of your mother. While your husband and your mother are off in the other room watching *Casablanca,* turn to good old Dad for solace.

Having said that, you'll want to keep an eagle eye on the relationship developing between your husband and your father. At first, like dominant males in the wild, they'll do a lot of posturing around each other. Your dad has been your protector since the day you were born, and it's not easy for him to give that up just because some young guy scrounged up enough money to give you a wedding ring. It takes years for most fathers to develop true respect for a son-in-law. But eventually, the two of them will discover they have something in common—golf, hunting, aviation history, the art of cooking meat—and then settle into a relationship of mutual tolerance. Respect will follow; just be patient.

Brothers and sisters are always interesting. Their interaction with your husband produces too many personality combinations to name, but a few of the most popular are: the unmarried older sister whose jealousy spurs a love/hate relationship with your husband, the angry musician brother who thinks your husband's a dork, the younger brother who loves it when your husband swings him around by one arm, the younger sister who writes your husband love notes, the football player brother who tells your husband about his one-time vow to beat to a pulp any boyfriend who mistreated you, and the baby sister who flings mashed potatoes at your husband every Thanksgiving.

The reason family visits are so fascinating, and exhausting, is that all of your relatives' various behaviors come into play. What seems like an innocent celebration of Uncle Lou's birthday quickly transforms into a domestic soap opera. There's Mom, teaching you the finer points of cupcake decoration. And Dad, telling your husband how he survived for six days on his belly in a Vietnam swamp eating nothing but palm fronds and grubs. Turn around, and there's your husband tolerantly carrying on his back six of his new nieces and nephews. It appears they think he's a camel.

In the kitchen, your big sister tells you your husband just insulted her: "Is green *really* your color?" he benightedly asked. At dinner, your father tells everyone what's wrong with this country—that too many people do whatever it is your husband does for a living. Your mother defends your husband, which pisses off your dad; your sister's so mad at your husband, she can't eat; and your eldest nephew, for no clear reason, is viciously kicking you under the table.

Everyone's exhausted, and after what feels like two hours of good-byes, you and your husband make it out the door. But not before Mom gets in a parting shot: "Think maybe you could come see us more than once every four months?"

Keep in mind that, to you, this is just the normal insanity you grew up with. To your husband, however, these family visits are a bit of a challenge. Let him know you understand what he's going through. After all, you experience the same thing every time you visit his family. If he balks entirely at the familial visits, there are a few techniques that may help.

First, don't spring the visit on him. Give him a few weeks' warning, and he may warm up to the idea. Second, set parameters. If you're going for an entire weekend, allow time for the two of you to get away together, and make sure your parents know, for example, that Saturday night you're going to the movies—alone. If you're just going to your parents' home for dinner, let your husband know there's light at the end of the tunnel by saying up front, "We'll get there at six and leave no later than nine P.M." Third, be partners, not adversaries. Let him know that these visits are tough on you, too, and his presence is very much needed.

We've found that, in order to survive each other's families, many successful couples also make deals. One couple allows each partner to skip one family event per year, sort of a sanity exemption. Another couple faces each family as a team, leaving each other's side for only ten minutes at a time at the most. That way, they face any incoming family pressure together and present the very picture of blissful solidarity.

One couple simply told each of their families that they don't travel during the holidays. They said they would rather spend that time carving out their own family niche, at first just the two of them, then with the children that followed. Since they laid down this law in their first year of marriage, their parents got over it very quickly. As a result, they've never had a bad holiday. (See the "Holidays" chapter for more tips.)

As time goes on, you'll develop your own strategies for surviving your family. The experience, believe it or not, can and will make you a stronger couple.

The In-laws—His

Are the stereotypes true? Is the terrifying mother-in-law image we grew up with from *The Flintstones* and *Bewitched* reruns really what the average couple experiences? Is every mother-in-law a rolling-pin-wielding, giant-suitcase-carrying, loud-mouthed husband-hater?

The couples we polled for this book said no. Typically, the men said they get along with their mothers-in-law (though some felt Mom tends to overstay her welcome when she visits). The tricky relationship, according to these guys, is the father-in-law.

Not that most guys had a problem with their father-in-law. It's just that your wife's dad can be a little cranky now and then. He worked all his life to buy everything his daughter needed. He did whatever was necessary to protect his little girl from all the creeps who wanted to sleep with her. When he finally broke down and decided to trust you, he had to fork over thousands of dollars for the wedding so that you could have legal sex with his daughter. How happy would that make *you*?

Sure, it's easy to make fun of your wife's dad. In fact, it's no great task to make fun of fathers in general. They wear funny shorts. They'd rather put another thousand dollars into their '79 Oldsmobile Custom Cruiser than buy a new car. They think Pat Sajak is a pretty funny guy. But when you take a moment to remember what you've done to your father-in-law's daughter, and to his checkbook, he's kind of got a point about you.

That's why many guys try to buddy up to the old man. For instance, one couple turned a potentially scary in-law encounter into a lasting positive relationship. When this particular prospective groom first met his future father-in-law, the man was in his living room cleaning his gun collection. Intimidation tactic? Maybe. But the enterprising young fellow immediately suggested a target shooting expedition, a bonding experience so successful that the two men began to schedule regular hunting weekends. By the time marriage came up, they were old buddies, which just goes to show that first impressions don't mean a whole lot.

Chances are, if you're reasonably successful at your job or at least demonstrate that you're willing to work for a living, your father-in-law will give you his stamp of approval. Also, remember that your wife has complete control over her father. If she convinces him you're capable of making her happy for the rest of her life, he'll give you the thumbs-up.

But even after your marriage receives the parental okay, visiting will always be an adventure. Every time you venture into your in-laws' house, you get that stranger-in-a-strange-land feeling, made even more disorienting by the fact that these people now want you to call them Mom and Dad. It's the same feeling you used to get as a kid when you spent the night at your best friend's house—strange smells, strange food, strange bed—only now it's where your second mom and dad live, and that means you're supposed to treat it like a second home.

I wish I could promise you'll get used to visiting your wife's parents, but a little part of you will always feel a bit out of place. That's okay, you can rest easy knowing that, whenever your in-laws come to visit you, you have every right to ask them to sleep in separate beds. Your house, your rules.

On a more serious note, no matter how hard they try, some people never do find a way to get along with their in-laws. Or, citing irreconcilable differences over religion, politics, or just plain personality, you or your wife may choose to never associate with certain family members, or entire families, again. This is an extremely difficult decision, especially if the conflict involves a parent.

There are no quick and easy solutions, but there is one point of view that may help you or your wife get your priorities straight. You did not choose your family, but you most likely *did* choose your spouse. You're planning to live with that person until death do you part. And the decisions

---

SEVEN SURVIVAL TIPS FOR VISITING THE IN-LAWS

1 Know your football. Your father-in-law isn't interested in any pansy who doesn't understand the basics of gridiron play.

2 Eat what's in front of you. Unless you want to insult your mother-in-law and cause a major interfamily incident.

3 Always ask for seconds. See above.

4 Compliment your mother-in-law's dress. Scores major points.

5 Exercise sexual restraint. Your father-in-law doesn't give a tin poop if you're married, you're not doing anything to his daughter in his house.

6 No complaints. Your father-in-law walked four miles to school every day naked with razor blades for shoes in twenty-eight feet of snow. So quit your whining.

7 Wash the dishes. While your father-in-law may assume elves do it, your mother-in-law will never forget what a courteous young man you are.

that affect you are yours to make, not your family's. So whatever you decide to do, keep your personal happiness and the success of your marriage firmly in mind, and you'll find a way past any family problem, large or small.

In-Laws—Hers

Any woman who has survived her first year of marriage will tell you the brutal truth. Minor husbandly irritations aside, it's all about Sucking Up to the In-Laws.

In reality, in-laws are never as bad as cliché makes them out to be (though our surveys for this book brought in some truly horrific mother-in-law stories). Your husband's family members are probably great people, just like the members of your own family. And it's likely that you're pretty comfortable with them by now—even close—particularly if you and your husband dated for a long time before your marriage.

Still, when you visit someone else's folks, it's a little like entering a foreign country. Your husband's family has its own language, history, and sacred traditions, all of which are completely alien to you. Over the course of the next twelve months, you're going to have to put together your own Fodor's guide to navigating In-Law Land. In some foreign countries, it's considered incredibly rude to blow your nose in public: similarly, you'll need to uncover your in-laws' behavioral tics. With tact and finesse, your job is to get a fix on the interpersonal dynamics in In-Law Land so that you can insinuate yourself among the natives with minimal disturbance to the peace.

Warning: Don't trust your translator. Your husband was born and raised in In-Law Land. Though he means well, his perspective is unreliable at best and biased at worst. When his dad sits down at the piano and starts belting off-key show tunes, your husband is allowed to act like it's hurting his ears, but you are not. Your husband will tell you that you are, and that it's a running joke in the family, but until you're firmly entrenched in the family culture, you should instead refrain from criticizing any creative endeavors pursued by in-laws.

Once you've gotten a thorough understanding of In-Law Land and can pass for a native there, your task is to actually enjoy being a part of it. This is harder than it sounds. You're going to have to develop a strategy, not only for coping with, but for *relating to* every member of your new husband's family. Starting with the toughest nut to crack, let's explore Sucking Up techniques that will create the emotional bonds you need with each and every in-law. (Note: Since I have in-laws of my own, it should be clearly understood that I use the phrase "Sucking Up" in a strictly light-hearted manner. The techniques themselves are genuinely intended to strengthen one's interfamilial relationships.)

Your Mother-in-Law.   Also known as the Mistress of Metaphor. Whatever she says, there's another layer of meaning beneath it. What she comments: *"I thought maybe you and I could go to the mall later. Maybe we could pick out a nice embroidery project so I could give it to you for Christmas."* What she means: *"I want a grandchild, please. My schedule will allow me to be crocheting baby booties by December."*

How to cope? Kill her with attention. Go to the mall together. Call her for advice on cooking a turkey. If she's standoffish, approach her on common ground: Engage her in conversations about your husband's childhood. Ask her to show you old family pictures. Tip: Always speak positively about your husband to her. Even if it seems she's initiated some lighthearted ribbing at his expense, beware of joining in, and if you do, make sure to stay in the good-natured zone. Nothing will chill the in-law air more quickly than an impassioned outburst on your part about how he leaves dirty pots on the stove for days.

Your goal: Get to know her. Really. Underneath all the double meanings, there's someone there who's just as great as your own mom.

Your Father-in-Law.   Also known as The Man in Charge. Possibly the easiest in-law relationship. The two of you pose absolutely no threat to each other and, in fact, are likely to provide mutual refuge from your mother-in-law. How to bond: Let him do nice things for you even if it goes against your self-sufficient grain. You may be perfectly capable of carrying that heavy suitcase upstairs, but you'll score points by letting The Man in Charge take care of it.

Your Brother-in-Law.   Whether it's an older or younger brother, you may run into bonding resistance if he's not used to seeing your husband a happily committed man. How to cope: Most brothers relate to each other like good friends, so read the "Friends" chapter for survival techniques.

Your Sister-in-Law. She's seen all his previous girlfriends, and you may not be her favorite, but you are here to stay. This relationship may resemble your relationship with your own sister(s)—it can be really close, or fraught with tension and competition, or both at the same time. How to cope: This is largely a matter of chemistry. If the chemistry is good, terrific; if it's bad, there's not a lot you can do. Try to find common ground on which to approach a sister-in-law. With a mother-in-law you can always talk about your husband, but chances are your sister-in-law will be more interested in things like shopping, cooking, books, careers, or kids.

Nephews and Nieces. They want to play with you, and they want to play NOW! Be warned: As a new addition to the tribe, you'll likely be overwhelmed by demands for entertainment from the youngsters. More important, your in-laws will begin judging your mothering potential by how you interact with the small fry. How to cope: The more attention you pay, the better. Use playtime with these kids to determine when and if you want your own.

Assorted Wives and Husbands of Siblings. Your knights in shining armor. They know exactly what you're going through; they've been through it themselves with your husband's family and will probably welcome you with open arms. How to bond: As the newest addition to the family, you're low-in-law-on-the-totem–pole. Respect the superior position of the other husbands and wives. Use them like libraries: They possess a wealth of in-law experience and will be more than happy to share coping secrets with an ally.

The more you perfect the art of Sucking Up, the more you'll develop a real affinity for your new family. Someday you'll realize you're actually looking forward to your husband's annual family reunion. In-law love sneaks up on you that way.

Holidays—His

Remember when you used to enjoy Thanksgiving? You could smell the turkey basting all day. Catch back-to-back-to-back football games. Help Mom by sliding that tube of cranberry sauce out of the can. Watch eagerly as Dad sliced up the turkey with the old electric carver.

Well, forget it. Never again will Thanksgiving be a day of relaxation. You've got three families now—the one you had, the one you married into, and the one that consists of you and your wife—and that means that every fourth Thursday in November will be Eating and Driving Day.

From now on, you'll wake up Thanksgiving morning, eat, then drive to Parent A, eat, then drive to Parent B, eat, then drive home and pass out. Heaven help you if either of your parents is divorced and remarried, a situation that adds to the mix Parent C and possibly even Parents D and E. If you have brothers and sisters who have families of their own, you might as well check into the asylum now.

The point is, everybody wants to see everybody during the holidays, which would be much easier if the holidays lasted more than one day. If you're Jewish, you're in luck. Both Hanukkah and Passover allow you to spread the pain over several evenings. But everyone who tries to celebrate Christmas with both families on the same day will find afterward that they need a holiday from the holiday.

It's not that these occasions aren't still fun. There are presents and free food, and your brother can still make your sister snort milk out of her nose. It's just that the logistics now seem . . . well, a little bit like work, especially when you're at your in-laws'.

Spending part of a holiday such as Christmas at the home of your wife's parents may at first feel a little awkward. But don't let her family's tradition of square dancing after the meal throw you. Sure, it's different, and maybe a little weird. But she's thinking the same thing at your parents' house after ten straight hours of opening presents and passing around every sock, game, and cookie tin for each person in the room to inspect. You'll get used to it, and you may even eventually enjoy it, as long as you and your wife stick together and help each other through the rough areas.

Over time, you'll find that taking turns is a good solution to holiday overload. If you spend Thanksgiving at your wife's parents' home, work it out so you spend Christmas at yours. To keep it fair, switch off the following year. Or, if you live near both sets of parents and they (or you) insist on a visit each and every holiday, spend the night before at hers and the day itself at yours. Christmas has an eve, so why can't Thanksgiving?

About mothers. Holidays aren't what they used to be for them either, for the simple reason that you're not always there. Mothers may therefore act a little crazy when you do visit, as their emotions may be close to the surface. Here are a few basic rules for keeping Mom happy during homecomings.

1. Stay out of the kitchen—that's her territory, and you don't belong there unless there are dishes to be washed.

2. Hug her a lot—she needs to know she's still your mom. That Oedipal stuff pops up big-time on holidays.

3. Take out the trash—it shows you retained the courtesy and manners she taught you.

4. Have a date in your mind to visit again—she can put it on her calendar, and that makes mothers happy.

5. Tell her she's a great cook—she fed you from birth on, and the least you can do is thank her for it. Sure, you left for another woman, but let her know you'll always return for her stuffing.

Other than that, stay away when she's holding sharp things, and you'll make it through every holiday with Mom, wife, family, and your own mental health intact.

Holidays—Hers

Your husband has no clue how tough the holidays are. By this I mean that a lot goes on he doesn't know about, because he's never really needed to know.

For example, the Christmas season. Even if your mate says he's got the gifts for his side of the family covered, you still have to worry about them. Now that you're officially his wife, his family thinks you're the official gift-buyer. They'll sneak up to you and make suggestions, which you somehow have to implement. And they'll make comments on past gift choices he made before you were even in the picture, comments that you have to keep entirely to yourself.

Your wifely abilities will be evaluated. Holidays showcase a woman's cooking, cleaning, and child-relationship skills. No matter how lovely his family is, they will have certain expectations in these departments—which you cannot ask your husband to translate for you.

He'll tell you his mother said it's not necessary to bring food to Thanksgiving dinner. Translation: It is. The only question is whether she wants you to bring dessert or a side dish. You may be a successful career woman, but your culinary offering will be judged in relation to his family's traditional dishes—and it will pale in comparison. If he tells you his mother is adamantly opposed to Mother's Day gifts, you must come out with a "Yes, dear" or a "Sure" and arrive at her house laden with flowers—one of several ways mothers-in-law can be made into allies.

Holidays also throw reproductive issues into stark relief. You're not sure when or if you're having kids? Be prepared for a barrage of innuendo and oh-so-subtle hints, like "Look at those little devils tear into their gifts. I expect you'll be getting more presents than usual this time next year!"

Also, as the most recent woman to join the family, you'll be expected to help with all the clean-up duties, even though you'll be told outright to sit back and relax. Don't look to your husband for help here either. Sitting back and relaxing is his middle name. When in doubt, rush to assist. It will take years before you truly understand the culture and dynamics of his family. Aim to please at every opportunity, and you'll eventually get the hang of it.

Holidays spent with your family are infinitely easier—on you. Chances are, your husband will have the same fish-out-of-water feeling you had sitting around the table with his folks, so your job is to ease his way. Don't leave him alone for too long, unless he's really and truly bonded with the members of your family. Present a united front at all times (same goes with his folks). Don't dig at each other, and don't put your relatives in a position of taking sides, ever.

When visiting either of your families for the holidays, remember to be loving and considerate of their feelings. Your mom and dad may still be adjusting to the fact that you're truly "on your own." They may be missing you more than you think. So while it's important for you to see close friends and other relatives while you're in town, make a point of spending plenty of time with the 'rents.

Friends–His

You probably thought you were marrying just one woman. Foolish man! You're marrying an entire entourage, starting with your wife's family, continuing through her pets, and extending to all of her friends. One thing you better get used to is that her best friend knows nearly everything about you, from all your annoying habits to how you were in bed last night. (If that's not an incentive to perfect your technique, I don't know what is.)

If you like your wife's best friend, then you really don't have a problem. If you think she's the wicked witch of the west, the challenges are just beginning. The last thing you want to do is give your wife an ultimatum: you or her friend. Naturally, her friends are important to her, just as yours are to you, and you can't demand she give one up unless you're willing to make the same sacrifice.

So what happens if one of your wife's good friends happens to be—gasp—a man? Or—even bigger gasp—an ex-boyfriend? In our wedding, Wendy invited two men to stand on her side of the party as "bridesmen." What did I do when confronted with this outrage? Nothing, really. I'm fortunate enough to like all of her friends, even

SEVEN SURVIVAL TIPS FOR DEALING WITH THE DIFFICULT WOMAN YOU DIDN'T MARRY

1 Extend an olive branch. Spend time talking with your wife's best friend. Once you get to know her better, you may find out that she's not always the embodiment of pure evil.

2 Buddy up to her boyfriend or husband. Then you can hang out with him while the women do whatever it is they do.

3 Ask your wife not to share intimate secrets with her friend. Unless you tell her exactly what you consider private, your wife may think all information is public domain.

4 Don't set up the friend with one of your buddies, unless you want to see even more of her.

5 Be nice to her. When she calls for your wife, ask her how she is. When she comes over, give her a hug and a kiss. Turn an enemy into a friend by smothering her with kindness.

6 Avoid playing competitive board games with her. Nothing kills an evening faster than arguing over who was the first to scream out "Toenail scissors!" in Pictionary.

7 Ask your wife nicely to reduce her best friend's visiting frequency. If it feels as though this friend is constantly in your home, you have no place to retreat, and that's not fair.

the male ones. My suggestion is that you get to know your wife's guy friends. They're probably great people. And in most cases, there's absolutely no reason you should feel threatened by these relationships. After all, you're the one she married.

Now, if your wife's not crazy about one, some, or all of your friends, think about why that might be so. Do they come over and drink a lot and make you do dumb things? Do they think she did to them what Yoko Ono did to the Beatles? Do they hit on her friends, or worse—and this does happen—do they hit on her? Or are they just loudmouths with wide-ranging definitions of courtesy?

The point is, there must be a reason. Talk to your wife about your friends, and find out what's at the root of her objections. Set ground rules for how your friends should treat your house when they come over. If you both go out with your friends, make sure you do things your wife enjoys. Don't expect her to be excited about season tickets if she hates football.

Most couples find that, during the first year of marriage, the concept of "his" friends and "her" friends evolves. You'll start to spend more time with other couples and less time out with the guys. It makes sense if you think about it. When you were a single guy, you spent more time with other single guys, most likely in the pursuit of single girls. Now that you're married, you relate differently to your single friends.

Your goals have changed, as may your idea of fun. If your single friends are having trouble handling this, don't worry. The day they get married, it will all become clear.

Friends—Hers

Men, like dogs, travel in packs. The alpha dog, or pack leader, is the most single man—the man furthest from commitment. When you and your husband got married, he lost a whole lot of pack status.

So during your first year of marriage, you have your work cut out for you. Your husband will still want to run with his buddies, so you'll be seeing a lot of those old dogs. But you can make your life a lot easier if you get yourself declared an honorary member. This involves feeding your husband's friends and playing with them (no tummy-scratching necessary). Keep their favorite food and drinks around, and you may even get the ultimate compliment: "You're all right. You're just like one of the guys."

Your husband will need your help in adjusting to being a part-time, rather than a full-time, pack member. He's a happily married man, but he'll still have lots of single friends tugging at his sleeve to go do single things. What should you do? Let him go. The more you resist your husband's single activities, the more you'll find yourself falling into the role of a ball and chain. Your husband's single friends will make fun of him, and then he'll try to spend more time with them to reestablish his sense of belonging. Use reverse psychology and encourage him to go out; you'll win the eternal admiration of his buddies, and they may even voluntarily include you in their activities.

If your husband's a good guy (and he is, of course), he'll understand this innate conflict between you—the newcomer—and the established regime. He'll probably even have a sense of humor about it. Chances are, there are guys in his group whom even he doesn't like. Try to find out ahead of time which buddies you can make fun of, and which you can't.

Eventually, however, even if you've done your best, you may find you just can't stand one or two of his friends. Chalk it up to bad chemistry, then find out how good a friend this guy is. Once you determine the extent of your spouse's loyalty, you can judge your actions accordingly. Stay calm if your husband's friend is actually a girl or, worse yet, his ex. This does happen, and if it bothers you, you should check out the "Jealousy" chapter. Actually, this scenario can be sort of fun for you—there are times when two women can gang up on your husband and make good clean sport of him. Be careful not to cross the line, though. He'll laugh as long as you keep the jokes above the belt, but anything else borders on emasculation.

When you plan social activities for you and your husband with other couples, make sure they're fun. Shooting pool might be a better choice than a formal dinner since a little healthy competition tends to accentuate each couple's togetherness. Eventually, you may be able to train your husband to look forward to couples' activities as enthusiastically as he envisions single-guy outings. It's possible, unfortunately, that the couples you hang out with may split into irritating gender factions. This means the guys will look on your foursome as a chance to sit on the porch, howl at the moon, and remove beer caps with their teeth while the womenfolk cook dinner or go shopping or do other "girl" things.

All the women I talked with had the same advice: Fight this like the devil. Get out on that porch and wrap your teeth around some beer caps, or in ten years you'll find yourself clearing mounds of dishes after a dinner party before bringing coffee and dessert to the boys glued to the TV set watching football. Remember that foursomes don't always work. When you decide to do stuff with another couple, consider the friend's spouse. You both have to be able to tolerate both members of the couple if you want things to work out.

While men love to go out and run with the big dogs, women have a harder time separating their mates from relationships with their friends. How do you deal with your personal pack? What if they don't like your spouse? What if he doesn't like them? What if they can't get used to you as part of a couple—or, worse yet, if they start leaving you out of single-girl activities?

First of all, if your friends don't like your husband, they will politely keep their feelings to themselves, if they're good friends. But if you sense in your nearest and dearest pal a deep animosity toward your mate, try to find out if there's a real underlying reason. Does your friend believe you've made a mistake? Why? Is there something you should know that she's trying to spare you? Maybe he just reminds her of the guy in second grade who tickled her till she wet her pants.

If, on the other hand, your husband doesn't like your friends, you're pretty much stuck with it. But if you build him up in your friends' eyes, he may see them reacting more positively toward him, and he may stop running away when they come over. If this doesn't work, then there's no reason you can't remain friends with them; you just won't be able to truly enjoy the company of your friends and your husband at the same time. Your friends might grow on him over time, but you will probably end up shooting yourself in the foot if you try to force both parties to be nice to each other.

If you're on the early end of the marriage curve, it's common for your single friends to have problems dealing with it. Be patient. Include them in your married life: Don't relegate them to bottom dog in the pack. You may have to see them for Saturday lunch instead of Friday night, but when you're with them, be fully present. Leave your husband at home physically and mentally.

Make time to do the things with your friends you used to. Relationship maintenance is as important as keeping up with the yard or making sure the car gets regular tune-ups. Remember that old Girl Scout tune: "Make new friends, but keep the old/One is silver but the other's gold."

Babies—His

Who wants you to have a baby more, your wife or your mother-in-law? I usually give the edge to the mother-in-law, but frankly it's difficult to tell when they gang up on you.

If you've been married for any length of time, you've taken a few hits from this mother/daughter tag-team. Your wife begins the wrestling match with the subtle but effective "I saw the cutest thing at Baby Gap the other day" ear pull. Like lightning, your mother-in-law tags in and applies a "My daughter's not getting any younger" choke hold. She deftly switches to the "I want a ton of grandchildren before I die" full nelson, while your wife lines you up for the dreaded "My mother has promised to stay with us for at least a month after the baby is born" pile driver.

Before you know what's coming, your wife pins you with the highly illegal "I drew up a list of names, what do you think of 'Scarlett' and 'Rhett'?" flying scissor-kick. You retreat, aching and disoriented, to your den, which has been converted from a masculine workplace to a frilly pink and blue nursery, with Barney bellowing "I Love You!" from your stereo and the wallpaper teeming with Smurfs.

If your wife isn't ready to become pregnant yet, her mother will seek another suitable partner with whom she can apply the pressure. *Your* mother is a prime candidate. One phone call between the two is all it takes, and the mothers, itching to be grandmothers, will begin a grueling campaign of hint dropping and heavy sighing designed to eat away at your defenses. Your friends might even get in on the act, especially if you've moved into a place with an extra bedroom. You just got through writing thank-you notes from the wedding/housewarming, and suddenly *everyone* is asking what you're waiting for, parentally speaking.

The strange thing about all this pressure is that, out of all the newly married couples we spoke to, more than 80 percent—both the women and the men—wanted to have a child within five years. Chances are you would love to have a baby with your wife—sooner or later. So why is everybody so eager to send you down the road of fatherhood *right now*?

Could it be that everybody loves other people's babies? Might it not be pleasant to hold babies, rock them, play with them, then hand them back to their parents and go home to your own babyless life? And in the case of mothers, isn't it possible that your relative incompetence in caring for your first child allows them to come to the rescue, bearing all kinds of maternal wisdom? Could this represent one last chance for your mother and mother-in-law to help their kids through another difficult stage of growth?

All of these emotions probably come into play, and the thing to remember is that every one of your friends and every member of your family has the best of intentions when they ask, "So when are you two going to have kids?" Try not to think of their urging as pressure. It's not like they're asking you to get busy right there on the living-room floor. They're just wondering when two of their favorite people are going to produce more people, because that gives everybody something interesting to talk about and a good reason to visit. They'll be perfectly happy whenever you decide to have kids, whether it's in nine months, nine years, or just an unqualified "later." And even if you decide not to have children at all, your family and friends will probably have a bunch of their own to fawn over. Which gives you good reason to visit *them*.

If you were married within the last year, it's a good bet that many of your friends, being of similar ages, are either recently married or soon to be. Things like this seem to happen in waves, and having babies is no exception. One friend breaks the ice, and then WHAM! everybody you know is breeding. While it does take the pressure off you, this influx of new life means added responsibilities for you and your wife.

The day your friend's baby is born, it's time to leap into action. There's a new birthday to be remembered, so write it down on your calendar and make sure you spell the child's name right. This is one of the few times it won't be awkward to ask. There's a visit to be arranged. There's a present to bring or send. There's a new father to congratulate: your job is to pat him on the back and get that glazed look off his face. When visiting new parents, one couple we spoke with always brings—in addition to a baby gift—a six-pack of beer for the shell-shocked father. There are ceremonies to attend such as christenings and brisses, and roles to play—you may be asked to be the child's godfather. There are religious gifts to bring to these occasions as well.

It may seem like dealing with other people's babies is almost as much work as having kids of your own. But in the end, you can still go home and get a good night's sleep. When you do have your own child, you'll find out just how much work it is, but you'll also discover that it's one of the most rewarding things you and your wife will ever do. New parents find joy in the oddest places. If you've ever seen a father beaming with pride when his son leaves a healthy mess in his diapers, you know what I mean.

Babies—Hers

One day, during your first few years of marriage, you'll look around and realize that babies are rolling into your life in astonishing numbers. Your friends and colleagues are having them by the dozen. You wish Hallmark offered congratulations cards in a super economy pack. You've wrapped so many adorable little baby outfits that even the teensy socks don't look so cute anymore.

Everyone your age who hasn't just had a child is either expecting or is trying to get pregnant. And into this miasma of fertility enter the veteran mothers: Yes, your mother and your mother-in-law. When you come over, they've rented *My Cousin Vinny,* and they insist on replaying for your enjoyment the scene where Marisa Tomei complains about the ticking of her biological clock. "See," they say sagely, "this could be you in a few years."

In this vein, Sherri told us about visiting her parents nine months after her wedding. Both her brother and sister had just had babies, and so, Sherri said, "Every time I turned around, there was an infant being plopped down on my lap. They'd study my reactions and whisper among themselves. It was as though they were hoping I'd catch the I-want-a-baby bug just by holding one—like they were drug pushers giving out samples of speed in the hope that I'd become an instant addict."

If you're reading this chapter and you and your husband know you want to have kids right away, we understand that the good far outweighs the bad. Let's say, however, that one of you wants to start a family immediately and the other doesn't. Among the couples we interviewed, it was often the wife who was more eager to have children. If this holds true for you, you can probably talk your husband into sharing your enthusiasm without too much difficulty. His biggest concerns will be "How will we afford it?" and "What will happen to our social lives?" If you make an effort to spend time with friends who have kids but still have social lives, he may see that even if you have to hire a sitter to spend a night on the town, you can still be the same fun people you were prebaby.

If your husband is more ready than you are for children, you can probably talk him into waiting a little while. Most husbands realize that having kids is not just an enormous life-change, it's a tremendous physical and emotional strain, particularly on a woman. So in many cases they will defer to your wishes.

Recognizing this, it's entirely possible that having children may be the furthest thing from your mind during your first year of marriage (and in successive years, too). There are so many things to worry about, as our survey respondents told us:

- Change in the relationship between you and your husband
- Loss of independence
- Loss of identity
- Loss of sexual desire
- Fertility anxiety
- Weight gain and other physical changes
- Cost of raising and educating a child ($211,830 from birth to young adulthood alone)
- Space
- Your parenting ability

With so much to think about, it's no wonder many couples decide to treat their first year of marriage as a time to get to know each other before bringing another life into the equation. You have years and years in front of you, after all, and the most important thing about deciding to have a baby is making sure you're comfortable with all the above issues. No amount of pressure from family or friends should make you rush into the enormous responsibility of parenthood.

If you're having a baby urge, give your emotions a productive outlet by spending quality time with other people's babies. These parents will appreciate the help as much as you'll appreciate the chance to experience motherhood on a temporary basis. Also, use this time to sit down with your husband and draw up a list of how you both feel about certain important child-raising issues. Agree on your future parenting styles: how many hours of television will your child be allowed to watch, and which channels? How permissive or restrictive will you be about keeping junk food in the house? Talk through your respective attitudes toward discipline.

Remember, having a child is the one life commitment you can't undo. Everything else is, to some degree, "returnable." But when it comes to starting a family, it's crucial to balance emotion and reason so that you have a child (a) because that child will be truly wanted and (b) because you're absolutely ready to have it.

The Relationship Sketch-O-Matic Quiz

Here's a little pop psychology drawing exercise to amuse and enlighten you both. Find a piece of 8½" × 11" paper and two pencils, one for you and one for your spouse. As you draw, be sure to finish each image before you move on to the next.

Imagine that the paper is a vast, empty desert.
Draw a palm tree anywhere in your desert.

Then, draw a lake.

Now, draw a bird.

Next, draw a cloud.

Then, draw a ladder.

Finally, pick a number from one to ten, and draw that many coconuts.

Once you've finished, read the following.

The palm tree represents you and how you see yourself in the world. The lake is your parents. The bird is your spouse. The cloud is your in-laws. The ladder represents your friends, and the coconut(s) represent your children. Now examine the relationships among these people as you've drawn them. How close is your spouse to you? Are your in-laws providing nourishing rain or deadly lightning? How far are the coconuts . . . ah, babies, from the tree? How tall and sturdy are your friends? Compare your drawing with that of your spouse, and use them as a starting point for a discussion about the importance of the relationships among you, your family, and your friends.

SEX AND ROMANCE

Sex—Where and When–His

*F*or most couples these days, the wedding night isn't likely to hold many surprises, since living in sin doesn't carry the stigma it did forty years ago. According to a recent study published by the National Opinion Research Center at the University of Chicago, two-thirds of the couples surveyed lived together before marriage. As a result, newlywed couples are often already experts at making love to each other.

Unfortunately, the fact that you're married may take some of the fun out of sex. I mean, even your parents approve of it now. How else are they going to get grandchildren? Even the purpose of birth control has changed. In your single days you used it to prevent a problem. But now, if the diaphragm springs a leak, it's not a disaster, it's an adjustment to your ten-year life-plan.

Remember when you wished for the freedom to have sex whenever and wherever you wanted, without the threat of being interrupted by midnight-snacking parents or grumpy roommates? Remember when you used to dream of making love to a beautiful woman all night, waking up next to her, and starting over again? Well, you woke up next to her this morning, and now you can have sex anytime the mood strikes you. So how come so many of us get married and settle into the same old routine, making love at the same time every time, in the very same bed?

Because the grass is always greener on the other side of the marriage license. Before you were married, it was stability and comfort you craved. Now it's danger and excitement you miss.

The cure for the sexual blahs is simple. Now that you're free to have sex, explore the limits of your freedom.

> **FUN FACTS ABOUT MARRIED SEX**
>
> - Married people age 18–29 have sex twice a week on average. They spend more than twenty hours a week watching TV.
> - Married people age 60–69 have sex less than once a week on average but watch more than twenty-three hours of TV a week.
> - From ages 30 to 49, couples have less sex (1.25–1.5 times per week) and watch less TV (17–18 hours per week).
> - Married people age 18–29 have almost twice as much sex as their unmarried counterparts.

Meet at home for a quickie at lunchtime. Warm up with a long romantic dinner. Wake your wife in the morning by nibbling on her ear. Jump in the shower with her before work.

Every time you make love doesn't have to be an epic masterpiece. For every *Gone With the Wind*, there's a commercial break that's just as pleasurable. Try not to let little things get in the way of your passion. So what if one of you just came back all sweaty from the gym? What's a little morning breath between lifelong partners? Are you really going to get fired if you're a little late for work?

You may also find yourself in the rut of making love in the same place every time. Have you tried every room in your house? How about the backyard? Sure, someone might see you, but that's part of the fun. To help get your creative juices flowing, here are the top-ten out-of-the-ordinary places the men we polled like to make love.

❶ The bathroom of an elegant restaurant (men's or ladies', pick a stall that locks, no McDonald's please)

❷ In your office at work (cubicles make it difficult but not impossible)

❸ On a train, late at night (if you don't think it's romantic, rent *Risky Business*)

❹ Sneak into a swimming pool at night (invigorating, and there's no need to shower afterward)

❺ In the car (like high school, only now you know what you're doing)

❻ Anywhere in the rain (feels like a cocoon of sound and water)

❼ At night on a golf course green (no hole-in-one jokes, please)

❽ On an airplane (the Mile-High Club is looking for new members)

❾ In a movie theater (sit in the back, and watch out for the guys who caught Pee-wee Herman)

❿ On top of a historical landmark (make your mark on Stonehenge; the druids would be proud)

With some thought and an adventurous spirit, it's easy to keep it exciting to make love with your wife. Of course, these suggestions assume that you're both in the mood for love. As a card-carrying red-blooded male, you may be hard-pressed to think of a time when you're *not* in the mood, so the real determining factor is your wife.

What do you do when you want sex and she doesn't? You could beg, but that's never pretty. A far more successful method is to start things slowly by stroking her hair or giving her a back or foot rub. Women generally need more time to become aroused than men, who are often aroused anyway for no good reason at all. Your wife can successfully initiate sex by saying, "You. Naked. On the kitchen counter. Now." You, on the other hand, cannot. Give your wife the time and attention she needs and you're far more likely to get your way.

Just be sure to put some heart into it, and mix in a few different techniques from time to time. Nothing kills the mood faster than a wife who blows your cover by noting "Oh boy, here comes the obligatory five-minute I-want-to-have-sex back rub!"

Sex—Where and When—Hers

*I*f you're reading this book as a newlywed or prenewlywed, you probably thought you'd skip this chapter altogether. After all, you already know that the answers to the questions "Sex—Where and When?" are "Wherever" and "Whenever."

Those are great answers. Stick to them, and your relationship will be as wonderfully intimate fifty years from now as it is today. As they say, the best sex in the world is married sex. There is nothing like the pleasure of giving yourself over to a person you love and trust completely. But you need to be conscious of the fact that your first year of marriage is still an emotional and physical learning period. It's a time to become comfortable with each other and with your commitment.

And these days, because couples have such busy schedules, sex has a tendency to drift into routine. Your task during this first year is to develop the skills that will allow you to recognize when making love is no longer magical, and to realize that you may be just going through the motions, as nice as those motions are.

If you do discover that you've been settling for the same old song and dance, there's no need to panic. Try these tips to break the routine:

- Location, location, location: You know what it's like in bed, but have you tried the stairs? The roof? The patio you just built together? Under the Christmas tree? A locked bathroom at a party? Extraordinary sex can happen anywhere. A suggestion from one of our survey participants: If you're going to do it outside, make sure there are no policemen around.

- Timing is everything: Many couples tend to limit their sex lives to the period between getting into bed at night and falling asleep. But men are actually at their mental and physical peaks first thing in the morning. Why wait all day for the watered-down version?

- Rent a sexy movie: Lots of the couples we interviewed got a kick out of making life imitate art.

- Don't go all the way: Touching doesn't have to be a prelude to intercourse. And making love doesn't have to end the same way every time. In your single days, you probably had a whole repertoire of exciting alternatives. Dust them off and use them.

- Break your record: Stay in bed one weekend morning. Pick a day that's rainy so you won't be in any hurry to go out. Forget your appointments, forget your friends, and if you get hungry, incorporate food into your lovemaking.

- Communicate: If sex has become routine, ask your husband if he feels that way, too. Sometimes men aren't even aware they've slipped into a predictable pattern. To them, even the most common sex is still pretty darn great. Tell your husband what you want and what you don't.

- Make sexy kissing a regular part of every day. Not pecks hello and good-bye. Real kisses.

- Experiment: This means toys. Trick handcuffs aren't just for Halloween. Tie your husband up and tickle him. (They hate that, but you can do something to make up for it.)

- Don't let him finish a phone call: While he's jabbering away to a baseball buddy, make it impossible for him to remember Willie Mays's batting average in 1958.

- Go freestyle: We may never know why, but telling your man you've forgotten to wear underwear provokes dramatic results. Go figure.

- Spend time by yourself. Do something to feel good, inside or out. Spend a night on the town with a bunch of friends; flirt, have some wine. Go to the gym, then get a great haircut and have your toenails painted fuchsia. Your husband will reap the benefits of your boosted self-confidence.

Several more first-year issues came up in our surveys. Believe it or not, there are times when you may want sex and your husband doesn't. If he's tired or worried about work or if he feels pressured for emotional closeness, making love may be the last thing on his mind. Don't take it personally. Leave him alone and find something else to do. Of course, the opposite situation occurs as well. According to a DuPont Comforel Pillow Poll, 50 percent of the men surveyed said that having sex was their favorite thing to do in bed, other than sleep. Just 20 percent of the women agreed. Most said they preferred reading.

Marriage is a time when many couples reevaluate their method of birth control (or start using one). It may be time to switch to a more permanent method—like the pill or Norplant inserts—or to one that's more easily reversible—like condoms or a diaphragm—if you're planning to start a family sometime soon.

Finally, there's the afterglow issue. The stereotype is that women want to spend more time cuddling after sex, men less. But it's been hypothesized that the problem has less to do with a man's reluctance to hug and more to do with fear. For all some men know, "afterglow" means holding you until sunrise with the arm they've placed under you turning blue from blood loss; constantly wondering if it's okay to fall asleep or if you're waiting to pounce on them for their insensitivity. You can spare your husband some anxiety by telling him specifically what you expect. Make a deal: After he holds you for five minutes, you can both drift off to sleep.

Keep these suggestions in mind, and your sex life can always seem as fresh and new as your marriage is now. They say there's nothing sexier than being naked except for your wedding ring. With a little effort, that will be equally true on all your anniversaries to come.

Romance—His

If your high school English teacher never forced you to read Jane Austen's *Pride and Prejudice,* allow me to summarize the plot: Middle-class girl meets upper-class guy, he's rude to her at first, then he falls in love.

This love eats him up until he can't stand it anymore so, ignoring the fact that she's way below him in status, he asks the girl to marry him, to which she says no because . . . well, he's rude. He waits and waits and waits, until she realizes, after she sees his gazillion-dollar estate, that he's not that rude after all. He does some gallant things for her family, and 612 pages later, he asks her to marry him again, at which point she finally says yes. Then they kiss for the first and only time in the whole book.

I say the moral of this story is that a gazillion dollars can make any doofus look like Sir Walter Raleigh. My wife informs me that the book's lead male character, Mr. Darcy, is one of the most romantic fictional men ever created. His undying love transcends adversity and societal barriers, and he eventually overcomes his arrogant pride, making him the very definition of a gentleman.

Okay, I think most men can see why a woman would be enamored with someone who professes his love and then spends a very long novel proving it with little or no encouragement. And just because the author of this book was a woman doesn't mean that men like Darcy are purely products of the female imagination. Shakespeare created some equally romantic characters, one of whom, a lad by the name of Romeo, took his own life when he learned of the death of his beloved Juliet. Of course Romeo was only about fourteen. And *Pride and Prejudice* ends right after the wedding, so we're left to wonder if Darcy remains quite so romantic in Austen's unwritten sequel, *Marriage and Maternity.*

My point is, the typical woman possesses a certain image of a romantic man. And then there's her husband. Over the course of a year of marriage, these two images will likely grow farther apart. Since you are now playing the role of husband, it's important for you to understand your wife's need to keep Darcy alive in some way. In other words, if you don't find tangible ways to spontaneously demonstrate your earth-shattering love, your wife may become quite unhappy.

How common is this problem? Look at the covers of the major women's magazines. You'll see headlines like "How to Make Your Man More Romantic," and "10 Easy Ways to a More Loving Marriage." Unfortunately, since these magazines are almost exclusively purchased by women, more often than not they're preaching to the converted.

You may jump to the conclusion that magazine pieces like these are written for desperate women, women who weren't lucky enough to marry men as thoughtful and sensitive as you. Here's a news flash: Those articles were written for your wife, and for all the wives of all your friends. They reappear month after month because every woman feels she could use a bit more romance in her life, and every man has at least a little trouble delivering it.

So let's assume you want to make your wife extremely happy by upping the level of romance in your marriage. Where does a man turn for romantic ideas? Easy. Put down this book and turn to your wife. Not only has she read all of those articles in the grocery-store checkout line, she's the only one who knows what her personal vision of romance is. She'll tell you exactly what you can do to be more romantic, from little things like lighting a candle when you eat meals together to big stuff like sweeping her off to a secluded bed and breakfast next Valentine's Day.

Once she gets rolling, you may be inspired enough to add a few ideas of your own. But be sure to run them by her first. The last thing you want to do is surprise your wife with your idea of a romantic gesture if you're out of practice. Anything that comes off as automatic or obvious (flowers on her birthday springs to mind) can have the opposite effect of what you intended. Any guy who has ever given his wife flowers only to see her burst into tears can sympathize.

If you do decide to venture down the romantic road without your wife's assistance, keep in mind a few basic guidelines.

Be original, because if you've done it before or if one of your friends just did it, your wife will be unimpressed.

Be chivalrous. Holding the car door open for her is always a welcome gesture—even in this age of remote automatic locks and women's rights—as is helping her with her coat and pulling out her chair at a restaurant.

Be courteous. Remembering to call if you're going to be late and brushing your teeth to keep your breath fresh may not seem particularly romantic, but they contribute to your wife's overall impression of you as a considerate, loving man.

Keep track of special occasions. Get up right now and go to your calendar or datebook. Write yourself a note on your wedding anniversary, Valentine's Day, your wife's birthday, and if you're feeling really romantic, the anniversary of the day you first met. Then go back at least a week before each date and write yourself another note to start planning something special for each big day. Then you'll avoid that last-minute call to 1-800 FLOWERS that wins so many of us the Jerk of the Year award.

And finally, *do for your wife whatever creative thing you do best.* If you're a great cook, make her dinner often. If you write poetry, write her as much as you can, and e-mail her a poem at work. If you sing, serenade her; if you play guitar, write her a song. Even if your interests don't tend toward the artistic, any special effort on your part will be appreciated.

Stick to what you know, and use your personal passions to demonstrate your passion for your wife. You may never reach the wuthering romantic heights attained by Darcy or Romeo, but that's okay. All she really wants is a somewhat romantic you.

Romance–Hers

*T*he period before your marriage showcased your new husband at his romantic peak. First, he was courting you. Then he had to propose to you in a way that had never been done before, by anybody, so that the event would pass into the Girlfriends' Oral History of Great Engagement Stories. Next, he spent a year or so lavishing attention on you to keep you sane during the planning of the wedding. Finally, he declared his love for you in public. Now, brace yourself because, in the immortal words of Seals and Crofts, "We may never pass this way again."

In your first year of marriage, the era of Voluntary Romance gives birth to the dawn of Enforced Emoting. Sadly, your husband may have been ripped off at birth in the romance department. Science tells us that estrogen boosts short-term memory. So while you're a walking, talking repository of every detail of your relationship, he's usually hard-pressed to recall what movie the two of you saw last night.

Here's the problem. Our hormones make us four, count 'em four, different sexual personae at different times of the month, ranging from avid to frigid. The male sex drive operates on one constant level: Men are always in pursuit. While women can be completely unpredictable—a seductress one day, an ice cube the next—men generally want sex regularly and assume that everybody else does, too. Since our sexual desire is to a large degree wrapped up in emotions and moods, and since the best way for a man to swing our emotions his way is through the art of romance, how are you both going to get what you want when your husband is romantically inept?

Thank goodness romance can be learned. With a little work, you can rebuild your husband. I'm not saying he'll turn into a giant of spontaneous sentiment, but it *is* possible to train him not to give you socks for your birthday. The secret is to make romance palatable and meaningful rather than a threatening, abstract concept.

In other words, you have to make it seem like a sporting event. If you haven't seen the movie *Bull Durham,* tell your husband it's about baseball and rent it tonight. Both men and women agree that Kevin Costner's character, Crash Davis—aside from being the minor league leader in career home runs—epitomizes romance with class. In the movie, Crash creates the Bull Durham Paradigm that women covet across the country. What does Crash have that you want? He is:

- Spontaneous. He shows up at Annie's door with flowers. And he didn't bring them to apologize, he brought them . . . just because.
- Thoughtful. Even though he takes off in the morning, he leaves Annie breakfast in bed and a note.
- Patient. He's in no hurry for sex. He wants to *make love* to Annie: He'd rather not have sex at all than have bad sex. Tell your husband to pay particular attention to the "long, slow kisses" speech.
- Uninhibited. He dances around Annie's living room in a bathrobe.
- Creative. A bathtub and a zillion candles.
- Strong yet gentle and in touch with the feminine part of his nature. See the toenail-painting scene.

Not only will this movie show your husband what romance is all about, he may be inspired enough to develop his own romantic techniques. Go through the tenets of the Bull Durham Paradigm with him, and tell him to learn it, love it, live it. Before you know what's happening, you'll have a husband who plans things for the two of you, who's sensitive, who's on time, who remembers birthdays and anniversaries and your deepest wishes—you'll basically have Kevin Costner, only with no Oscars and without all that pesky money.

If all else fails and you're still given sports gear for Christmas, try taping helpful hints to your husband's favorite beer mug. And if even that doesn't give you the infusion of romance you crave, supply your husband with the form love letter below. Give him fifty copies and tell him to send you one a week.

Dear [your name here,]

I cannot put into words how much I love loving you. The way you [something you do that's really cute] and your beautiful [the body part

*you're most proud of] are etched in my mind so I can scarcely concentrate
at work. I wish we were together now at [your favorite place] enjoying a
glass of [your favorite drink] and the moonlight over the waters of [there
must be water near you somewhere.] When I see other beautiful women, I
imagine them with your face (so you're pushing it a little, he won't read
down this far anyway), and when I sleep at night, I dream only of you. I'm
counting the minutes until I see you again.*

Love,

[a space for your husband to sign his name.]

*P.S. [A space for your husband to write something truly romantic from his
own mind, should he start to feel guilty about sending you this form letter
all the time.]*

Don't forget, romance is a two-way street. If you find you're taking
your husband for granted and giving him less than his romantic due, surprise him with sweet little gifts like a
book, a CD, or a great bottle of wine.
Send a no-occasion "I love you" card to
his office. Let him know how much you
care about him. Hold his hand: Some
studies show that men crave affection
even more than sex.

Buy him a really expensive present,
like those high-end speakers he's always
wanted, even if you have to save up for
a year or two. No matter how comfortable the two of you are together, don't
go to bed every night in your rattiest
T-shirt with a face full of assorted lo-
tions and creams. Keep all necessary
parts shaved: 75 percent of women age
16–55 say they slack off on shaving in
the winter—and their romantic lives
probably slack off accordingly. Present
your husband with a wife he'll *want* to
feel romantic about, and he will respond in kind.

Warning: By nature, some men are
predisposed to strong emotional behavior
and the expression of sentiment. If you've
married the emotional type, use the Bull
Durham Paradigm sparingly, or you may
push him over the edge. Exercise caution if:

1 Your husband goes through more tissues
than you do at the end of *Steel
Magnolias.*
2 He hugs any member of your family for
more than sixty seconds.
3 He owns a highlighted copy of *The
Bridges of Madison County.*
4 His Christmas gifts to you were better
than yours to him.
5 He makes a toast to love and friendship
at your family's Thanksgiving dinner.
6 In public places, he sings to you loudly in
Italian.
7 He feels you don't cuddle long enough
after sex.

Physical Appearance—His

*I*f love isn't, as the saying goes, blind, it is most certainly nearsighted. Men appear to be the primary beneficiaries of this rule, a theorem in evidence every time a gorgeous female movie star marries someone like Lyle Lovett. He's talented, to be sure, but no Adonis.

There's no need for me to pick on Lyle in particular, because the vast majority of men can be less than easy on the eye. Receding hairlines, copious body hair, and giant Adam's apples don't exactly add up to the stuff of dreams. But in accordance with love being astigmatic, when women search for men to spend the rest of their lives with, they place more importance on personality than on personal appearance. At first glance, physical attractiveness does come into play, but over time, what wins women over is a sense of humor, confidence, talent, or inexhaustible kindness.

Ask your wife if she thought you were gorgeous or handsome when you first met. If she's honest, she may say, "No, but I definitely do now." That's how love is. It's an ocean that slowly erodes people's surfaces and pretenses, until you, an ugly hunk of sandstone, begin to look like Brad Pitt—at least in the eyes of one woman.

We men like to hang out in that ocean, too. But unfortunately for women, we spend more of our time splashing around in the shallows. A woman's physical appearance seems very important, and during the dating process we're most consciously aware of it. Which is how many of us fall in love without knowing exactly why. Here you are, just having fun with a woman you think is attractive, and suddenly you realize you can't live without her. Not because she's beautiful, but because she's smart, funny, interesting, inspirational, or whatever else you're a sucker for. You started out surfing, but now you're in over your head.

By your first year of marriage, love has effectively demoted personal appearance to a secondary spot on your and your wife's list of concerns. While it's perfectly acceptable to take advantage of that security—you'll probably gain a few pounds and shed a few head-hairs; your wife may gain a few pounds and a few gray hairs—you should draw the line somewhere.

I highly recommend that you continue to brush and floss your teeth, for instance. Toenails should remain clipped and the clippings properly disposed of (that is, not on the carpet). Check your back for acne. Yuck.

Shave frequently, or if you have a beard, keep it neat. The basic rule is, wherever hair looks funny, trim it. This means anything growing in your nose and ears, and those strange tufts that sprout on your shoulders and toes. Whatever hair is left on your head needs regular maintenance, too. Don't be afraid to change your hairstyle occasionally. And every once in a while, would it kill you to comb your hair, put on nice clothes and aftershave, and take your wife out to dinner? If you want a marriage that will last forever, now and then you've got to remind your spouse that she married one good-lookin' hunk of man.

This means you'll have to watch your weight, too. Before you began living with your wife, you had to forage for food. You enjoyed a liquid dinner with the guys, and you skipped breakfast in favor of a few extra minutes of sleep. But now that you're married, the refrigerator contains more than beer, bread, and ketchup, and you probably have enough disposable income to buy more than a slice of pizza for dinner. Add to that the fact that your metabolism will change as you grow older, so you'll no longer be able to eat the twenty-taco value meal without noticing it around your waist.

Your exercise habits will probably change as well. You'll play fewer pick-up football games on the weekend, and you'll have less desire to haul out the mountain bike. You worked out regularly before your marriage, and it worked: You got yourself in great shape, and you got a wife. But now a chunk of your motivation is gone. There's no need to go out and toss around the old pigskin when you can lie on the sofa, caressing your college football and watching your alma mater fight the good fight on TV, knowing your devoted wife is securely ensconced in the next room. Just watch for these warning signs, and keep an eye on your weight, or else your wife will be in the next room simply because she can't fit in the same room with you.

It's reasonable to expect that your wife should take care of herself, too. You can reinforce this behavior by telling her frequently that she looks nice. Encourage her when she wears makeup, perfume, or clothes you like, and pay attention when she gets her hair styled. Tell her she looks great when she makes an effort to lose (or gain) weight, and let her know when she wears a particularly flattering outfit. Honest compliments are not only an invaluable tool for keeping your wife happy, they also keep her beautiful in your eyes.

Physical Appearance–Hers

Remember the "freshman 15"—those fifteen pounds everyone said you'd gain in your first year of college? You'd tried so hard to forestall the inevitable results of all that beer and those late-night runs to 7-Eleven by exercising like a madwoman (when the spirit moved you) and substituting Ultra Slimfast shakes for every possible meal. But why was it so important to keep off those pounds? And how important is it now that you're happily married to the man of your dreams?

As single women, we obsess about our weight because, in a society where one-third of the population is clinically obese, we're assaulted by images of featherweight waifs who seem to lack an ounce of body fat—or muscle tissue for that matter. Today's standards of female physical perfection are narrowing while the vast majority of women continue to expand. We have always been afraid of not making the cut.

Now that you're married, though, your weight may not seem as important. You're confident knowing that whatever you look like, your husband will love you. Occasionally, however, men get society's rules mixed up with their own tastes. This may cause your husband to ask, as he stares at a photo of Kate Moss clothed in a scrap of fabric, "Why don't you dress like that?" It's possible he has no concept of the ramifications of this insensitive remark; he's simply lying in bed next to his wife with whom, it is dawning on him, he will be spending the rest of his life. He sees a glamour shot of the latest supermodel and wonders, innocently enough, why the woman next to him doesn't look like the woman shown in the magazine he's holding.

Never mind the hours you spend at the gym or on the treadmill in the living room, trying to make less or more of the body you were born with. Forget the times you suffered watching your husband devour a foot-long cheese steak sandwich while you pushed a spinach salad around your plate. Your spouse wants to know why you don't dress like Kate Moss.

"Because nobody dresses like her" is one of the answers that comes to mind. "That's why she's a supermodel and not your wife, who's lying here next to you." Or you could launch into a full-length tirade. "Why can't you hit a baseball four hundred feet? I'll tell you why. Because twenty guys in the world can do that with any regularity. And they'll be washed up by the time they're forty. That's exactly what's going to happen to Kate Moss. Sometime around the magic four-oh, she'll be in an infomercial at three in morning teaching other women how to be beautiful."

Or perhaps you'd be better served by answering your husband's ill-advised question with a question of your own. Turn to him, smile, and ask, "Honey, do you love me?" He'll answer the only way he possibly can: "Of course I love you, dear." To which you'll say, "Then throw the magazine away, lay your head down on the pillow, and ask yourself, 'Why did I just ask my wife such an unbelievably stupid question?' "

The funny thing is, even if your husband wonders why he's not married to a supermodel, he probably adores your body. Men love the female physique in all shapes and sizes. They're not just being nice when they say, "Of course those jeans don't make you look fat. I don't see the slightest bit of fat on your body!" With weight, as with household dirt and chores, men have a much higher tolerance level. Carrying around an extra five pounds may make you feel less attractive, but your husband probably doesn't even notice it.

Many women spend a lot of time working out, not just to be attractive to men but for their own self-image. In fact, we may actually spend more time exercising after marriage. We have a desperate fear of becoming matronly; we want to retain our desirable single-girl physiques, not to mention our self-esteem. For women, single or married, it can be harder to enjoy physical intimacy if we don't feel good about our bodies. Exercise makes us feel sexier, more alive, more energetic, and not as stressed. Research has shown that people who exercise regularly are less depressed, anxious, and angry—vigorous aerobic movement releases mood-elevating chemicals like serotonin and endorphins into the brain.

Now, if only we could use this scientific evidence to convince our husbands that sixty minutes of exercise each day feels a lot better than channel surfing and snack-food snarfing. As guys settle into marriage, they're capable of letting the pounds creep on, one after the other, with little angst. If the waist on their pants is too tight, they think it's time for new pants. Try to picture your husband not wanting to make love because he "feels too puffy." This obliviousness is good in some ways (there's only so much room in the typical relationship for body-image problems), but not so good in that a few months into your marriage, you may wake up and find yourself laying next to Orca.

It's hard to imagine your husband not being the love of your life—but what if he were to become (gasp) less physically attractive to you? First of all, stop feeling guilty for being "superficial." If your spouse has a bad attitude about his body, it could reflect a lack of respect for himself and for you. Plus, all the chicken wings, pizza, and beer he likes to consume are coagulating in his veins, shortening a life span that's already statistically briefer than yours by about ten years. Ever spent time in a retirement home? The residence lists usually contain the names of four hundred women and two men. If you want to even the odds, you'll need to get your husband off the sofa.

He may resist going to the gym or doing anything that seems like exercise because he's secretly feeling bad about his physical appearance. If you disguise activity as fun, he may not notice what you're doing. Take him Rollerblading. Organize an Ultimate Frisbee match on the weekend, or pull together a tennis doubles team. Encourage your spouse: Instead of saying, "Why don't you get up and do something for a change, you gigantic, *Seinfeld*-watching slug?" tell him how attractive he looks when he's outside being active.

The real kicker is, even if your husband decides not to take care of himself, the society that created Kate Moss will still embrace him. While you spread out, your husband will get more substantial. That's why women run a perpetual race against the ravages of time and gravity, while men just let nature take its course.

I'd like to believe that someday elective plastic surgery will go the way of the Hula Hoop and that men will learn to love natural breasts out of love for the women they are attached to. Of course, part of me also wants to see the tables turned, a world where men are expected to have perfect chests, sculpted arms and abdominals, luxurious hair, strong chins, and adventurous Australian accents. But since most women can't agree on whether all these things combined are sexier than a great personality, I wouldn't count on it.

Jealousy and Flirting—His

Chances are, if you were the flirtatious type before your wedding, you'll go right on flirting for the rest of your life. There's no reason to stop, because there's really nothing wrong with it. Flirting with women doesn't necessarily mean you want to sleep with them. It just means you want them to like you, to be interested in what you have to say, to laugh at your jokes.

Eliciting this positive reaction from members of the opposite sex bolsters the male ego. Unfortunately, most of the time, it has a different effect on your wife.

That's understandable. Out of all the complete jerks out there (think of some of your friends), she managed to find a partner she can be with for the rest of her life. Now he's across the room ogling some stick-thin model wannabe with EEE implants. Your wife's first thought is "My husband thinks she's more attractive than I am." Her second is "I have to get him away from her," which is followed quickly by "I'm going to kill him."

But it never has to get to that point. You can keep jealousy from rearing its ugly head in any situation by doing one simple thing: Flirt with your wife. When you go to a party together, treat your wife like the most important person in the room. That doesn't mean you can't leave her side; go ahead, split up. Mingle. But every fifteen minutes or so, make an effort to see how she's doing. Put your arm around her, touch her hair, support the stories she tells. Then, after you've given her ego a lift, go off and boost your own with Twiggy.

When you're talking to a woman and your wife approaches you, show that you're happy to see her. Put your arm around your spouse. Introduce her to the woman, and shift the conversation to something you can all discuss intelligently. That way you let your wife know that, although you like to talk to other women, she's the one you'll be with forever. Convey this message when you go out, and you won't find yourself fighting on the long drive home.

As for flirting when your wife's not around, go for it. Just remember, you're married and there's no reason to hide it. You're allowed to look nice when you go out with the guys, but only a total Neanderthal would take off his wedding ring. I don't care if you *do* have a rash on that finger. And if you don't want to end up in the doghouse—or even worse, divorce court—keep this in mind: You can talk, you can laugh, you can look, but never, ever touch.

And what if your wife's a flirt? Well, that's probably how she got you in the first place. Still, when she giggles moronically at every word her muscle-laden personal trainer utters, you probably feel like a swift kick in the glutes would do him some good.

Forget it. Go over and introduce yourself, or just take a deep breath and ignore it. Sure, you work hard to pay attention to her in social situations, and it's fair to expect the same in return, but if she'd rather talk to Buff Biff than you at the moment, give her some slack. You know it doesn't mean anything when you talk to some other beautiful woman; show the same confidence in your wife's devotion to you.

Over time, if her flirting becomes a genuine problem, don't embarrass her by making a scene in public. Wait until you get home to talk about it. Working together, you can set some ground rules for flirting that you, your wife, Twiggy, and Biff can all live with.

Jealousy and Flirting—Hers

Now that you're married, you're planning to spend the rest of your life with one man. It doesn't matter if you're 19, 32, or 56, this can be a rough life sentence if you're not allowed a certain amount of harmless flirtation with the opposite sex.

Key word: *harmless*. Harmless to you (don't charm the socks off some bruiser in a pool hall who won't take it so lightly when he notices your wedding ring). Harmless to your husband (flirting to cause jealousy is not a pretty thing, and you really don't want to have to clean him up after you've made him fight for your honor). And harmless to the bruiser in the bar (no one likes to be toyed with).

Personally, I believe that nonserious flirtation—which basically means friendliness with evidence of your married status in full view—is perfectly fine. Flirting makes us feel great and lets us say to ourselves, *"Look what I can still do!"* Our ability to appreciate men other than our husband, and our husband's ability to respect that, is a huge sign of the healthiness of the relationship. Fully trusting that the two of you share a bond unlike any other relationship in your lives will enable you to delight in other people while deepening your appreciation for each other.

If your husband has trouble with your gentle, no-results-intended flirtation, having your own male friends is the perfect way to help him get over it. He'll get used to seeing that you can relate to other men while remaining utterly true to him. Even better, if your guy friend gets along with your husband, then you've got a mutual friend with whom you both can do things individually or together.

That said, flirtation can harm your marriage even if it never crosses the line to cheating. One woman recently wrote in a magazine article about something that happened between her and her male best friend. The two of them were both incurable flirts, and sometimes they'd spend evenings together that involved all the key elements of romance—dinners with wine and deep eye contact, followed by long phone conversations recapping the night's events. "Nothing happened," she wrote, "but I still felt guilty."

She discovered she had been caught up in something that's not uncommon among married people: a mental affair. She and her friend never swapped spit, but their evenings together weren't something she was going to describe to her husband in full detail. The guilt of that secrecy weighed on her mind, and the emotional energy she was putting into the mental affair started to get in the way of her primary relationship—her marriage. So she thought about her options, asked herself some tough questions, and decided the mental affair had to end.

Where do *you* draw the line with flirting? Sometimes it's difficult to tell, but if strong or persistent feelings of guilt are involved, it's probably time to start questioning what you're doing.

Now, what about *his* flirting? Hmm. A relationship is a two-way street, so just as your husband should learn to trust you, you should trust him to understand the parameters of harmless flirting. Most men can appreciate a gorgeous woman walking down the beach without feeling any less devoted to you. It's a little hard to take, but I've been told that men can even fantasize about another woman without (a) wanting to act on the fantasy or (b) feeling any less in love with you. Ouch.

SEVEN SURVIVAL TIPS FOR LIVING WITH A FLIRT

1 Check your husband's shirt collars nightly. No lipstick, no worries.
2 Never send him out to walk the dog alone, especially if you have a cute dog—or worse, a puppy. Women love dogs, and your husband loves women. Enough said.
3 Give him a T-shirt that says, "Friendly but Married."
4 If he goes out, ask him to call in at some point and tell you when he'll be home. It won't prevent him from flirting, but it'll give the woman he's been talking to all night at the bar a chance to get away.
5 Convince him that there's no need to keep wasting money on Rogaine now that he's married.
6 Tell him to eat a lot of garlic because it's good for him. You'll get used to it, but his breath will ward off other women.
7 Learn to trust him. He knows he's married without you reminding him all the time, so let him have fun as long as he lets you do the same.

The Married Sex Quiz

❶ When you arrive home before your spouse, you:
  a. Turn on the TV and take a nap.
  b. Start to cook (or order in) dinner.
  c. Turn on some music and open a bottle of wine.
  d. Strip naked and hide behind the couch.

❷ When your spouse asks if you want to try something a little different to spice up your sex life, you say:
  a. "You mean, like, without clothes?"
  b. "What exactly do you have in mind?"
  c. "Anything you want, baby!"
  d. "Great, I'll invite the neighbors."

❸ You catch your spouse flirting with someone very attractive. So you:
  a. Smash his or her face in the cheese dip.
  b. Leave them alone, you'll catch up later.
  c. Introduce yourself and join in the conversation.
  d. French kiss the next babe that saunters by.

❹ How many times have you made love (presumably with your spouse) in the last month?
  a. Does thinking about it count?
  b. Quite a few times.
  c. Every chance we get.
  d. We're having sex right now.

❺ How many places, other than beds, have you and your spouse made love?
  a. You don't have to do it in bed?
  b. Three or four.
  c. Fifteen or so.
  d. Okay, let's just use the process of elimination.

❻ When is your favorite time to make love?
  a. Just before we go to sleep.
  b. Right when we wake up.

c. We try to mix it up throughout the day.
d. Now.

7 You start to pick up clues that your spouse may have been unfaithful. What do you do?
a. Ignore it, and it'll go away.
b. Try to catch him or her in the act.
c. Approach the issue honestly, and ask your spouse about it.
d. Have him or her neutered or spayed.

8 You're not getting everything you want out of your sex life. How do you plan to make it better?
a. I married this person for who he or she is, why change?
b. Ask your closest friends for advice.
c. Talk to your spouse openly, and tell him or her what you want.
d. Invite the neighbors.

9 What's your idea of a romantic evening?
a. Being together, in front of the TV.
b. Dinner, dancing, expensive wine.
c. Bubble bath for two, strip poker, edible fingerpaint.
d. You, me, naked, now.

10 How would you rate your partner in bed?
a. Exactly what I expect.
b. Very nice, very tender.
c. Perfect, original.
d. Run for your life!

If you answered all A's, you're in serious need of a session with Dr. Ruth. All B's are perfectly reasonable, but it wouldn't kill you to go nuts once in a while. All C's indicate that your married romantic life is extremely healthy and fulfilling, and if you marked all D's, it might be time to cut down on the caffeine.

BELIEFS AND BIG ISSUES

Decision Making—His

Getting married may have been the first big decision you and your wife made together. But it sure won't be the last, and as the two of you begin to work more often as a team, you'll realize that there are four ways a couple makes decisions about anything: (1) You both share the same opinion strongly, and you make decisions based on mutual confidence. (2) Your wife convinces you to see something her way, and you agree to make a decision based on what she wants. (3) You feel strongly about something, and you convince your wife to defer to you in making a decision. (4) You create an integrated decision, with both people contributing what they can.

Healthy marriages display a balance of all these processes, but couples usually find themselves most satisfied with decisions made using Method 4. Think of making an integrated decision as looking through a pair of binoculars. Each eye sees a slightly different image, but when these images are joined together, you not only get a clear view, you get remarkable depth perception, too. When a husband and wife contribute both their individual points of view to the decision-making process, they feel a strong depth of vision. And when they work together to blend those feelings, opinions, and solutions into a decision made by the couple and for the couple, they are typically happier with the results.

Unfortunately, many couples find that one partner falls into the habit of almost always controlling or submitting to the other. Everything from "What do you want to do tonight?" to "Should we buy a house and have a baby?" requires a decision, and the more your answers come out as either "I don't care, what do you think?" or "We're seeing a movie, buying a condo, and having 2.6 kids, and that's final," the more you move away from a partnership and toward a dictatorship.

I'm not saying this is always wrong. As long as there's an intelligent discussion involved that takes both your opinions into account, it's great if one of you gets his or her way. In the end, the important thing isn't who convinced whom, it's the decision itself. That's something to keep in mind during every discussion you have with your wife. Whenever a situation involves one partner who is trying to convince the other partner to change his or her point of view, power is involved. The power of persuasion is very enticing, and so is being right, but if you allow every discussion to drift into a power struggle, you're going to lose sight of the goal—which, if you remember, is to make a decision that will make you *both* happy.

It may seem ridiculous to imagine that a discussion over whether you should get pizza or Chinese takeout could turn into a battle for dominance in your marriage. Yet little power struggles do add up, and the skills to deal with them and keep them in perspective are essential when the stakes are higher. One couple, Joel and Mary, spent the majority of their first year of marriage with real estate agents. Weekend after weekend, they looked at houses without ever seeing one that Joel was completely comfortable with. Finally, Mary found a great house and fell in love with it, but Joel thought it was just okay. He had grown tired of looking; he felt bad about always being the one who said no; and so after a week of Mary's persuasive speeches, he decided he would give her this one. They bought the house.

Unfortunately, two months later Joel saw a beautiful house with a For Sale sign out front. It was well within their price range, and when he took Mary to see it, she thought it was great, too. But they didn't have enough equity to sell the house they had just bought, so they watched helplessly as their dream home was sold to another couple. All because Joel made a decision based on impatience and the false impression that his wife was unhappy with his previous judgments. Mary later told Joel that she didn't mind him being choosy, she just wanted a house in which they could both be happy. If she had known she was persuading Joel to buy a house he really didn't want, she wouldn't have pushed him so hard toward that decision.

Before you make major decisions, regrets can often be averted through a simple discussion of what you and your wife are really feeling. Decisions are never about who wins and who loses when the goal is for both of you to come out on top.

Decision Making—Hers

*L*ike driving, the ability to make decisions is something for which women have gotten a bad rap over the years. "Women just can't make up their minds," it's sometimes said. But we know the truth: Women *can* make up their minds; they *do* make up their minds; and whether they do it quickly or slowly, they make them up well.

Women tend to be more self-analytical than men. I'm generalizing here, but we really do seem to spend more time thinking about who we are and what we want in life. When a choice presents itself, to the untrained eye we may appear indecisive, but scratch the surface of a woman hesitating over a decision, and you'll find a steel-trap mind computing potential permutations and future implications. By the time a woman determines a course of action, she's mentally supported it with a file-cabinet-full of fail-safe reasons.

Odd, isn't it, since men are said to be the rational ones, while women operate on emotional impulses? Most of the couples we surveyed for this book, however, reported the opposite to be true. Newlywed husbands tended to make fast, from-the-gut decisions and then stand by those decisions come hell or high water. For example, Will and Denise had been searching for an apartment for months. They finally found a place they both liked, and Will insisted on putting down a bid "so as not to lose the place" while Denise was still writing a pros/cons list.

Their bid was accepted, and they moved in a few months later to discover they now lived on one of the loudest streets in town. "Noise" with a question mark had been at the top of Denise's "To be researched" list. As time went by, Denise grew more and more aggravated over the racket from the street, not so much because of the decibel level but because she hadn't strongly communicated from the very beginning how much she was bothered by noise. Will and Denise decided to move again two years later, this time with a clearly thought-out list of likes and dislikes and a more patient approach to house-hunting.

As this example illustrates, a couple often learns by trial and error how to make decisions together. Over time, you'll discover how to deal with your partner's techniques of decision making and persuasion and how to most effectively present your point of view. In the past, having and asserting a point of view may not have been high on a wife's list of priorities. Now, most women learn these skills in school and on the job, and they apply them readily to decision making within their marriages. Yet even today, some women have trouble speaking up when a decision involves them, and so they defer to their husbands on certain matters of importance. If you occasionally fall into this category, there are many good ways to hone your decision-making ability and enhance your powers of persuasion.

Take a class. Community colleges offer classes in everything from macramé to tai chi, so I'm sure you can locate a nearby institution that offers a course in the art of negotiation. If not, stay up late one night and sit through a few TV infomercials. Repugnant as they may be, you'll probably be able to order an effective learn-at-home program for the low, low price of $19.95.

Practice decision making in other areas of your life. One of the best ways to prepare yourself for confronting tough decisions at home is to study your technique in a place where there's no question about your ability. For some, it's at work. But it may be somewhere as mundane as the mall. Go to your favorite store, try something on, and make a purchase. Then—here comes the hard part—*don't return it*. Practice making your decisions final, and you'll give more weight to each one you make.

As long as you and your husband stick together, allowing each person to say his or her piece, you'll be able to conquer any decision that stands in your way. But if all else fails, we do have one last resort:

The How to Get Your Way Flow Chart

Ask nicely

↓

Nag

↓

Whine

↓

Throw hissy fit

↓

Beg

↓

Offer sex

↓

Deny sex

↓

Hog bathroom

↓

Take clicker hostage

↓

Cry

Make lists. Whenever you're faced with a decision, find a quiet place and write down the pros and cons involved. Include practical and emotional points on both sides. Then think about the issue from your husband's point of view, and make sure you've considered what the pros and cons might be *for him*. A list like this prevents you from dwelling on only one aspect of a decision, and it lets you see at a glance all the repercussions of that decision. The list functions as an organizing tool; it should not make a decision for you. Even if the pro side clearly has more going for it than the con side, you don't necessarily have to pick that option. Ultimately you will use your head, your heart, and your husband's input to come to a resolution.

Take a course together. Many of the programs we list in the back of this book teach couples valuable techniques for making mutually beneficial decisions. You'll learn that neither one of you necessarily has to compromise to reach a conclusion. When working properly, the most successful decision-making process for couples is *additive:* Both spouses add pieces of the puzzle by expressing opinions or proposing solutions until the decision is made.

Problem Solving—His

Ask a hundred men what their ideal relationship would be like, and you'll hear the same adjectives over and over again. *Easy* is a big favorite. *Comfortable* is another. *Flexible* is in there, too. I've never heard of a man falling in love with a La-Z-Boy Recliner, but all indications point to it being a perfect match.

As a married man, you already know the bad news: In every relationship, there will be problems. The most successful marriages benefit from healthy doses of adjectives like *tolerant, supportive,* and *understanding* long before they get to the easy-chair stage. Don't get me wrong: I'm a firm believer in the possibility of love at first sight, but an instant attraction doesn't mean two people will work smoothly together right from the start.

In fact, according to recent research, married couples who have fewer problems are not necessarily happier than those who have more. Happiness in marriage seems to be related more closely to a couple's ability to successfully *resolve* their problems. In other words, a relationship in which there are several conflicts a day, each one being solved in a mutually satisfying way, may be healthier and happier than a relationship in which there are relatively few sources of conflict, with ineffective approaches being used to resolve them.

Facing relationship problems doesn't come under the heading of Easy for most guys. We are much more likely than our wives to avoid bringing up an issue. Often we know it's there; we feel it coming; but we refuse to quantify it in our minds, preferring instead to linger at work or go out with our friends or turn on the TV—anything to avoid the inevitable difficulties a problem will bring.

Sometimes the problem gets worse, our wives get angrier, and we get more distant. Then we blame our wives for what's about to occur. "I know what's going to happen," you might say to a buddy. "I'm going to go home, and she's going to light into me about the fact that I'm spending too much time with my friends, and that when *I am* home I just turn the TV on and don't say anything. We don't talk enough, blah, blah, blah."

Well of course she's going to say those things, because that's how she sees you reacting to whatever the real problem is. By the time you cut through all the smoke and mirrors you've surrounded the problem with, you'll be too tired to actually solve it. So you go on avoiding it until your wife finally blows up at you, a situation neither of you wanted and that could have been avoided.

A better approach is to not avoid problems in the first place. Ask yourself three questions every night before you go to bed, or every morning in the shower: "What are the major areas of concern in my marriage? Did I say or do anything today or yesterday that might have made my wife unhappy, or vice versa? If we could solve one problem in our relationship today, what would it be and how could we solve it?"

If you have trouble answering any of these questions, ask your wife to help out. Maybe she's noticed a problem that you haven't. Maybe she has a solution that didn't occur to you. Or maybe there's absolutely nothing wrong between you and your wife, and you can go about your day in your usual happy-go-lucky manner. The point is, at least you'll know. Isn't sixty seconds of deep thought in the shower worth a full day's peace of mind?

Let's say you've identified a problem in your marriage. Now what? Well, you and your wife have to find a way to solve it as a team. First things first: Explain the problem to her and see if she's as concerned about it as you are. As you then discuss possible solutions together, keep in mind these basic do's and don'ts of problem solving:

Do communicate clearly how you feel, using statements that begin with "I" rather than "You."

Don't start off by laying blame on the other person. Through honest discussion, the source of the problem will become clear.

Do lay out the problem fully before trying to find a solution. Understanding it is half the battle.

Don't force solutions on your wife. A man's typical first impulse is to fix things quickly to make the problem go away. But the best answers aren't always the easiest.

Do listen closely. A deeper problem or a solution may be hidden in the things your wife says, or doesn't say.

Don't assume you know what your wife is thinking. Rather than trying to interpret something that's unclear, ask her exactly what she means.

Do empathize with your wife. Discuss similar situations when you felt the same way. If you understand exactly how she feels, say so out loud: "I understand."

Don't change the subject. One problem at a time is enough for any couple to tackle.

Finally, to make sure your discussion is ultimately productive:

Do make a plan. Once you've reached a solution, agree on a way to implement it. Give it a month or so to see if it works, and fine-tune it frequently until the problem stops recurring.

Don't walk away from a discussion without agreeing to do something about it, or at least agreeing on a time to discuss it again. Identifying a problem is half the solution but it's only the first half; the problem will always be there until you resolve it.

Problem Solving—Hers

*I*magine what happens when the average woman goes to her husband with a problem she has at work or with a friend. He listens politely for a few seconds, then offers four possible solutions in a tone that lets her know just how stupid she is for not having thought of those things herself. "Problem solved," he figures, and he goes back to doing whatever he was doing before. She, however, is stuck wondering whether he didn't understand the problem or just didn't care.

Chances are, the husband of this prototypical woman really does care. He probably just hasn't developed the skills to listen to her thoroughly and help her solve her problem reasonably. That's unfortunate, because research has shown that many women, when asked about key positive events in their current relationship, point to a situation where their partner helped them deal with an emotional, physical, or financial problem they were facing.

If only more men knew how important this aspect of a relationship is! It's not that we need our husbands to solve our problems for us; it's just that we want them to get intimately involved discussing them. Problem solving in pairs can actually create intimacy. It builds confidence and trust in both partners, and because it lets a male partner feel like he's coming to the rescue, it allows him to show how much he cares in a manly way.

Not only can solving individual problems together strengthen your marriage, it may be *essential* to your relationship's survival. Researchers at UCLA say that one of the biggest indicators of marital dissatisfaction and divorce may be how adept partners are at offering support when dealing with each other's personal problems. If your husband keeps flunking Support 101, you may want to give him a cheat sheet to use the next time you come to him with an issue. Here's one my friend Jennie tried out on her husband (slightly modified):

- The answer to "Do you understand?" is "Yes." To prove you know how you arrived at that answer, you will be required to show your work.

- A problem is not a race. It's acceptable to solve it slowly.

- Sometimes there is no solution. I may just want you to listen to my problem and hold me.

- I am not a man. The answer is not "Clock him/her over the head if he/she says that again."

- Listen to me. Not to the TV, the car radio, your colleagues outside your office door—me.

- My timing may not be perfect. To cope with a problem, you may have to miss a chunk of the *Star Trek* film festival on TNT.

- If you score particularly well in helping me with my problem, you may choose from the following extra-credit bonuses:
    1. I'll cook you dinner.
    2. I'll give you the best back rub ever.
    3. I'll make passionate love to you.

You may be surprised how well your husband performs when he hears about the extra credit.

Women are certainly not the only ones who have personal problems. Your husband has them, but they may be harder to spot. When you ask him how his day was, he'll probably say "good" and leave it at that, because he doesn't want to spend any more time than he has to thinking or talking about his problem. He may even feel the problem isn't important enough to talk about, or that it will go away by itself. Maybe it throws his masculinity into question, and as a result, he doesn't want to share it with you.

To some men, having a personal problem is a sign of general weakness. Deep in your husband's psyche, society may have implanted the idea that males are supposed to be strong, courageous, and stoic. They should solve problems, not have them. If your husband is having trouble getting ahead at work, managing his finances, dealing with his friends, or dealing with you, then the problem is itself making him feel helpless and angry, and the fact that he has the problem to begin with is making him feel inadequate. That's a tough combination.

While your husband can do wonders for you by simply holding you while you cry, you will probably need to give him more vocal and emotional support. First, of course, you'll have to dig the problem out of him. How can you tell something's wrong? Taciturn behavior is a good indicator. Lack of energy and oversleeping are other signs. Asking your husband what's up may not do the trick, so you'll have to do some detective work. What has he told you lately about his job? Has he complained about anything in particular? Is he angry at you about something? You'll probably have to ask a number of pointed questions before the real issue comes out. Stay focused until you pin him down.

When he finally does clarify what's bothering him, many of the do's and don'ts mentioned in the previous pages will come in handy for you, too. But there are a few techniques specific to dealing with men. At every opportunity, reinforce your husband's sense of personal competence. Tell him how much you rely on him and trust him. Bring up success stories from his past. Avoid assuring him that it's okay to fail, for example, or that you'll pick up the slack if he loses his job. These things may be true, but hearing them may make him feel worse. You're better off doing little things to relieve his burden a bit at a time.

As Dave said, men tend to rush to solve their partner's problems, and it's no different when they're solving their own. We can help by slowing down our husbands' minds a bit, helping them understand what their problems are all about, and guiding them toward solutions that may make them—and ourselves—happier.

Fights—His

*D*id you notice that June and Ward Cleaver never argued on their show, but Lucy and Ricky Ricardo fought on every single episode? On and off the TV screen, you'll find both kinds of couples, probably among your own family and friends. Is one type of relationship healthier? We have a tendency to assume that couples who fight constantly are unhappy and destined to break up. Then again, we also assume that couples who never fight are just internalizing their anger and are sooner or later going to bust out with the granddaddy of all arguments.

The real concern for most couples, however, is not how often they fight but how they do it. If you and your wife have never had a real argument, don't worry that there's something missing. You're not weird, you're just . . . happy. But if you do fight with your wife, either occasionally or constantly, you should be sure you're doing it for the right reasons and in a constructive way.

Certainly, no one looks forward to a fight. It's not something you can plan for, although most couples know when an argument is brewing and that when it does break out, civilities like courtesy and logic can go right out the window. But in spite of this emotional chaos, fights between two people who love each other should have definite ground rules, and these rules should be based on mutual respect.

As unpleasant as it may be, this is something you and your wife should talk about. Pick a quiet, conflict-free day and have a discussion about what makes a fair fight. Then make yourselves a set of ironclad rules, and agree that, no matter how angry you get, no matter what the situation may be, there are certain lines neither of you will ever cross. To get started, here are a few of the more common argument guidelines we've heard:

- **Listen.** Approach an argument with an open mind, and speak your own mind calmly and respectfully.
- **No name calling or put-downs.** It's okay to express your anger by telling your wife, "I'm angry at you because . . ." But the only

reason you would call your wife a jerk, or worse, is to humiliate her. Self-defense experts say that if you're ever attacked or mugged, shouting profanities or calling your assailant a bad name can produce a palpable feeling of rage and possibly escalate the urge for violence. Shouting nasty words at your wife will make things worse and will also prove that you don't have anything intelligent to say.

- **No hitting or shoving.** If you actually hit your wife in the heat of an argument, you need to seek counseling immediately. Domestic violence affects one in four couples in the United States—four million women in any given year will be assaulted by a domestic partner. That's a plague that must be stopped one family at a time. Physical force of any kind will not convince your wife to see things your way. Talking is a much more powerful method of persuasion.

- **No arguing in public.** Again, this route leads to humiliation. Fighting is best left to the privacy of your own home.

- **Don't go to bed angry or without a plan.** This is a time-honored rule, and a good one. Address an issue before you go to sleep, and you won't give it a chance to develop into a serious problem. Both you and your wife will wake up with one less worry to deal with the next day. Some problems obviously can't be solved in a single evening, so you may need to make a plan to talk more tomorrow night, and the next night if need be.

- **Never give up.** Withdrawing or leaving is a quick way to end a fight, but a bad way to resolve one. Men are especially guilty of withdrawing in the face of a

SEVEN SURVIVAL TIPS FOR FIGHTING

1 Remember, as a team, you can move beyond the immediate problem.
2 Let your partner fully express what's on her mind. Don't interrupt if she's still talking, even if you think you've gotten the point already.
3 Try to see things from your partner's point of view. From time to time paraphrase what your partner says so that you clearly understand it.
4 Dig out the real issue underlying a seemingly superficial conflict.
5 Express your feelings without placing blame, criticizing, or speaking contemptuously.
6 Focus on solutions for the couple, not just for your individual needs.
7 Always work toward mutual resolution.

difficult relationship problem. Keep in mind that your wife is the person you love most in the world, so respect her enough to let her have her say, and tell her what's on your mind. Discuss your opinions like adults; if the argument gets too hot for your tastes, suggest that you take a break and schedule another time to continue the discussion.

- **Be honest.** Lies and deceit are not the basis of a healthy marriage. If you're wrong, admit it. It takes more strength to say "You're right" to your wife every now and then than to go through life thinking you're never wrong.

- **Don't answer one insult with another.** This will only escalate the problem. Take the high road and deflect an attack by ignoring it or by asking your wife not to do it again.

- **Don't be a mind-reader.** You don't know what your wife is thinking until she clearly expresses herself to you, so try not to jump to negative conclusions.

- **No tit for tat.** "You forgot to take the garbage out." "Yeah well, you forgot to get a job." Needless to say, this is not a constructive exchange. Address your wife's complaints directly, not by piling on your own.

If you currently fight a lot with your wife, it may not be cause for great concern. For some couples, fighting is an effective way to work through differences and let off steam. If you observe reasonable ground rules and pay attention to how you fight, your bouts of venting may never lead to total meltdown.

Fights—Hers

*D*oes this sound familiar? It's eight P.M. on a Tuesday; you and your husband are calmly discussing your respective days; then all of a sudden the two of you are fighting over something meaningless. How did this happen?

Well, the progression probably went something like this. Neither of you had any preference for dinner, so your husband suggested going out. But money's a bit tight these days, so you decided to stay in and cook. The kitchen's too messy to cook in, however, because it was your turn to do the dishes last night, but you had so much work to do that you were too tired when you got home to clean up after the meal your husband made for himself. While he was waiting for you to get home, your sister called, and he forgot to give you the message until five minutes ago. Boom, a fight starts.

A logical escalation, given the number of points of tension going on. How many can you count? Answer: five. Financial pressure; conflict over domestic chores; career issues; resentment over a lack of time for each other; family dynamics.

Arguments between couples—whether they're giant issue-related discussions, innocuous conversations that suddenly blow up, or those countless bickering disagreements that are so commonplace you almost don't notice them—tend to follow patterns that are predictable both in their origins and in their resolutions. Time and again we find ourselves arguing about the same old things. Dave and I, for example, know that doing laundry inevitably triggers some sort of argument. We also understand that these fights are not really about dirty underwear; they're about some hidden issue.

One of the several programs recommended at the end of this book teaches couples about the three main types of issues that underlie arguments: concerns about caring and closeness; concerns about respect and recognition; or concerns about power and control. These are all wrapped up in the T-Rex of all hidden agendas: acceptance. Many problems bring two or more of these issues into play. In the case of our dirty laundry,

Wendy and I have power issues over whose turn it is, control issues over how to fold my shirts, respect issues about not putting her spandex in the dryer, and closeness issues about how much of the laundry process should be performed together. If it sounds complicated, it is. And recognizing that is an important step away from the hot button that started the fight, toward a deeper solution.

Your particular hot buttons can be anything from a bed gone unmade to a thoughtless comment made at a party. And if hurricane conditions already exist in your home, any act or word may be enough to make a howler rise up. Even if all seems well on the surface, some incident may exacerbate differences between you and your husband that are benign under normal circumstances but malignant when combined with hidden issues and extramarital stress.

Psychologists have found that many couples get into trouble because they can't deal with negative feelings. De-escalating a conflict, after all, goes against our natural instincts to either attack or run away from trouble. Managing conflict is a learned skill. The patterns we learned from our parents are the ones we carry into our current relationships, and many times these approaches are not effective in dealing with a particular partner. Maureen, for example, came from a family in which the modus operandi was to smooth over conflict at all costs. Her husband Jay, on the other hand, grew up in an environment that fostered a get-it-all-out approach. Jay tends to be much more emotional and quick to anger, while Maureen is likely to feel defensive and resort to self-preservation.

When they argued, Maureen and Jay found their arguments falling into a predictable pattern: Jay would do all the talking, and Maureen would do all the apologizing. Neither ever felt a problem was truly solved. Only through understanding each other's history and developing the skills to explore their distinct feelings and reactions to conflict were they able to argue on equal terms. Maureen and Jay didn't stop fighting; they simply learned how to fight effectively and how to reach more mutually satisfying resolutions.

This chapter seems like an appropriate place to talk about crying. Studies show that men and women cry for very different reasons. For instance, some women cry to get their way, while men often cry to express pride and joy. A woman may cry in response to something being said or done to her, while a man is more likely to shed tears because of what he's experiencing in his body. Women cry about four times more often than men and for longer periods of time. Men are less likely to sob and generally produce fewer tears.

All these facts put together provide insight into why our husbands rarely cry, and the effects our tears have on them. While we usually have little control over when we start to cry, it's important to understand that men may interpret crying as a manipulative gesture designed to end a fight without giving him his say. You may therefore have to explain to your husband what you're crying about, even if it's obvious. As always, clear communication is the key.

If your ultimate goal is to eliminate the worst fights in your relationship, researchers have come up with all kinds of techniques for preventing marital distress before it starts. "You can't have a hurricane," they reason, "if certain atmospheric conditions aren't present." Any of the various relationship-counseling programs listed in the Appendix will be an enormous help if you want to learn how to truly listen to each other and focus on the hidden issues behind your disagreements.

Illness and Injury—His

What's the only thing that makes it bearable to be stuck at home with a sandpaper throat, a head full of snot, and a nagging cough? Having your wife there to wait on you, of course. When you've got a cold or the flu, you usually look so miserable and whine so pitifully that she's more than willing to bring you warm socks, cook you a nice hot meal, give you lots of fluids, answer the phone, take out the trash, and do anything else you tell her you're too weak to do.

Honestly, don't you wonder why everyone doesn't *want* to get a little bit sick? When you have a cold, you get to stay home from work and watch TV all day. It's like being unemployed, only with job security. People are extra nice to you, and you get to sleep as much as you want. Need a nap at three P.M.? Why not? When you're sick, you need all the rest you can get.

If you take advantage of cold and flu season more freely than your wife does, you're not alone among men. Your wife will say things like, "Men are the biggest babies in the world. One little sniffle, and suddenly they're too weak to get out of bed. When I get a cold, I tough it out, march straight to work, and go on with my day." But before you know it, she's whipping you up a nice batch of chicken noodle soup, brewing hot tea, and giving you kisses on the forehead to make the fever go away.

I say we guys are the smart ones. We wouldn't be babies about getting sick if it weren't to our advantage to act that way. As long as our wives are willing to do wonderful, comforting things for us, we're willing to accept that kindness with whatever situational strings come attached.

A problem arises only when our wives see through the scam. It happens when you push their sympathy just a little too far. Try a line like "Honey, can you give me a sponge bath? I'm too weak to stand up in the shower," and the jig is up. You'll be making your own soup and getting your own medicine, and not just for this cold and flu season, but for every season well into the next century, until your wife forgets what a jerk you were. And when *she* gets sick, you owe her big-time.

Funny how, no matter who's caught the latest bug, there's never enough of the right cold medicine in the house to get either one of you through it.

You don't buy the stuff when you're not sick—who wants to think about having a cold before it happens? So every year, when you get the same flu you always get, either you or your wife has to run out and buy medicine in the middle of the night. Play your cards right, and you can almost always get her to do it. Here are some sure-fire techniques that'll have your wife out the door and on her way to the twenty-four-hour drugstore in no time:

- Volunteer to get more medicine yourself, even though you can barely choke out the words past your horribly swollen tonsils.
- Babble incoherently. That'll scare her good.
- Go to the bathroom, lock the door, and pretend you're throwing up. When someone close to you is vomiting, you want only two things: to help them stop, and to get as far away from them as possible. For your wife, going to the drugstore achieves both goals.
- Start writing your will.
- Remember *E.T.*? Hold a thermometer next to the lightbulb for a minute. When your wife sees you have a temperature of 105 degrees, she'll run to the pharmacist posthaste. (Don't go overboard with this, though. A 110-degree temperature will land you a three-hour wait in the emergency room.)
- Cry. This makes women melt. Shed tears, and she'll do whatever you ask.
- Pretend you're delirious and call her "Mommy." She'll want that to end as soon as humanly possible.
- Cough loudly once every five seconds. Drive her crazy, and she'll drive to the store.
- Roll your eyes up into your head and fall down. This looks serious.
- Tell her you're going to the store, then open the hall closet and walk in. Stay there for a good long time. When she comes over to check on you, pretend you're asleep.
- Ask her to go to the store. This one may sound strange, but on some parts of the planet, asking politely for help has been known to work.

Illness and Injury—Hers

You don't really know your husband until you've seen him when he's sick. That same man who is brave enough to squash gigantic insects is reduced to a whiny little child at the first hint of a sore throat and a cough.

Of course, your husband may not break down completely in the face of illness. He may think he's handling the situation like a true stoic, keeping a stiff upper lip and going about his day. But he'll still operate on a principle that exists only in Manland: Being sick exempts you from everyday household duties. "Oh, honey, I'm sick," he'll say, "so won't you *please* take out the trash?" "I know it's my turn to do the dishes, dear, but—*achew! sniff . . . sniff*—I just don't feel up to it." Oddly enough, his 99.9-degree temperature makes it impossible for him to make the bed, but he's still able to stagger to the couch and manipulate the clicker. What a unique ailment he must have! Someone call *The New England Journal of Medicine.*

If you haven't married Baby-Me Fred, you may find you've gotten hitched to Never-Sick Ned. You could fry an egg on his fevered brow; a purple rash has spread over his entire body; and still, though he lost his voice a week ago, he'll manage to croak out the words "Nah, I'm not sick. Healthy as a horse. I'm always this pale." All of which translates to "Yes, I am a grown man, but there's no way I'm going to see a doctor, because doctors have cold hands and they put them in sensitive places."

Doesn't sound familiar? How about Hypochondriac Harry? Signs and symptoms that you've married this type include:

- What once was a reasonable, daily multivitamin habit when you were dating has turned into a cabinet full of vitamins A through Z, aspirin, shark cartilage, snake oil, rhinoceros horn, and Native American herbs.

- He's circled twenty entries in *The Dictionary of Deadly Diseases* that he's convinced apply to him.

- When you watch *ER,* he's positive he's contracted whatever he sees on the screen: measles, irritable bowel syndrome, Ebola virus.

The difficulty in dealing with someone who is chronically worried about becoming sick is that it's difficult to tell when he is actually seriously ill. So many illnesses have symptoms that closely resemble everyday aches and pains that it's fairly easy for you or your husband to mistake something minor for something serious. Or vice versa.

Take chronic fatigue syndrome, a malady that affects nearly two million Americans. With symptoms like extreme tiredness, lack of enthusiasm, and a general absence of energy, it's easy to overlook this problem and chalk it up to the everyday blahs. Until recently, many doctors believed chronic fatigue syndrome to be a mental, rather than a physical, condition. Now it's classified as a serious but treatable disease.

I bring up this particular illness because, strangely enough, the closer you become to someone, the more likely you are to take that person's complaints for granted. No wife wants to hear that her husband is too tired to go out and have a drink with her and her colleagues after work. You also don't want your spouse to sleep until noon when you're up and ready to go at seven A.M. But unless one of you is a doctor, you can't assume you can make an accurate diagnosis of the problem—even if you know each other better than anyone else in the world.

No matter how much of a whiner your husband is, if he believes he's seriously ill, get him to a doctor and find out what's wrong. If you're not satisfied with that doctor's conclusion, get a second opinion, or even a third. That isn't to say you can't make fun of your sick husband for being a big wallowing crybaby. You can rib him at will when he's obviously turning a touch of the flu into an affliction on the scale of a biblical plague.

Fortunately, during your first year of marriage, the most serious thing your husband is likely to face will be a broken arm or leg from too much weekend football and not enough real exercise. Forget how much it hurts *him*, this is one of the most excruciating things a wife can go through, especially if you were there to see him get maimed. But this is an experience you'll have to get used to if you plan to have kids. Whether you like it or not, children get injured and sick, sometimes seriously. As a mother, you'll have to be there when the doctor administers that tetanus shot, shoots those X-rays, and sets those broken limbs back into place.

God willing, neither your husband nor any other member of your family will be seriously hurt this year or ever. But if they are, remember, you have to be strongest when things seem the worst. Most women are amazed at how well they hold up under the pressure caused by the illness or injury of a loved one. Our husbands may be the only ones with the stomach to kill bugs, but you and I know that women are the true bravehearts of the family.

Time and Pace—His

*T*ime management is one of those ugly terms that brings to mind sterile work environments, 1980s-era business theory, and *Dilbert* cartoons. But it also happens to be one of the more common trouble spots among newly married couples. If, during a typical day, both you and your wife wake up, take showers, go to work, have business lunches, go to the gym, go out with friends, read for an hour, and then go to sleep, when do you participate in your marriage?

There are two good ways to approach this problem. One is to recognize that you and your spouse have to *make* time to spend together. Even if it means sitting in your living room with your calendars open scheduling each other in. *Lunch, Friday: wife* sounds very impersonal, not exactly the kind of romantic, spontaneous relationship you thought you were building. But romance isn't in the planning as much as it is in the execution—nobody said you have to actually *eat lunch* on Friday at noon.

The other approach is to list all those things you typically do alone and consider making an effort to do them with your wife. Normal things count: shopping, car washing, housecleaning, cooking, and commuting to work. As do, of course, intimate things like showering, rubbing lotion on dry hands, and . . . changing the oil filter on the car. Well, you know what I mean. If something is important enough, you'll find time to devote to it. I think you'll agree that your wife belongs in that category.

Pace, on the other hand, is something that most couples aren't aware of until it becomes a problem. But your individual sense of time, and the pace at which you do things, may be very different from that of your wife. Do you walk faster than she does? Do you suck down a whole sandwich in the time it takes her to put mustard on hers? When getting ready to go out, have you learned to wait until her hair is fully coifed and she's put on at least one shoe before you even begin to get dressed, knowing you'll both still be ready to walk out the door at the same time?

You're not alone. Many men find that their preferred life-pace is faster than their wives'. What's interesting to think about is which person gets annoyed in which situation. When you eat faster, she probably tells you to chew your food like a normal person. When she takes longer to get ready, you probably complain about being late. When you spend five minutes cleaning the bathroom, she questions the thoroughness of your job. And when she spends too much time in that very same bathroom, you're inclined to bang on the door and shout, "Are you counting the tiles in there or what?"

It all seems to boil down to this: When you're preparing to do something, the slow person is wrong, and when you're actually doing something, the fast one is wrong. Fortunately, you spend half your life preparing to do things and the other half doing them, so no matter what your life-pace is, you're guaranteed to be right 50 percent of the time. But before you were married, you were on your own, so no matter how much time you took to do something, you were always 100 percent right.

Now, common courtesy requires that you adjust to your partner's time and pace, and naturally she should take steps to accommodate you. If you find that you finish your meals well before she does, it's probably because you're not stopping to talk. And if you don't get anything else from this book, at the very least you should understand the basic principle of a successful marriage: Talk is good.

Tomorrow, during lunch, practice talking while having a meal—preferably with another person present so those around you don't think you're nuts. Take a bite, put down your fork, chew your food, swallow, say something, repeat. Before you know it, you'll be a sparkling conversationalist who can dine with the best of them.

In the same way that two people sleeping next to each other will adopt similar breathing patterns and heart rates, you and your wife will eventually develop a complementary sense of time and pace. You'll each find comfortable times to wake up, come home from work, eat dinner, and go to bed. You'll learn to live with differences in timing that simply can't be fixed.

You'll reconcile yourself to the fact that your wife will never take just five minutes to get ready, not in your lifetime. If I asked you to go somewhere right now, you could probably pull yourself together and be at the door in five minutes, easy. Your wife will also say she'll be ready in five minutes. But she'll actually take closer to half an hour. You'll cut your toenails, warm up the car, brush the cat, mow the lawn, and she's still in the bathroom doing whatever it is women do in there. Ask her at any point how much longer she'll be, and you'll get a painful but all-too-common answer: five minutes.

Here we have a classic case of the difference between male and female time. Your wife really thinks she's only going to be another five minutes, and even worse, she thinks you should believe her. In her mind she's telling the truth, and essentially she is, only her math is off. During your first year of marriage you'll learn to convert the amount of time she tells you she needs into the amount of time she'll actually take. For now, keep this handy table in your wallet:

Just a second = 10 minutes

5 minutes = 30 minutes

15 minutes = 1 hour

Half an hour = Find a good book

At 8:00 = Somewhere around 9:30

Hold your horses = 5-minute penalty

You're annoying me = 10-minute penalty

Just go without me = If you do, I'll kill you

As you can see, there are dangers to messing with your wife's math. The more you ask her how long she'll be, the longer you're going to have to wait. When she says, "Five more minutes," your natural inclination will be to reply, "You said that five minutes ago." Not only is this ineffective, she may tack on an additional five minutes.

When preparing to go out with your wife, it's best to simply leave her alone. Focus on getting yourself ready, and then find something constructive to do. The floor could always use a nice coat of shellac, and what the heck—you've got five minutes.

Time and Pace—Hers

Time, like money, is something you may have thought you would gain when you got married. Two people, each with twenty-four hours in the day, would combine their efforts, eliminate redundancy, and thus have plenty of free time to spend together, right? Wrong-O. Now that you're married, you probably have less time than ever, and you have to deal with the added burden of needing to agree on how to spend the time you do have.

Suppose you want to go out on the town more often, and your husband wants to work late every night. The Prevention and Relationship Enhancement Program (PREP®) in New York City recommends you approach this, and all time-management issues, with the ABCs of problem solving. First, set an Agenda. Limit the problem to something specific, such as "He wants to work/she wants to play." Don't stray into "Why won't you ever clean the toilet?"

Next, get two pads of paper and two pencils, and Brainstorm ways to solve the problem, no matter how stupid. Look over each other's notes, reach a Compromise, and form a Contract. You may decide that, next week, your husband will work late three nights and go out two nights, if you arrange the entertainment plans. Agree to stick to the contract for a certain amount of time, say a month, and when the contract period is up, evaluate your results.

You can use this process to work out most time-management issues in your marriage, including the "He wants to watch TV/she wants to get out and exercise" problem and the "He wants to eat before he dies of hunger/she wants to shop till she drops" conundrum.

Speaking of which, shopping happens to be a perfect example of the differences between how men and women view time and pace. Many women believe the closest thing to heaven on earth is shopping. When we shop, we lose virtually all sense of time. We can spend hours in a factory outlet, days in a dusty antique shop, and months in a major department store. One day we will probably find Amelia Earhart wandering between Petites and Casuals in the Bermuda Triangle Macy's.

The owners of clothing stores know that women forget about time when they shop, and being good business people, they encourage it by creating shopping environments that resemble the interiors of casinos. Bright lights, seductive displays, no clocks, and in many stores no windows. Women who enter these temples of retail seduction can shop to their heart's content, unaware that night has fallen and their husbands are home sticking a Swanson's aluminum TV dinner tray into the microwave.

Unfortunately, your husband's sense of time while shopping is vastly different from yours. If he spends fifteen minutes shopping with you, it's fifteen minutes too long. Tell him you'll only be ten minutes longer, and he'll time you with a stopwatch. He'll say or do anything to get you out of the store—even if he knows you're just going on to the next shop. Time moves unbelievably slowly for him when he's doing something he hates to do. And the same is true for you.

Case in point: sporting events. He invites you to go see a baseball game, which, compared to watching it on TV, seems like it might actually be fun. Unfortunately, he wants to get there early so he doesn't miss anything. Such as the players standing around and spitting while the grounds crew waters the infield. And two grown men, who make more money than any female sports star ever will, warming up for their strenuous "job" by playing a leisurely game of catch.

Not only can your husband not miss batting practice, he's got to see the entire game. Even if it starts to rain. Even if it's 14 to 2 in the fifth inning. Even if the home team is being beaten so badly their shortstop is pitching. He paid full price for his tickets, after all, and by gum he's going to get a full

> **SEVEN SURVIVAL TIPS FOR PASSING THE TIME ON SUPER BOWL SUNDAY**
>
> 1 Wait until the second quarter, then grab all the women in the room and go shopping. The guys will never notice.
> 2 After every play, shout "Touchdown!" as loud as you can.
> 3 Put the clicker in your pocket. Change the channel at strategic moments, then look around like you don't know who's got the remote.
> 4 Every time the guys talk about how great a football player is, mention that you heard he was gay.
> 5 Tell your husband you're off to the postgame party and walk out the door in a cheerleader outfit.
> 6 Ask a bunch of questions like "How many points do you get for ripping a man's head clean off?"
> 7 Rig the Super Bowl pool so you win every time.

evening's entertainment. Besides, he reasons, once the fair-weather fans leave the stadium, there'll be less traffic by the time you drive home.

After the first two hours of this, you start counting the number of people in the stands wearing red hats. You amuse yourself by throwing peanut shells at your husband's head. Can you make one land in his ear? Then you enter the ridiculous-question phase: "What if the mascot tried to steal second, and the scoreboard suddenly exploded and toppled over into center field? Would the runner take an extra base, or would that qualify as delay of game?"

At least when time is going slowly for women, we are able to find ways in which to entertain ourselves. Personally, I always bring a book to sporting events. At first I worried that it would seem rude—but then I realized, who am I kidding? Who's going to notice the book on my lap at a baseball stadium except another bored wife, who'll probably ask to borrow it when I go for a walk after the third rain delay? But men become very whiny when they feel their time is being wasted. They whine when you shop too long. They whine when you take too long to get ready. They whine when you ask them whether the fourth dress you've tried on makes you look fat. Can't they realize that any time you spend together is quality time?

Maybe someday, in a perfect world, men and women will learn to do the same things, at the same time, in perfect harmony, without being ruled by the dictatorial musings of Father Time, lost in a timeless meadow of perpetual baseball and shoes that fit perfectly . . . nah.

Change—His

Men hate change. We hate to change our cars, our couches, our houses, and our lives. We hate to change our underwear. We never change our clothes because we never notice when styles have changed. We won't change toothpaste even if ours has been proven to *cause* tooth decay.

We don't want to change our shoes, our hair, or our minds. Just about the only thing we will change regularly and with abandon is the TV channel, and that's not really change as much as it is a rational need to sample the entire available scope of sports and action programming. It's not easy to change from a single man to a married man, but once we decided to do it, nothing was going to change our minds.

This is the fundamental difference between men's and women's approaches to change: *While men are incredibly slow to accept change, the minute we do, the change is a done deal.*

Nothing will stop us from seeing a life-altering decision, once made, to its fruition. Any other course of action would be changing our minds, and as we just established, that's out of the question. Most women, however, will change at the drop of a hat, pick the hat back up again, then change their minds again and drop it, pick it up, drop it, pick it up, until some outside force causes them to finally make a decision they have to stick with. That force is usually us. Of course, these are all biased, sweeping, gender-based generalizations, but now that they're down on paper, I really don't want to change them.

The most frustrating thing about our wives' willingness to change is that most of the time, they're right. Women have an uncanny ability to sense the right time to make changes, both minor and major. Men, on the other hand, have a tremendous capacity for sleeping through the crucial crossroads of our lives. This may stem from the fact that women tend to look at the benefits and results of completing the change, and men tend to worry about the painful logistics of seeing a change through.

For instance, imagine that, in your first year of marriage, your wife suggests the two of you should move to a bigger home. She's thinking how great it would be to have more space. You're thinking of what a pain it will be to move all your junk. When she suggests you get rid of the old TV and buy a new one, she's thinking, "Great! Better color, bigger screen." And you think, "Oh, *great,* now I have to see if I can sell the old one, then we have to comparison-shop for a new one, haul it home, hook it up, and make sure all the clickers work together."

Once you agree to make a change, big or small, you're already well on your way to planning the completion of the project, which is why it's incredibly annoying when your wife decides you can't afford a new TV after all. But it may be equally frustrating for her to suggest a change and put up with your complaints all the way through it, only to finally get what she wanted and have you say, "You know, honey, you were right. That was one change we made for the better."

So what have we learned? Men hate change but do it well. Women welcome change but exercise it poorly. What a revelation. Since the attitude of both sexes is equally annoying, it's a wonder anything changes at all.

Change-Hers

The old joke goes: Men spend nine months trying to get out of the female body and the rest of their lives trying to get back in. This is only half true. If men had their way, they would never come out in the first place. The male fear of change starts at conception and solidifies at weaning, a process that is known to take longer on average for boys than for girls.

Maybe it's just a trick of evolution that causes men to lag behind at almost every crucial juncture of life. Girls grow faster, reach puberty more quickly, and marry younger than boys (age 24.5 for women as opposed to 26.5 for men). Of course, men reach their so-called sexual peak much earlier than women do, but then they hold on to their sex drive long after it has any practical use. Doing otherwise would involve—oh, horror—a *change*. Imagine if men were the ones who had to go through something called the change of life.

Aside from the biological evidence that men hate change, you probably notice this tendency in your husband every day, in little ways. You can tell a lot about a man by his underwear: Shorts are essentially the tea leaves of the male psyche. I have an interesting assignment for you, though you may not like what you find.

Go to your husband's dresser, open the top drawer, and lay out all his underwear on the bed. Now count the holes. If there are none, congratula-

> **SEVEN SURVIVAL TIPS FOR CONVINCING YOUR HUSBAND TO CHANGE**
>
> 1 Threaten to invite your mother over for a week unless he gets rid of that ancient flannel shirt.
> 2 Tell him you'll find him more attractive if he would change his underwear more than, say, once a week.
> 3 Four words: My boyfriend's doing it.
> 4 Want him to move something? Leave a trail of beef jerky from the object to the place where you want it moved.
> 5 Tell him you'll change into something more comfortable (wink, wink) but only after he changes all the curtains from the winter to the spring set.
> 6 Need to change a few of his bad habits? Try a cattle prod. It trains monkeys; it's got to work on your big ape.
> 7 Sit down with your husband, have an open discussion, and tell him why it's important that he make a particular change. Boring, but probably the most effective technique.

tions. You're the proud owner of a man who isn't afraid of change, maybe even one who welcomes variety. His ability to purchase new underwear and discard the old is an admirable trait. One to five holes indicates a fairly typical pattern of male change aversion. Six to ten signifies a change-o-phobic, and eleven or more means your spouse is probably still *in* the bed, underneath the covers and piles of underwear, avoiding the dawning of a new day. Underwear is, for change-resistant men, a garment that has seen his most intimate parts, and he's reluctant to let it go out in the world where it might end up as landfill.

Your husband's fear of change is also evident in his need to make plans. When you agree that you'll go to the grocery store and he'll go to the place that sells six-hundred-pound bags of dog food, there is no room for error. Any deviant decisions you make on your own are an affront to the established structure.

You probably don't realize that your spouse has timed your arrival home from the store at precisely 3:30 P.M., whereupon the chocolate sauce he asked you to purchase is going to go straight on top of the bowl of ice cream he's scooped out at just the right moment so that it's ready to eat when your car pulls into the driveway. Oblivious to his agenda, however, you've taken a detour to the mall and lingered in the shops deciding what piece of clothing you would buy if you could afford to buy anything this month. You arrive home to find the man you love slouched in his favorite chair, a spoon in one hand, a bowl of lukewarm white liquid in the other.

Then you fight. Not over the real issue, of course, but over the skirt you just bought. After an hour of arguing over clothes and money, it dawns on you that this is really an argument about change. Don't you see? You *changed plans.* Plans you didn't know you had. How dare you!

Note: Not every husband on the planet is averse to change. Every once in a while you find one who's happy-go-lucky and spontaneous, hurling away his worldly possessions and moving from town to town in restless, romantic, Jack Kerouac fashion. Unfortunately, every few months these types tend to find their marriages a burden, and so they toss away wives like so much hole-ridden underwear.

Is there a happy medium? Can you have a fulfilling marriage with a man who's open to change (as you are) without thriving on it like a drug? Possibly, if you work on him with relentless determination. You'll just have to give him good reason to include you in his personal changes every day of his life.

Religion—His

When a couple with similar religious beliefs marries, one potential source of tension is completely eliminated. But personally, I find interfaith marriages more interesting. It's heartwarming to watch two people exchange vows of deep, undying love despite having completely different views on the nature of God and the origin of the universe; differences that have been responsible for countless wars and deaths over the course of human history. It's enlightening to witness the collision of cultures and the collage of beliefs that are created when representatives of two faiths preside over a wedding ceremony. And it's fascinating to see two people work out the specifics of raising a child in an interfaith household.

The problem with discussing the effects of religion on marriage in any specific way is that there are so many different religions in the world, which can produce a seemingly infinite number of marital combinations. Add to that the fact that there are so many facets within each religion; millions of shades of belief that are at the root of what we do, say, and feel in everyday life.

You and your wife may struggle to reach a mutual decision about when or how often to attend a church, synagogue, or mosque, only to find you hold different views on the right to life versus freedom of choice, the death penalty, or prayer in schools. These issues may seem more political than religious, but they're based on the concept of morality with which you were raised, and if you think religion isn't involved because you're not fighting over whether there really was a great flood that lasted forty days and forty nights, you are sorely mistaken.

Hopefully, you and your wife hashed out differences in your basic religious beliefs before you got married. But if you're just finding out now, in your first year of marriage, that you're having a real problem with something that's a cornerstone of your wife's religion, there's no need to panic. It can be worked out through calm, open-minded discussion, understanding, and a little self-education. Take time to read your wife's religious books, and learn more about her faith before you condemn an idea that may be the product of hundreds of years of human thought. You don't have to swing around to her way of thinking, and she doesn't have to abandon her beliefs, but you can find ways to deal with a religious issue that's bothering you, perhaps by just agreeing not to discuss it. As long as you make an effort to understand both your feelings and hers, you can protect your marriage from this all-too-common source of tension.

Religious pressure is much more likely to come from your families than from you or your wife. Some parents find their children's interfaith marriages absolutely unacceptable. Others may be just a bit disappointed, extending their best wishes because their children are so clearly in love. Fortunately, by the time you reach your first year of marriage, you've already worked your way through the difficulties of obtaining parental approval—probably with the help of a hard-fought, soul-searching compromise, such as "Okay, son, the marriage is fine with us, as long as you raise nice Catholic [Jewish, Hindu, Moonie] kids."

Guided by a desire to find common ground, the steady march of time will probably bring you, your wife, and your families together, regardless of differences in faith. But even if your family never accepts your decision to enter into an interfaith marriage, the important thing is to not let their beliefs interfere with the new family you've created. After all, you're living your life, not theirs.

Religion—Hers

While you were in your umpteenth "discussion" with your future mother-in-law about the guest list for your wedding, by any chance did you experience one of those dark nights of the soul when you wondered why the heck you hadn't eloped months ago? It's almost impossible to plan a wedding these days and not experience a crisis of some sort. And chances are, whether your prewedding problems had to do with finances or inter-familial relationships, they involved the kinds of big issues that will likely pop up again sometime during your postwedding life.

Religion is one example. One of the first decisions you and your husband had to make concerned the nature of your wedding ceremony. Would it be of your faith? His faith? Both? Neither? Even if the two of you are of the same faith, you still had to choose whether your family's religious leader or his would perform the marriage. Both of your parents probably had strong views on this subject, which may have engendered some discussion between you and your husband on the meaning of faith and the role you envisioned it would play in your future.

These issues won't go away during your first year of marriage. Questions will keep coming up: Will you attend his church or temple? Yours? Both? Neither? If you're of the same faith, how often will you worship? How involved will you get in your local religious community? If you're planning to have children, you'll need to work out the role of religion in their upbringing. Then, from the child's earliest days, you'll have to play by those rules.

The key here is communication. The compromises you and your husband made before your wedding were great practice for the discussions you're having in your first year of marriage. Difficult as it may be, it's important to rank the aspects of your religion in order of their importance to you. If you don't mind reducing the frequency with which you attend church, but you feel your children must absolutely be raised Catholic, then you know where you're willing to bend and where you need to stand fast.

One couple we spoke with—both Catholics when they married eight years ago—are to this day still trying to resolve their religious issues. Brian had let his faith lapse while Elizabeth had not. She had read studies proving, to her mind, that children raised in a religious household are more socially well adjusted than are secularly raised children. Their child is now old enough to begin attending church—but with which parent? Both? How often? And what about Sunday school? In order to answer these questions in your own marriage, you'll first need to agree upon whether children should be brought up in a specific faith at all, or allowed to choose their faith of their own accord once they've reached an age when they can reason it out for themselves.

These are heavy topics, so they shouldn't be discussed lightly. At the same time, they shouldn't be avoided. Every time a holiday comes along, every time you attend a wedding, and every time a friend's or relative's baby is born, questions of religion will arise. You have to resolve them with your husband as soon as possible, and more important, the resolutions should be yours and your husband's alone. You are your own family now, and you should be the sole proprietors of your family's religious environment.

I'm not saying you should ignore the advice and teachings of your parents and friends, only that you should use it intelligently rather than accepting it blindly. Organized religion has molded many an unsuspecting mind. You and your husband may find you're better off shaping religious concepts in order to fit your marriage, rather than the reverse.

Politics—His

A recent cartoon in *The New Yorker* magazine depicts an elderly husband and wife talking to their daughter. The wife comments, "Even after all these years, I still find it very exciting using my vote to cancel out your father's."

Politics may make strange bedfellows but, from what we've found, not altogether uncommon ones. If you searched the whole country, you'd be hard-pressed to find another person who holds exactly the same political views as you do. So the odds are astronomical that the woman who shares your life will share your every opinion, too. Most likely, you'll find key areas of common ground, the sort of agreement on social issues that attracted you to each other in the first place.

One thing the two of you will notice, not necessarily in your first year of marriage but long-term, is that over time your views begin to merge. It's not uncommon to see fundamental liberals become staunch conservatives after living for a few years with a self-styled Ronald or Nancy Reagan. Conversely, many folks make the move from right to left under the influence of more liberal spouses.

The word *influence* here shouldn't be construed as negative. Rational husbands and wives don't force each other to change political beliefs. Times change, issues evolve, and a decision to back a political candidate is based on a lot more than partisanship. If your friends tell you they think your wife changed your politics, it's really beside the point. Your wife changed your entire life. But it was you who chose to marry her, you who chose which candidate to believe in, and you who chose which way to vote on which issue, even if your choices may seem inconsistent over the years.

Also, with time you may be surprised to discover that your wife holds strong political beliefs you never knew about. More startling, you may not know the real reasons behind those views she does express frequently. If you're bored one evening and looking for an interesting discussion topic, try giving each other the following political beliefs pop quiz:

❶ Where do you stand on abortion?

❷ What do you think of the current president? Governor? Mayor?

❸ Do you think every political position should have a term limit?

❹ What's more important, lowering taxes or reducing the deficit?

❺ Do you think the death penalty is a deterrent to crime?

❻ What would you do to improve race relations in this country?

❼ Would you sacrifice your own Social Security benefits for the larger economic good of the country?

❽ Is the federal government spending enough on the environment?

❾ Should we further restrict immigration to this country?

❿ If we legalized drugs like marijuana, would it make the nation's drug problem better or worse?

⓫ What do you think about the welfare system in this country, and how can it be made more effective and egalitarian?

If you already know what your wife's answers will be to each question, ask her why she feels that way. Play devil's advocate and give her a series of "What ifs?" For instance, if she says she's against the death penalty, ask her how she would punish a lunatic who murdered her parents. If she's for saving the spotted owl, ask whether her thinking would change if her only income came from working at a lumber mill. At the very least, these questions can create interesting dinner conversation and teach you and your spouse a little more about each other. You'll begin to ask questions about your own beliefs, and perhaps open your mind to new possibilities.

The great thing about this quiz is that it's nonbiodegradable, which means it's just as interesting to take during your fifth year of marriage as during your first. By giving the quiz to each other periodically for the rest of your lives, you can keep track of your evolving political beliefs. Then you won't be quite as shocked come Election Day 2008 when your wife starts sporting an "I Love Dan Quayle" button.

Politics–Hers

Many men love to talk about politics. Blessed by the same authority as Moses on the mountain, with the Ten Commandments in hand, your husband is ready, willing, and able to entertain any social gathering with his sparkling oratory on the finer points of our constitutional rights. *Snore.*

Hey, everybody's got political beliefs. Some of us prefer to keep them quiet until we're safely behind the curtain at the voting booth. But people express their political opinions in a variety of ways, and if your husband doesn't fit the description above, he's likely to fall into one of the following categories:

- *The Zealot:* He's got a stubbornly strong opinion about every issue, and no matter how much you "discuss" it, he's right and you're wrong. He pulls out statistics and acts of Congress you couldn't possibly refute because no one in his right mind knows whether they're fact or fiction. Did Eisenhower really spend $53 million on national highway development? Maybe. But how, exactly, does the Zealot know that? He also likes to throw in the far-out conspiracy kicker: something like "It's a little-known fact that Ronald Reagan privately gave millions to Greenpeace out of his own pocket."

- *The Silent Majority Member:* He has opinions but rarely expresses them until a Zealot enters the room. He reads quite a bit but doesn't retain enough facts and figures to enter into an in-depth political debate. He believes what he believes, and as political climates and his position in life slowly change, his beliefs change with them.

- *The One-Issue Wonder:* He doesn't much care for politics and politicians in general, but there is one thing that really gets him fired up. It's usually something emotionally charged like abortion, the death penalty, or welfare. He'll march in the parades, he'll carry the signs, he'll wear the buttons and display the bumper stickers, and when voting time comes around, he'll pick his candidates based upon their stance on his issue of choice.

- *Mr. Clueless:* He failed high school social studies and has no intention of delving back into it in his adult life. When asked who he voted for in the last presidential election, he's likely to say either Mickey Mouse or

Bugs Bunny, depending upon his classic cartoon preference. He finds spirited political debate humorous at best and tedious at worst, chuckling to himself as he watches people grow increasingly heated over issues he isn't familiar with and couldn't care less about.

This political typecasting certainly applies to women as well as men. In fact, you may want to evaluate yourself in this spectrum and see how you match up alongside your husband. Any combination of these categories can work in a marriage, although two Zealots had better share extraordinarily similar views if they're going to get any peace. By understanding your partner's *approach* to politics, regardless of what those politics are, you can avoid a lot of trouble spots in your marriage. If you feel uncomfortable when you visit your friends and your conservative husband launches into an aggressive political debate, you should ask yourself, "What's making me unhappy here? Is it his conservative beliefs themselves, or the fact that he's expressing them so confrontationally?"

If your husband's politics truly bug you, you don't have to try to change him, or your own beliefs, in order to get along. James Carville and Mary Matalin, for example, are a couple who have expressed very different views in a very public way, and in the process, they've demonstrated how a strong marriage grounded in mutual respect can support even the most deep-seated emotional and intellectual differences. They probably do argue about trickle-down economics and deficit reduction, but my bet is that neither one pulls off the gloves to convince the other that he or she is wrong.

What's the point? Both members of a couple believe different things. That's fodder for an intelligent discussion of the facts, not proof that one person or the other is a dolt. The important thing is that you love and respect the man you married, even if you find it hard to love his politics.

SEVEN SURVIVAL TIPS FOR PUTTING AN END TO A HUSBAND'S POLITICAL DISCUSSION

1 Bring up baseball. It's like watching a cat eating Meow Mix discover a small flightless bird sitting next to the food dish.
2 Tell him he should write down his thoughts and e-mail them to someone who cares.
3 Put something in his mouth, like a large piece of fruit or a chew toy.
4 Tell him if he doesn't shut up, you'll be exercising your line-item veto on sex tonight.
5 Bring the discussion to a vote.
6 Yawn for a full minute.
7 Shout, "Ladies and Gentlemen! The President of the United States!" and start applauding.

Drugs and Alcohol—His

Most people of legal age are inclined to have a few drinks now and then. Anyone who has indulged in more than a few will feel a number of things the next day: head pain, nausea, dizziness, cottonmouth, and, if you smoke (or don't but the demon liquor convinces you that you should), the phenomenon known as scorched throat. Anxiety over things you may have said and done will come back to haunt you, and you'll experience regret for continuing to drink after you knew you were inebriated. Hand-in-hand comes penitence—a ridiculously sincere promise to never drink that much again. And finally, a numbness of the brain that causes you to watch nothing but the Cartoon Network for the next twenty-four hours.

Now that you've entered your first year of marriage, you can add a new feeling to this list: guilt. Example 1. You go out with the guys and arrive home late. Very late. Your wife opens the front door because you've woken her up trying to unlock it with your car key for the last half hour (the only good use for it since, even in your state, you weren't stupid enough to drive home). You come in, kiss her good night, and pass out on the bed fully clothed, smelling like an ashtray and snoring like a fifteen-year-old Pug with asthma.

Example 2. You go to a wedding or some other event with your wife, and you consume your body weight in free drinks. You jump onstage with the band. You win the limbo contest. You're the life of the party. Your wife remained sober in order to drive you home, and once you arrive there, you turn into Dr. Love. She gives you a look that chills your heart and sends you off to take a cold shower. You have bad dreams all night anticipating the worst morning of your life.

Situations vary, but the results are the same. You drank too much, your wife didn't, and now you have to pay for your indiscretion with a motherlode (or should I say wifeload) of guilt. There is only one piece of solid advice I can give you here, and that is: Wait until you sober up to work it out. If you argue while you're still drunk you will (a) lose badly, say the exact wrong thing, and make it worse, (b) look so pathetic that your wife won't be able to stand the sight of you, or (c) the double whammy, both at once.

When you've sobered up, you'll have a better command of necessary tactical skills. Practice this mantra: "Honey, I know I'm drunk and I'm being a jerk. I think I should sleep it off, and we'll talk about it in the morning." Rehearse these words now so your muscle memory will take over when you're in the bag. In addition, if you're planning a night of liberal libation, check out the "Fights" chapter. You'll need this information to make it alive through the morning after.

Now suppose your wife is the one who comes home drunk and stupid and unusually amorous. Well . . . great! I mean, c'mon, you're a guy, and this is your wife, and she really wants you, and so what if she's a little drunk, unless of course, this becomes a regular thing. Try not to give her the third degree about where she was, who she was with, how much she drank, and if any guys hit on her. She went out, she had fun, and she came home to you, so enjoy it!

Now drugs, being illegal, aren't a topic we'll go into in detail here. But suffice it to say that when either of you is under the influence of some controlled substance, it's best not to enter into an argument of any sort. Fortunately, many pharmaceuticals tend to neutralize your bickering synapses, so your need to eat an enormous amount of snack foods may outweigh your need to fight. There's a good reason a certain group of modern recreational drug users coined the phrase "Make love not war." Of course, many drugs leave you too stupid to make love—or make anything, in fact, other than microwave popcorn.

Finally, a word on that most insidious drug—cigarettes. Is it worse being a smoker married to a nonsmoker spouting constant health statistics and complaining about your smoky breath, hair, and clothing? Or is it worse being the nonsmoking spouse of a cigarette addict, whom you care deeply about? Either way, smoking can be a major source of marital tension, and it won't disappear of its own accord. If you don't want to be puffing away in the exile of the garage when you're sixty, our advice is to talk about it and reach some sort of resolution now. Most of your life is still ahead of you. If you smoke, and you make a resolution to stop now, your future will be healthier and your spouse will be eternally grateful.

As we've said, a healthy marriage is one in which two individuals enjoy doing a variety of things together. If drinking, smoking, and taking drugs are not among the things you *both* like to do, then quit or cut way back. Regardless of whether these activities are right or wrong, if they're getting between you and your wife, you can find better ways to have a good time.

Drugs and Alcohol–Hers

Medical research on drug and alcohol abuse has uncovered something called the "marriage effect." A recent study showed that, when young adults got married, marijuana use dropped on average by more than a third and cocaine use by more than one-half. When former drug users went through a divorce, the marriage effect reversed. One proposed explanation is that the sense of commitment that comes with marriage encourages spouses to get control of behavior that could harm their partners. In addition, marriage means there's now someone in the abuser's life who's astutely aware of the problem.

Even for those who don't have problems with substance abuse, normal ingestion of alcohol is such an integral part of social occasions that it could possibly become an issue for you and your husband from the earliest moment of your marriage. Before and during their weddings, couples can get a first taste of their family's differences regarding alcohol. Will the bar be open or cash? Will there even be a bar? Serious discussions probably hinged on who was supposed to pay for all the liquor, and the person who got the bill was probably the one who felt most strongly about drinking in the first place.

Now that you're married, the question is, how do you and your husband feel about drinking? It's not unusual if you've never actually discussed this issue. Many couples don't address the effects of alcohol or drugs on their marriage until a real problem pops up, such as a major fight.

How can you avoid that argument, or at least address it in a calm, sober manner? Try sitting down with your husband and asking each other the following questions:

- Do you think I drink too much/take too many drugs?
- Do you like me when I drink/get high?
- Do you wish I would drink or do drugs less? More?

- How much money do you think we spend on alcohol/drugs?

- What would you say if I asked you to stop drinking/taking drugs?

Tough questions, but I guarantee you'll learn something valuable by asking them. You'll find out exactly how important drugs and alcohol are to your spouse; you'll find out whether your spouse has been putting off confronting a potentially difficult issue; and you'll find out how much of your joint budget is being spent in this area of your lives. Be warned, however, that this kind of face-to-face soul searching could actually start an argument between you. But it's better to work it out under controlled circumstances than to wait for a problem to explode when at least one of you is drunk and irrational.

So now you have the tools you need to nip major drug- and alcohol-related problems in the bud. What about smaller problems? Carla had been married for four months when she realized that her husband Evan always did something really annoying when they went out. He could never, ever leave a beer half finished. She would say, "Hey, let's go," and even if he was ready to go, too, he would respond, "Okay, just let me finish my beer."

Carla couldn't figure out why he did this. Did he love beer that much? Was he hell-bent on getting his money's worth from that bottle of Heineken? Or was it a way to hang out a little longer?

If you feel that you or your wife has a serious problem with drugs or alcohol, here are a few national sources for information and assistance:

Alcoholics Anonymous
Regional chapters everywhere; check your local listings
http://www.alcoholics-anonymous.org/

Narcotics Anonymous
Regional chapters everywhere; check your local listings
http://www.wsoinc.com/

The National Council on Alcoholism and Substance Abuse Hotline
1-800-662-4357

Betty Ford Center
1-800-854-9211
http://www.bettyfordcenter.org/

Hazelden
1-800-257-7810 in the U.S. and Canada
http://www.hazelden.org/

Online Recovery Resources
1-800-604-6149
http://www.recovery.org/

Recovery Related Resources
http://members.aol.com/powerless/recovery.htm

She finally asked him point-blank, and the answer was, he didn't know. He just had a vague compulsion to finish what he started.

Once Carla pointed out the problem, Evan decided it was a little silly to finish a beer just to finish it. He made a concerted effort to leave a bar or a party when he wanted to leave, not when a bottle told him he was finished. Because Evan made this compromise, Carla started making an effort to say "I'm ready to go" only when she saw that Evan was nearly finished with his beer. This is a great example of a couple working together by using honest communication and compromise to keep a small annoyance from turning into a big problem.

Another issue might center on tolerance levels. Due to a combination of body weight, food consumption, and drinking experience, one partner in a marriage may become intoxicated considerably faster than the other. The less drunk partner may develop negative feelings: "Why can't he hold his liquor?" "Why is she making such an ass of herself?" "Looks like I'm going to have to carry him home again." These reactions are typical in a relationship that's been thrown temporarily out of balance. Instead of judging the condition of your spouse, you may find it more effective to solve the problem logically. Say to your spouse, "I understand that I get tipsy faster than you do when we go out and drink. So maybe I should slow down, pace myself a little better, or eat more while drinking."

In the end, your best solution may be to stop drinking altogether. Or to do it only within reason. We all become different people when we drink or get high; under the influence, your husband may not be quite the person you intended to marry, and vice versa. While alcohol and drugs may heighten a social or romantic moment, intoxication that's more than momentary may put a sobering strain on a successful marriage.

Privacy and Independence–His

When we study a relationship, we often concentrate on the time a man and a woman spend together. We consider how they interact, the things they say to each other, and the things they do as a couple. However, in the same way that periodic silences are an essential part of a musical composition and negative space is crucial to a work of art, the time a husband and wife spend away from each other is an important component of any marriage. In this book, we offer a lot of suggestions about spending more time with your spouse, but it's sometimes in the best interest of your marriage to *not* spend time together.

This isn't meant to scare you, but in your first married year, the full scope of marriage and its effect on your life may not yet have sunk in. Not only is marriage forever, it's every single minute of every hour of every day from now until the end of forever. That's kind of an intimidating way to put it, but think about this. Before you met your wife, there were probably moments in your life when you were too often alone. At the time, you considered these to be periods of loneliness. But now that you're married, you may look wistfully back and call those periods by another name: privacy.

No matter how much you love your wife, it shouldn't surprise you if, now and then, you don't want to be in the same room with her. And privacy is not solely a male need. Your wife probably finds you impossible to be around sometimes, too. Somehow most married couples either develop methods for tactfully finding time alone, or they develop ways to be alone together. The first apartment Wendy and I shared consisted of a room and a kitchen with no door. The only room with a door was the bathroom. If I wanted to watch TV and Wendy wanted to read a book in peace, she had to bring a pillow into the bathroom and sit in the tub.

Speaking of the bathroom, it appears to be a safe haven of sorts for married couples. Many newly married men increase the amount of time they spend in the bathroom. We linger in the shower, take our time shaving, read the morning paper, make some phone calls, or just think for a while. The bathroom is reassuring in its tinyness; you can see all four walls and there are lots of knobs and handles that do things when you push or pull them. *Flush!* That's a comforting sound. The shower drowns out all the commotion from the outside world, and if it's not loud enough, you can switch on the little wet/dry radio hanging from the towel rack. The mirror is your friend. It won't tell you to take out the trash or clean the dishes. You can practice telling your boss to stick it in his ear. You can win the argument you lost to your wife last night. In the bathroom, alone, anything is possible, and I recommend going there as a minivacation in the middle of every stressful period.

If you're in the mood to be with other people but without your wife, that's fine, too. You won't want to make it a nightly thing, and those other people probably shouldn't be hookers, strippers, or your ex-girlfriend, but going out wifeless with your friends from work or college shouldn't be a source of tension in your marriage. See the "Friends" chapter for tips and ground rules. If your wife complains that you don't spend enough time with her, it could indicate one of two things:

❶ She has sacrificed too much of *her* independence to your marriage. Even in this day and age, many women settle all too easily into the role of "The Wife." She may have jettisoned friends you didn't approve of, or lost touch with them because she wanted to invest more time in her relationship with you. As a result, she considers your going out a form of abandonment, perhaps feeling that she's more committed to the marriage than you are. Inviting her to come along when you go out is a quick fix to this problem, although that doesn't take into consideration your need for independence. The best solution may be to encourage your wife to reestablish her relationships with old friends and to cultivate new ones by joining a community group or charitable organization.

❷ She's right. Maybe you are going out too much with your buddies. Are you avoiding something at home? Housework, perhaps, or a wife you feel is too demanding? Take a moment and think about whether you are going out *for* something or escaping *from* something. If you feel there's a problem at home, take the next few moments to talk to your wife about it. It may be something neither of you were aware of, something that's easily solvable.

Independence and privacy issues always seem more serious than they really are. The very need for privacy is what makes it difficult to have an in-depth, heart-to-heart discussion with your wife about why you went out alone four times last week. But if she senses there's something wrong, it merits discussion. The sooner you talk about it, the sooner you can step out of the bathroom and back into your marriage.

Privacy and Independence—Hers

During your wedding, you were asked a number of critical questions to which you answered "I do," "I will," "I shall," or a sentence with some other verb that essentially means "You betcha." The critical word in these affirmations, however, is not the verb but the subject: I. "I" is something that far too many women leave at the altar. Even in this age of enlightenment, a vast number of married women quickly subvert "I" for "we."

In her book *Marriage Shock,* Dalma Heyn explores this phenomenon by stating that even an independent woman can, upon marrying, fall under the spell of what a "wife" is supposed to be and change her behavior in order to conform to this ideal. A woman in a relationship may speak up less, hide her opinions more, and focus on other people's pleasure and happiness at the expense of her own. Perhaps this is because women, more so than men, believe that happiness is tied to relationship satisfaction. A woman may, therefore, invest more time in a relationship than in other aspects of her life. In simple English, this means married women may find it challenging to maintain a sense of independence.

The question you may be asking is "Why is it important to do so?" Marriage, after all, is a defining factor of life. But while it does require a certain amount of self-sacrifice, you should keep in mind that your "self" is a big part of what your husband married. If you sacrifice it, or discard chunks of it that are redundant now that his "self" is always around, you're taking a valuable ingredient *away* from the marriage. Your husband may find your loss of independence puzzling or unappealing. He may wonder what happened to the dynamic woman he married, with all her interesting friends and exciting hobbies. Here's how to keep her inside you where she belongs:

Make a concerted effort to keep up with old friends.   Look through your address book, browse your high school or college yearbook, search for long-lost familiar names on the Internet. (One great free site is www.switchboard.com.) Get e-mail at home or at work. It's a great, nearly free way to stay in touch with people you don't have the time or the inclination to speak with every day.

Make an effort to find new friends.   This is easy to say but increasingly difficult to do as you get older. In high school making friends was essential; in college it was easy. But when you're married, it starts to seem as though you should have already filled your lifetime quota of friends, and any gesture to acquire more may feel a little desperate.

It doesn't have to be that way at all. There are plenty of people who just want someone to talk to as they're going through their daily routines: the person in the next cube at work, that woman you always see at the gym, the couple that lives in the apartment down the hall. Strike up a conversation the next time you see them. Don't force yourselves to go to the movies right away—that kind of friendship takes time to build. Just continue to add to your outer circle of friends so you'll have an ever-expanding base from which closer friendships can develop.

Do things that have always made you happy.   Remember the activities you enjoyed as a kid? Maybe you liked to play softball or read comic books. Maybe you collected stamps, coins, or shells. Maybe you played an instrument or wrote stories that won prizes. Whatever it was, you did it on your own, and it didn't matter whether you did it well or not. If you're not still pursuing that interest actively as an adult, maybe it's time to take it up again. With interests, as with friends, you can't have too many.

Volunteer.   Community service is a hobby in and of itself; it's a great way to meet friends; it's helpful to society in general; and it's more personally fulfilling than writing a check to a charity. Nonprofit organizations are not difficult to find, and I don't know of one that has ever turned down a helping hand. First decide where your skills are most needed. Do you enjoy working with the elderly or with kids? Do you like to fix up houses, or would you rather try your hand at fund-raising? Pick something you enjoy, and tell your husband you'll be busy volunteering once a week.

Teach yourself how to do things around the house.   There's something satisfying about knowing you can handle the day-to-day jobs your husband may traditionally do. You don't want to find yourself calling your spouse on a business trip to tell him a lightbulb burned out and you don't know where he keeps the spares.

Consider the significance of your maiden name. Some women choose to keep their maiden name after marriage; they feel a strong connection between the name they were born with and their personal identity. Other women unquestioningly take their husband's last name, believing it solidifies their union. This may be a particularly easy decision if your maiden name is Stinkenblatt, but if you do, be prepared to take some grief from feminist friends. A third choice is hyphenation, though it's tough to fit "Mary Margaret Stinkenblatt-Fuskowitz" on a nameplate at work, and your children could wind up with names as long as that of Madonna's baby.

Take all necessary steps to feel good about yourself. Make time to go to the gym. Shop for clothing that makes you happy. Splurge on a really terrific haircut or a massage, or have your toenails painted purple. You deserve it.

The Pie of Life Quiz

Take a piece of 8¹/₂″ × 11″ paper, and draw two big circles of equal size on it. Under one circle, write "Me." Under the other, write "My husband" or "My wife."

Imagine that those circles represent pies, divided into all the big issues that you and your spouse think about on a day-to-day basis. Below is a partial list of these issues, but feel free to add any others that you feel are important.

Divide your pie into pieces representing each issue. The bigger the piece, the more important that issue is to you. Then divide your spouse's pie according to the importance you think he or she places on each issue. Your spouse should try the same exercise, then you can compare pies and see where your priorities are. The goal is not to aim for similar pies, but rather to understand why your and your partner's pies look the way they do. A working knowledge of your differences can be an invaluable tool throughout your first year of marriage, as can a clear picture of your own priorities.

BIG ISSUES

My Marriage	Sex	Hobbies
My Job	Money	Friends
Religion	Politics	Success and Failure
Physical Pain	The Future	Children
Eating	Physical Appearance	Exercise

Example

MONEY

Shopping—His

*T*here's nowhere your wife would rather be right now than in a store trying on shoes. It's an instinct similar to the way newborns reflexively grip fingers and men grip remotes. Try as you may, you'll never get your wife to go against her shoe-gathering instinct.

But you could accept that fact, if only you could avoid the shopping penalty box. That's the area of three or four chairs in every women's department where husbands and boyfriends go to slowly die while their significant others try on every piece of clothing in the store. In the penalty box, you'll get some half-hearted camaraderie—a knowing nod, a few eyeball rolls—and maybe you can borrow somebody's sports page. But the truth is, you've been dragged to a place you just don't want to be, and nothing makes a guy feel more stupid or caged-in than that.

The biggest problem with shopping is that things cost money. You can clip coupons; you can buy generic brands; you can compare cost per pound; but when you reach the checkout line, you'll still have to haul out your wallet. You and your wife can be spared a lot of pain if you give in to the reality of shopping before you enter any store: When it's over, you will have more things and less money. That's life.

While you may view shopping as a

SEVEN SURVIVAL TIPS FOR SHOPPING WITH YOUR WIFE

1 Agree to go only to men-friendly department stores. Remember the golden rule: If there's no chair, don't go there.
2 Take a magazine to clothing outlets. If your wife is feeling fat, take a book.
3 When your wife asks if you like something she's just tried on, don't point at the six-foot, stick-thin, part-time-model/saleswoman and say "I like *that!*"
4 Don't get pulled into the dressing-room area. You'll end up ferrying clothes back and forth from the rack to your wife. The other women will think you're a sicko.
5 Eat before you grocery shop. The bulk foods section of SuperFresh is no place to be suffering from low blood sugar.
6 Bring a list to the grocery store, and stick to it. You get two nonlist items a piece, and that's it. No cheating.
7 Do not argue. Your wife will ask your opinion, then ignore it when you give it. She'll tell you she's almost finished and spend another hour looking. She'll agree to a budget, then overspend with abandon. You can fight these truths, but you'll never beat them, so keep quiet and find a comfortable seat near the lingerie section.

way to acquire necessities, your wife sees it as self-expression. It's a female instinct. It's her way of hunting, and if she doesn't get it out of her system, she may be unpleasant to live with. Try to be tolerant of shopping and the bills it produces. Remember, it's her money, too. Even if she doesn't buy beer with it, she's allowed to feel as though it's money well spent.

How do you keep an eye on the bottom line and still stay out of the penalty box? First, before either of you shops, decide how much money each person will spend. If one of you feels the need to exceed that limit, agree that he or she will cut back in some other way to compensate.

Next, make a deal: Tell your wife you'll go shopping only when you plan to purchase something for yourself, for your home, or for someone you both know. Even so, once you're in a store, your wife may get caught in the powerful tractor beam of women's apparel or bathing suits. If this happens, ask her how much time she needs, then tell her you're going to get the car washed, or to the electronics department, or somewhere else you belong.

When you come back, you have every right to expect your wife to have finished her shopping. But at this point she might pull the "How does this look?" gambit. You will have no correct answer. If you say whatever it is looks great, you get to tack it onto the credit card bill. And if you say it looks terrible, she's going to want to know why. Here's a hint: You don't know the answer. Even if you think you do, you really, really don't. Why clothes do or don't look good is something only women know.

Diplomacy is the only way out. Tell your wife that if she wants a particular item, she should buy it, because *everything* looks great on her. But remind her that the money might be better spent on something more pressing, like food and shelter. If the cost of the purchase exceeds her preset limit, ask her if it's worth sacrificing some other expense. Your wife will eventually stop clothes shopping when you're around, mainly because then she can take her time, with no one there to remind her of the impending American Express bill.

Shopping—Hers

*T*here are three types of husband-and-wife shopping expeditions: (1) The two of you shop for *you;* (2) The two of you shop for *him;* and (3) The two of you shop for the two of you.

The first situation will never happen more than once (the very first time). After that you'll need to slip Valium into a hot dog and tie your husband to the passenger seat of the Subaru in order to get him to the mall. As for number two, he'll say anything to prevent it from happening: "This shirt still fits, pretty much." "But I look good in this." Pitiful signs of denial. You know the real story: His underwear looks like Swiss cheese suspended from a semidetached waistband, and he has fifty-two socks—none of which have partners. Number three usually takes place in a grocery or department store and involves a complex ritual of seduction and denial.

They say you can lead a horse to water, but you can't make him drink. Thus it is with men and shopping. You can suggest it's time to buy a few new things, but getting your husband through the door of a shop is the first obstacle. Try announcing that you're going out to buy him something, and suggest he accompany you so he can get his gift right away. Once in the store, a whole smorgasbord of challenges lies between the cash register and your new toilet seat cover, or the shirt of your husband's dreams (which he doesn't yet know about). Here's how to survive.

Let him take the lead. Follow your husband around as he picks things out, and praise his selections. Alternatively, try to anticipate his course and strategically place in his path those items you want him to select. It will be important for him to feel proprietary about the final purchase—"Look, I found it myself!" No man wants to admit to his friends that his wife picks out his clothes or food.

Don't leave him alone. Even if your favorite section is just a hop, skip, and a jump away, try not to shop for yourself while you're out shopping for him. He'll be finished much sooner than you will, and without your presence, your husband will end up buying six pounds of week-old kielbasa, or clothes that make him look like part of the cast of *Welcome Back, Kotter.* Then he'll whine like a baby for hours afterward about having to wait for you.

Once you've parked him safely in a dressing room or, say, the lighting department, let him start exploring items he has picked out. Then start mixing in things you've selected. Remember, you're in the company of someone who spends the majority of his life on the sofa but can't remember what color it is. Don't worry about him noticing which clothes were chosen by whom, or the fact that the Day-Glo lamp he was clutching has been replaced on the sly by something that won't fight with the wallpaper.

Once a man is wearing a shirt, he starts to think possessive thoughts. Likewise, once he puts that package of premarinated baby backribs into the cart, he's mentally begun to digest them. The solution is to remove bad selections as quickly as possible. Stall when your husband puts on a tasteful piece of clothing, in order to allow bonding to occur between him and it. Encourage a passionate coupling by telling him how good he looks, how sexy, how buff.

Making an actual purchase is a climactic experience. This leaves your husband feeling as though he's just had sex. He's signed the charge slip, forked over the cash, and now he's finished. He's thinking about a snack and a nap. While you may not yet have experienced similar satisfaction, you're going to have a hard time getting him to snuggle up to the idea of any further shopping.

Reinforce his good behavior with a treat. Let him pick out a piece of lingerie for you for every two pieces of clothing you pick out for him. A Hershey's Kiss for every can of Spam he puts back.

Keep it short. Your husband will be happy to volunteer an opinion on joint purchases, like furniture. But once again, when he's finished, he's finished. The male shopping tolerance level drops faster than a lead balloon. Try alternating fifteen minutes of clothes shopping with a rejuvenating trip to the frozen yogurt bar or the electronics department.

If you absolutely must shop for yourself while your husband is with you, for both your sakes, let him wander on his own. Just be sure to set a meeting time so you don't end up without a ride home. Keep M&M's in your purse and dole them out as needed to raise your husband's flagging spirits. You never know: You may even catch him having a good time.

Merging Your Money—His

With marriage comes his & hers towels, his & hers golf clubs, and his & hers oven mitts. That may be the reason it's so hard to let go of the idea of his & hers money. The thought that someone else has ATM card access to your bank account, even if it's the one person you trust most in the world, can send shivers down your spine. Remember the *Seinfeld* episode in which George refused to share his ATM password with his fiancée?

This is why some couples never combine their accounts even through fifty years of marriage. For instance, both before and after they were married, Adrienne and Frank kept a "his account," a "her account," and a joint account from which they withdrew household, travel, and investment expenses.

Most newlyweds, however, find that the benefits of the joint bank account far outweigh the temporary trauma of merging your money with that of your spouse. Before they were married, Janice and Jeff kept taped to the door of their refrigerator a running tally of his and hers expenditures. When they returned from their honeymoon, they ripped up the list with great ceremony. For them, a joint bank account was not just a procedural relief but also a sign of the freedom marriage brought to their relationship. Eric and Louisa pooled their accounts the very day they moved in together, and nothing changed when they officially tied the knot.

Once you've decided to merge your finances, you must deal with the Mystery of the Missing Money. Before you got married, it probably seemed you had a lot more cash to throw around. If you wanted something, you saved up for a while and bought it without consulting anyone else. But suddenly, the act of marriage seems to have put a serious strain on your disposable income, not to mention your consumer's freedom of choice. Surprisingly, your wife has the same impression. These feelings build up over time, until they find an outlet in the "You're spending too much" argument, in which each of you complains that the other is buying more than his or her share of personal stuff. Allow me to solve the mystery by identifying the culprit: It's not you, and it's not your wife; it's your marriage that's draining all the cash.

You see, there are three ways to spend money in a married household: His spending, Her spending and Couple spending. No matter how much time you spend budgeting your income, dividing your monthly spending allowance, and rationing out the money, you will never be happy with the amount that ends up in the His spending section of the budgetary pie. Where it used to be 100 percent, now it's only 33 percent.

The same thing has happened to your wife, which is why she's wondering where her monthly clothing allowance went. If you both have jobs, you may have thought combining incomes would actually increase the amount of money you would each have to spend. So it can be quite a shock to find that marriage increases only the amount of cash that goes to "community" items.

Welcome to one of the first big surprises of matrimony. Before you even add a child to the mix, at least one-third of your income will be going to support this union of two you've created. It goes toward stuff that doesn't feel like it truly belongs to either of you alone: vacations, furniture, table linens, rent on a house or apartment, even food.

Unfortunately, the bad news doesn't stop there for dual-income couples. The government wants a little piece of your marriage, which it takes in the form of the marriage penalty, a tax policy that forces you and your spouse to combine incomes as if you were one person making a higher wage, probably under a higher tax bracket. If you have no tax shelters, such as a home mortgage or children, this penalty can change an annual tax return into a big check written to the IRS. Even if you got married in December, you have to file your taxes as if you'd been married all that past year. If you're in this situation, you may want to calculate your taxes early and start saving up.

Now that you've agreed it's neither your nor your wife's fault that you don't have any money, feel free to make fun of the things she buys: facial creams, a rainbow of jogging bras, a new wardrobe for every season, a coat for every occasion. Even worse, she's probably put herself in charge of useless couple expenses like new valances and guest washcloths. If only she understood it's worth starving for a year so you can afford to wire the whole house so it runs off a single remote control unit. Unfortunately, at the mention of your electronic dreams, your wife will snort something like; "Oh great, so Jason and Suzanne will come over and say 'Great remote control system, but where the heck are your curtains? And I wanted to dry my hands in the bathroom, but there were no towels, so I just wiped them on your dog.' "

To which you can say . . . pretty much nothing, because you'll be forced to realize that maybe your wife is the one with the sensible spending habits after all, and maybe, just maybe, marriage is the best thing to happen to your standard of living since you discovered the self-clean setting on your oven.

You'll soon find that merging your money has an equally positive effect on your lifestyle. We've found that one of the great joys of being a wedded couple is the mutual freedom and responsibility of shared income. Wendy and I owe it to each other to spend prudently and respect our household budget; we trust that the other person will do so as well; we work as a team on major purchases; and we each want the other to enjoy life and have the ability to spend the money necessary to do so.

It took us an entire year of bickering over $150 worth of panty hose and a real-bargain-of-a-used-$3,000 stereo to arrive at this oh-so-mature financial attitude. Just do your best to avoid going bankrupt in the interim, and you'll get there, too.

Merging Your Money—Hers

A joint bank account is about trust. Imagine it to be an Oscar the Grouch cookie jar. You agree that you and your husband should both add cookies to the jar, so you're mutually responsible for keeping Oscar full. And you agree that each of you should be allowed to take cookies from the jar when your needs require it.

But we're all human, and the natural human instinct is to suspect you're doing a greater share of the cookie adding and less of the cookie taking. Your spouse is likely to feel the same way. What we have here is basically cookie-jar communism, and we all know how well that works in the real world.

Which brings us back to trust, the rock-solid foundation of any strong marriage. When you and your husband form a joint bank account, you're saying, "I know you won't skip off to Mexico with your secretary and all of our money." "I know you won't use our money to buy the dog a ten-piece set of designer Frisbees without telling me." "I trust you and you trust me, and we're doing this to reduce all the ridiculous paperwork in our lives." Believe it or not, hundreds of thousands of couples make the joint bank account work based on the strength of their trust.

Keep in mind that, just because you and your husband trust each other's judgment, a joint account doesn't guarantee you won't argue about money. Every couple argues about money, because no matter how much you have, it's never enough. So if you find yourselves arguing about who spent how much on which black dress that was totally on sale and fit perfectly, there's no need to question the value of a joint bank account. The account itself is fine. The real issue is money.

What threatens to crack the cookie jar right down the middle is the fundamental difference between the ways in which men and women look at spending money. Men get nervous about big expenditures that don't have buttons and blinking lights. They think nothing of spending $200 in one day if they spend it on four different things that cost $50 each. But they panic when faced with a $200 price tag on one item. Say the two of you have been looking for a comfortable chair for the living room. You both want it, and you both realize that the perfect chair might cost a lot of money. Then you find the chair, you agree on it, you look at the price: $300—and suddenly your husband balks. He's paralyzed with fear. Women, on the other hand, recognize that $300 is $300, no matter how you break it up.

On top of that, men don't have a clue what things cost. The average untrained husband would get his butt kicked on *The Price Is Right*. A vacuum cleaner? Shouldn't cost more than twenty dollars. A set of queen-size sheets with pillow cases? Fifteen. A brand new washer/dryer? What, like a hundred bucks? Your husband thinks things still cost what they did in the Depression. But that's no excuse for ignoring one very important economic principle: Spending money = saving money. Take the case of a discounted DKNY suit. When it's originally priced at $600 and I buy it for $400, I saved $200 in cash. Right? I mean, *duh*. One-third off is one-third right in your pocket.

Trust me, your husband will never understand advanced sale-shopping theory. But there are other strategies you can use to allow yourself to spend money freely. Understanding what makes our husbands panic has led women to develop finely tuned survival skills. Katie, for example, applies the ancient technique of Divide and Conquer. Rather than run the risk of her husband suffering heart failure after seeing a $150 charge from Nine West on the Visa bill, she puts one pair of shoes on the Visa and another pair on her MasterCard. Her husband—an otherwise intelligent man who understands that two plus two, in theory, equals four—can't see the Big Expenditure, thus camouflaged, for what it is. Similarly, Molly staggers her purchases according to when various credit card bills are due. If the American Express statement closing date is January 31, for example, she'll buy a jacket on January 30, put the pants on hold, and get them on February 1.

Before we get too cocky about women's superior sensibility when it comes to money, let's talk about the cash machine. If your husband has such a fear of big purchases, why is he perfectly comfortable withdrawing a hundred dollars at a time from the cash machine when we can only bring ourselves to take twenty? Your guess is as good as mine. Maybe we think that if we have it, we'll spend it, while men know that they're going to use it eventually so they take out more than they immediately need.

Speaking of ATMs, consider the case of Nadine and Kyle. Nadine didn't like to go to the ATM alone after work because she felt it wasn't safe, so she and Kyle opened a joint account and put him in charge of withdrawing cash. Nadine took from Kyle's wallet whatever she needed. This technique can be risky: Nadine told us that, at first, Kyle would yell at her when he opened his wallet only to discover, after he had already ordered his lunch, that he didn't have enough cash to pay for it. So they set some ground rules. Kyle keeps the wallet as full as he can, and Nadine always leaves at least twenty dollars in it.

Your husband may feel differently about you using his wallet as a bank. Some guys think their billfold should be their property, something they can predict and control. They don't spend a lot of time rifling through their wives' purses, and so they figure their spouses should just ask when they need cash.

The problem is that many women object to this "Here's your allowance" mentality. So we find alternative ways to make the joint bank account work. Some women pay with checks while their husbands stick to cash. Some couples rely on credit and keep a monthly pool of petty cash in the sock drawer. You and your husband will have to agree on which technique is best for you. But in the end, you will only experience the benefits of merging your money—less paperwork, more accountability, a greater feeling of togetherness—if you give yourself over to the kind of trust that marriage deserves.

Managing Your Finances—His

After you've merged your money, it's time to figure out how you're going to manage it. Evaluating your and your wife's credit is good place to start. Credit is an evil thing. It was offered to us all at a very young age, and many of us consumed it like candy because we *needed* that stereo, that rear spoiler, and that autographed poster of Charo. All too quickly we realized there's a reason they call it "credit" and not "free money."

Entering marriage, many men and women find that the only credit they have is bad. This can be a real detriment when the two of you try to buy a car or a home. Remember, now that you're married, your wife's credit is your credit, and vice versa. Now you both have to find a way to deal with the outstanding debt you've accumulated in your single lives.

There are only two things that can solve the bad credit problem. The first is time, and the second is good credit. Surprisingly, good credit is easy to come by. You earn it when you pay your heat and phone bills on time. Whenever you pay off a credit card, your rating goes up a notch. Needless to say, it's important to do all these things regularly. That means one of you should be in charge of paying the bills each month, presumably the one who can tell a checkbook from a matchbook.

First things first, though. You've got to divest yourself of old debts. If either of you is carrying a balance on a credit card with an interest rate of 15 percent or more, it doesn't make much sense to put extra income in a savings account where your money only earns around 4 percent. Slowly and steadily pay off each of your credit cards, and then cancel the ones you don't need. Try not to fall into the trap of signing up for new cards at a low introductory rate. Most of those rates only last a few months, and then you're stuck with another high-interest card to pay off. If you have several outstanding debts at varying interest rates, call around to a few banks and try to get a debt consolidation loan, which lets you make one low payment each month, usually at a reasonable interest rate.

Another useful resource in these credit situations is the Bank of Mom and Dad. Out of the couples we polled, during their first year of marriage, 75 percent asked their parents for some financial assistance, so there's absolutely nothing to be ashamed about. If your parents are willing to lend you the money, you should have no problem taking it. It essentially turns a high-interest loan into a no- (or very low-) interest loan, and because you use the money to pay off your bills, you demonstrate to the banks that you're making an effort to improve your credit.

Paying your bills on time and in full is not only great for your credit rating, it's a sensible way to manage your money. Once the bills are paid each month, you'll know exactly how much you have left over to spend on things that you want. Never treat bills as if they were optional—the sooner you pay them, the better off you'll be. To make bill-paying easier, call the phone, gas and electric, and cable companies, and ask them to bill you on a certain date each month. Then, when the bills arrive, sit down at the same time each month and write out all your checks.

Even if you feel as though these companies have control of your life, remember they're just service providers. If you explain that you want to pay your bills on time, they will be perfectly happy to help you. Many gas and electric companies offer an option that makes your payment the same averaged amount every month, so there are no surprises in the summer when your air conditioner uses more juice. Some cable companies give you a break when you pay your bill in full each January. You do have to bite the bullet up front, but in the long run it can save you a substantial amount of money. And since the cable company gets its money without having to bill you, you get pegged as a valuable customer.

If you work hard during your first year of marriage to establish strong credit and pay all your bills, you'll definitely see dividends when you apply for a car loan, insurance, a mortgage, or any other major family expense that requires a credit check. While these bits of advice may seem like the kind of common sense your father is fond of sharing, they are based on sound, time-tested principles of money management. And in the long run, following them can do wonders for your marriage's financial future.

Managing Your Finances—Hers

*L*et's face it, one of the reasons you got married in the first place was to say good-bye to bill-paying. Sure, you managed your checking account just fine when you were single, but was it fun? Of course not. We can bring home the bacon and fry it up in a pan, but sometimes we intelligent, self-sufficient women would rather let someone else baste the pork.

Managing household finances is one of those tasks women are perfectly able to do. But if someone else volunteers to take over, why not let him? The only catch is, boy will he take over. It's tough to go halfway when it comes to household money management, and if you try to make it a joint operation, either you or your husband will lose your mind. That's why one spouse usually ends up sticking his or her head in the sand and giving the other free rein with the accounting. There's only one drawback to being the ostrich: Since you don't know firsthand where the finances stand, you have no idea, in any given month, that you've spent your last dollar on Manolo Blahnik sandals.

Deciding who will handle the finances is easy if it's readily apparent that one of you is a numerical nincompoop. The warning signs: "Look, honey, everything after the decimal point matches what the bank says we have!" "I signed you up for another credit card—this way I can transfer the debt, and we never have to pay off the Visa bill I ran up in college!"

If it's not so apparent, there is another way to decide who gets to be the family financial manager: Get out your respective premarriage checkbooks. Start by laying them next to each other and judging them for accuracy, neatness, and overall composition. Then add up the total number of mistakes in each one to arrive at a letter grade.

The highest mark is A, which stands for Anal. You can only give an A to checkbooks that perform far and above the norm, those that are balanced perfectly each month, impeccably printed in indelible ink or even typed, annotated with every deposit, withdrawal, and check on a separate line, and topped off with each transaction date and place printed in the proper column. Very few checking-account holders reach this elite tier of organization. B is for Brilliant, still enviable, distinguishable from an A only by a certain lack of obsessive accuracy. In a B checkbook, successive ATM withdrawals may be combined on one line, and an occasional date may be missing.

Award a C for Casual to those checkbooks that are balanced within reason, accurate within limits, and overdrawn only once a year or so. In the graph of checking records, these constitute the top of the bell curve. D is for Disaster, a big hulking wreck of a checkbook with thick lines scrawled across the end of every month. These lines indicate that the user has started over each statement period based on however much money the bank says he or she has. Here you'll find inexplicable hundred-dollar leaps of faith, check numbers missing left and right, overdrafts beyond measure, and a unique capacity for butchering the principles of basic math.

What could be worse than a D checkbook? Why, an F, of course. F's reflect a Failure to keep any records whatsoever. Grade F people write checks and withdraw money until the ATM stops doling it out, so you could say that the F also stands for the Fickle Finger of Fate.

Now that you've arrived at an objective grade for your checkbooks, the next step is easy. The owner of the book with the higher grade wins the right to be your household's official treasurer. If your grades are the same—two B's, for instance—you'll have to hold a sudden-death tie-breaker right there at the dining-room table. Use the following questions: Who was the United States Secretary of the Treasury in 1956? What's 44 percent of 3,698 divided by 3? What's the national debt right this minute? Okay, what is it now? And finally, how old was Bill Gates when he was born?

If you win the tie-breaker, you have an awesome responsibility as treasurer. You must choose the right bank for your account, preferably one with free checking or low monthly minimums. You must devise a way for your partner to report transactions to you, such as sticking bank-machine withdrawal slips to the refrigerator with a magnet. And you must announce when the account hits the low-tide mark so that nobody runs out and buys that antique Turkish rug that would send the whole operation into the poorhouse.

And who gets to be the family treasurer if both your checkbooks score an F? Be kind to your money, and make your first shrewd investment. Pick up the phone and score yourselves a financial adviser.

Saving—His

Just about the toughest thing to do at this stage of your life is save money. If you're young and married for the first time, most of your major expenses are probably still in front of you. Car. House. Babies. College for those babies. Vacations. Furniture. Respectable stuff to replace all your cheap stuff. Retirement!?!

What in the world do you start saving for first? More important, how in the world can you save any money at all when you're already struggling to pay for the necessities of life: rent, clothes, food, and cable?

Unfortunately, there's no easy answer. The only way to start saving money is to just do it, and the best place to begin is at work. If you're working full time, your company probably offers a 401(k) savings plan, which allows you to put away a certain percentage of your pretax earnings each month. Even if your paycheck seems absolutely minuscule right now, you'll be doing yourself a big favor if you start contributing early to your 401(k). You probably know all the good reasons to do it: The money starts earning interest immediately; many employers will match your contributions; and you don't have to pay taxes on the fund until you withdraw from it, which in most cases, can be anytime after you turn fifty-nine and a half.

Maybe it seems silly to start saving for your retirement when you've got tons of other expenses to worry about. But ask any financial analyst, and they'll tell you that anyone who begins saving now, and plans to retire in the year 2025, will need close to $2 million in the bank in order to maintain a comfortable lifestyle for the remainder of his or her life. That's in addition to social security benefits (assuming you believe you'll be receiving them). The good news is that, if you start early and cut as deeply as you can into your paycheck, chances are good you'll save that much by the time you get your gold watch (assuming you think there's a company left that still gives them).

One more great thing about 401(k) plans. They build up more quickly than you think, and before you know it, they become equity. That means you can borrow from them when you want to buy a house or put a child through college. You will have to pay interest on the borrowed money, but the fun part is, you are the bank. You borrowed from yourself, so you're just paying yourself back with interest. Of course, you *do* have to pay yourself back over time. And keep in mind that if you plan on leaving your job, many companies insist that you pay back the debt, in full, right away.

Okay, so you've started contributing to your 401(k). What happens *tomorrow* when you want to buy a stereo or a new TV? Can you really save for retirement and put a little aside for essential electronic gear, too? Yes, but it's no fun. It means bringing a bag lunch to work every day rather than buying a sandwich at the deli. It means dumping your change into a big jar at night and occasionally putting it in rolls and bringing it to the bank. It means taking on overtime, freelance work, or even another part-time job. It means staying in every other Saturday evening and skipping a vacation or two. It means sacrificing some quality of life now in order to improve it later. Nobody ever said saving money is a picnic.

Before you and your wife start to save money, there are two things you should do. First, pay off any debt you may have, such as credit card balances and overdue bills. Second, agree on what you're saving for. Saving is much easier when you have a mutual goal in mind.

For instance, if you're saving for a down payment on a house, you and your spouse can police each other for breach of contract. If your wife comes home with one new dress too many, riddle her with guilt by saying, "That's a nice living room you're wearing." Beware, though. This road leads to retaliation. It won't take more than a few sarcastic comments like that before she starts nailing you for every infraction. "So you bought lunch at work today. Did it, by any chance, taste like wall-to-wall carpeting?" After a while, she'll stop even trying to be clever. "Nice hat. You'll need it when we don't have a roof."

Yes, saving money is tough on everyone. And right now probably seems like the worst time to start doing it. Bite the bullet, though, because there will never be a time when you have a big pile of money lying around with nowhere to go. Figure out why, how, and how much you're going to start saving. Then someday you'll have the pleasant experience of looking at what you saved and realizing, "Hey, that's a lot of money!"

Saving—Hers

Saving money. In theory, it's a good thing. In reality, well, it's a big, hairy drag. When you start thinking about all the things you'd rather be purchasing with the money you're socking away instead in some dull mutual fund—it's enough to drive you straight to the mall.

Especially as newlyweds. Think of all the places you want to travel with your beloved; all the romantic restaurants you want to experience together; all the Armani ties you want to drape around his neck. When you consider how much time you have ahead of you, it may seem ludicrous to begin saving now when money is so tight.

Unfortunately, if you've been swept up in the "live for the moment" rosy euphoria of newlywedhood, you need to slap yourself in the face; douse yourself with cold water; do whatever's necessary to accept the hard truth. In the next few months or years, you'll be making big purchases and life choices that will drain your finances dry. You may be buying a car or apartment or house, or even having a child who's going to need food, clothing, dance lessons, and schooling, not to mention those cool sneakers all the other kids have that light up when you walk.

Difficulty saving money when you're married crops up because two people with very different approaches to saving are no longer allowed to follow their natural instincts. There are as many different ways to save money as there are approaches to dieting, all having to do with whether you prefer your deprivation fast and intense (ripping the Band-Aid off all at once) or long-term and mild (peeling it off millimeter by millimeter). For example, one of you may belong to the Skim a Little Off the Top school of thought. If you need to lose weight, you cook with low-fat versions of everything; you're an expert at painless ways to get exercise by incorporating walking into your daily life rather than going to the gym. When it comes to saving money, you skimp a little every day; you buy generic aluminum foil; you brown-bag lunch instead of picking it up at the corner deli; and all the pennies you save this way gradually add up to a substantial sum. A thirty-five-year-old newlywed personal trainer at my gym is about to finish paying off his first home. How? He's been a skimmer since he was five years old.

If this seems like an agonizingly slow and ineffective method of saving, you may be more of a Quick Fixer. You like to bite the bullet and save money painfully. To lose weight, you throw yourself on the StairMaster for hours and starve yourself on four hundred calories a day. And when it comes to saving, you pay all the bills and then stick everything but twenty dollars "mad money" in the bank.

Whether you and your husband are Skimmers or Quick Fixers, the only truly satisfactory way to save money is to merge your saving styles in light of a mutually desirable goal. This is a three-step process. It may seem incredibly obvious, but you'd be surprised how much easier it is to save money when you take a methodical approach.

Step 1. Identify your goal. Discuss what you're putting money away for, and agree that it's something you both want. Obviously you won't be motivated to prolong the life of your panty hose with nail polish if you're only saving money for the pool table your husband has suddenly developed a yen for. Your goal can be specific or broad based, but if you have in mind something mutually acceptable, you'll be more motivated to sock away the cash.

Step 2. Figure out how much money you need to save. Are you working toward building a retirement nest egg, supporting a family, or starting a business? Or is your goal more specific and immediate, like buying a car or a stereo? If you're saving for a home down payment, for example, determine a rough estimate of how much it will cost. What's the average price of a home that fits your needs? What's the minimum allowable percent down in your area? How long can you wait to make your purchase?

Step 3. Create a budget. Ouch. This will hurt. You'll have to sit down and recognize exactly how much money you spend right now. Then figure out how much less you'll have to spend each day, each week, and each month in order to wind up with the sum you determined in Step 2.

Sounds simple, doesn't it? However, remember that when you're trying to save money, no matter what, you're still going to disagree over what constitutes an extravagance and what constitutes a necessity. But as long as you both firmly believe in your goal, you can handle anything—even bologna sandwiches seven days a week.

Salaries and Careers—His

*I*n the time before you and your wife have your first baby, the odds are good that you both will be working. Many couples in their first year of marriage continue to live on two incomes, mainly because, these days, you need more money just to get by.

But you probably don't work just for the money. More and more couples today are pursuing dual careers with equal ambition for personal growth and success. If your wife is building a career, it's essential that you recognize early on that her work is every bit as important to her as yours is to you. Even if she seems to hate her job more than anything in the world. Even if you make more money. Even if you advance more quickly. Even if it means postponing starting a family.

For the most part, this isn't too hard to come to grips with. It means you might have to make your own dinner when you come home. Neither of you will want to clean the house after working all day. You'll spend as much time talking about her career as you do about yours. Sometimes you'll have to go to her business functions and be introduced as her "better half."

These things aren't so bad, but there is one tough decision you may have to face, if not in your first year of marriage, perhaps within your first five. What if she gets transferred, or she gets a great job offer halfway across the country? You probably assumed your wife would follow you anywhere your job took you. Well, if your wife's career is equal in importance to yours, shouldn't you consider moving to help her advance? I have to say there's no easy answer to this problem. One couple we spoke with chose to live apart until the husband could find a suitable new job and a comfortable time to leave his old one. Another couple decided that his career *was* more important to him than hers was to her. If you're faced with a situation where one of you wants to relocate, you may decide a move will do both of your careers some good.

Now, if your wife makes more money than you, it may be a lot easier to support her career, but it may not have the greatest effect on your self-esteem. On average, women still earn only 72 percent of what men earn, and hold far fewer leadership positions, yet even enlightened men who consider themselves champions of working women's rights can still be intimidated by women who make more money than they do.

If your wife is the main breadwinner in your family, you may feel threatened or competitive. Instead of being grateful for the extra income and supportive of your wife's success, you might get edgy when she brings up her career in conversation, and less than sympathetic when she talks about her work problems. If you're comfortable with your wife's success, that's great, but if you feel resentful, the problem isn't with her, it's with you. Try focusing on your own career. Use your wife's success as an incentive to achieve your own. Eventually you'll come to terms with the fact that your wife is at least your equal in the job market. If she makes more money than you do, well, then you know how most women feel.

Of course, if you're both bringing in money, there's not a lot to complain about. Until you decide to have a baby. While there are certainly some stay-at-home dads, women are more likely the ones who have to decide between slowing their careers in order to raise children, or attempting to balance two full-time jobs. Many companies have taken aggressive strides toward supporting career women who want to have children, but the work still has to be done by someone, and new mothers can't always put in the long hours and overtime that today's jobs require. When you decide to start a family, should your wife quit her job and become a full-time mother? Should she return to work when your child is old enough for day care? These are incredibly hard choices for a couple, and especially a woman, to make. So whatever you do, no matter how much you want kids, you must respect the position in which motherhood will put your wife, careerwise.

However tough the family-planning issue is on career planning, it can be even tougher when the course of your career is decided for you—that is, if you or your wife loses a job. For many couples, unemployment = Trauma City. One of you will still feel the same pressures of office politics and getting ahead, while the other may grow depressed or withdrawn, staying up until three in the morning and sleeping in till noon. Downsizing can happen when you least expect it and can least afford it; for example, when you've just purchased your first home. The employed spouse may come home after work and wonder why the house is dirty and dinner isn't made. What in the world has the unemployed person been doing all day? The spouse who lost the job is probably sleeping late to avoid the heartache of watching his or her mate go off to work in the morning. And the last thing he or she wants to do is clean the house—that just adds insult to injury.

Unemployment necessitates sitting down and talking about these issues. Emotional support is required on both ends. Employed partners (and friends and family members) sometimes have a hard time remembering that looking for work can be a full-time job—and a depressing one at that. Most people have looked for a job at some point in their lives, and drawing from the emotions of that experience can be of great assistance in empathizing with an unemployed spouse.

During your first year of marriage, when you and your wife are trying to get settled in addition to perhaps pursuing dual careers, unemployment is the sort of major issue you're likely to face. And while it may seem incredibly stressful while you're in the middle of it, time has a way of smoothing out the ensuing marital conflicts. Through it all, it's vital that you work as a team, striving to set and achieve mutual goals and accommodating both of your needs to the best of your ability. Promise to support whatever your wife has chosen to do with her life, and she'll support you in turn—as long as your chosen field isn't professional couchwarming.

Salaries and Careers—Hers

We've come a long way, baby. Where once women were restricted to working as secretaries, teachers, or nurses, our job opportunities are now unlimited. Just like men, we can report the news, perform open-heart surgery, govern the state, sell stocks, and bring home the bacon.

Now if only we could bring home *as much* bacon as men.

It's a common story. If you work in an office, you can probably look around and find two or three guys who are doing the same job you do, and making more money at it. Why does this happen? Well, the top decision-makers in your company are still probably men. These leaders have likely created an atmosphere that encourages a "boys' club" dynamic; that is, an environment where young men, who act manly, aggressively express their opinions, play golf, squash, or poker with the boss, and tell dirty jokes in the workplace, are seen as promising workers. Meanwhile, women who pursue their careers assertively may be seen as "complainers" or "problem employees."

In some work environments, men are more easily accepted into the ranks of leadership while women are required to prove they can lead every bit as well as their male counterparts. When women try to do so, they are often accused of overcompensating. Caught in this no-win situation, many women sit back and try to do the best they can, with their careers idling as their husbands move more quickly up through the ranks.

If this isn't cause enough for disgruntlement, we are often humbled by those few women who are accepted as stars in their industries, the ones who beat the odds and claw their way to the top. We make up stories about them: "She slept with her boss at every level." "She has a powerful husband whom everyone wants to meet." Women wind up fighting each other for the right to hold select favored female positions.

After a full day of this, it's no wonder we sometimes come home in a bad mood. If you are a two-career couple, during your first year of marriage, your husband may feel you complain too much about work. "Be quiet and do your job, and eventually they'll give you a raise," he may say. "You're a business-person. You can't *cry* at work!" Of course, he'll say these things. That's how he gets raises. And he never cries, much less at work. Since he's probably a modern man who genuinely believes women deserve equal treatment, he may be under the mistaken impression that all men feel the same way and, therefore, that everything has been fixed, the ground has been leveled, the scales are balanced. Yet even after you explain to him that injustice does still exist in the world, it may be hard for him to empathize with your problems at work.

Let's take a common example from one of our surveys and examine how it plays out between a typical two-income newly married couple. Jeannie comes home and tells her husband, Terry, that she wants a raise but her boss hasn't given her one in two years. Terry assumes that Jeannie is asking him for his opinion about how to get a raise, so he tells her to do what he would do: Tell the boss all the reasons you deserve more money. Jeannie then says she can't understand why her boss hasn't given her a raise: She's done great work, and she's well liked. Terry says these are things she should say to her boss when she asks for the raise. Jeannie describes other people at work who get raises every year. Terry, thinking he's already solved Jeannie's problem for her, wonders why she's going on and on. Jeannie becomes annoyed. Terry doesn't seem to be listening to her, and all he does is tell her what to do. An argument breaks out.

Why are Terry and Jeannie fighting? Because Terry did a very male thing. He tried to solve a problem before he completely understood it. He leaped right to action without considering that the rules of the workplace may be different for his wife than they are for him. And Jeannie did a very female thing. She expected comfort, empathy, and emotion from her husband, not realizing that, for him, work is a battleground, a place where emotions make you "soft."

The solution? Teach your husband that there are still inequities in the marketplace. Ask him to simply listen when you tell him about a problem at work, or request that he help you lay out the problem before you both get into the solution. When you reach the point in a discussion where you want advice, signal it clearly by saying something like "So what do you think I should do?" If his words of advice are harsh or aggressive, let him have his say. Perhaps a direct approach *would* serve you better, and you could learn something about how men make business decisions. In the end, your husband can listen to you and enlighten you at the same time. He may be the enemy, but in time, he can make a pretty good double agent.

Finally, in a two-career family, it's twice as likely that one of you will be a workaholic. If you sense that one or both of you is putting more effort into the job than into the relationship, sit down, right away, and talk about it. Workaholism only gets worse if left unchecked. You don't want to wake up one morning and realize that the person sleeping next to you is a total stranger, his skin is pasty white because he hasn't seen daylight in months, and he's spent the entire third decade of life in search of his next promotion. If the workaholic is you, remember to put relationships first, and you'll likely wind up with a more balanced outlook on your career.

Buying a Car—His

Now that you're married, you and your wife will begin to make major purchases together. For example, many couples decide that one of the first things they need is a car. If both husband and wife owned cars before the wedding, chances are at least one of these vehicles is being held together by rubber bands, spit, and glue. Since it's only a matter of time before it will need a repair that costs more than the car's worth, you'll probably be in the hunt for a family car, one that both you and your wife will be comfortable driving, something practical in the winter, with room enough to accommodate kids should you have them in the next few years. In short, a mini-van.

Okay, you don't have to get that practical. But the car you buy should fit both your lifestyle and your budget. If you've never bought a car before, there are dozens of great books available to help you get through it unscathed. For solid advice and a broad overview of the many choices available to you, I recommend *Consumer Reports Guide to Buying a Car*. It's completely impartial—*Consumer Reports* magazine doesn't accept advertising or sponsorship from anyone—and it's updated every year with safety and performance ratings for every available model. Alternatively, every car magazine published today is filled with ads offering used car values for every make and model over the last ten years, and listings of each new car's invoice price—the actual cost of the car to the dealer. You can also find new and used car values on-line. Surf around the Internet, and you can get extremely up-to-date, unbiased car information, usually for free.

Once you know what a dealer paid for a car—or, if it's used, once you know what the car's actually worth—you're in a much stronger position to bargain. A dealer may tell you he's taking $2,000 off the sticker price as a special favor to you, but unless you know the original cost, you can never be sure you're getting the absolute lowest price.

Even if you're an old pro at buying cars, you'll find it's a whole different ball game when you try to do it with your wife. She may be perfectly comfortable giving her input on which car to buy and then letting you handle the actual buying. But many wives want to be an integral part of the whole process, and in fact, your wife might even feel that she can wrangle a better deal than you can. All things being equal, that may be so.

The sad truth, though, is that most car dealers in America still treat women like suckers, and unless your wife is extraordinarily forceful and knowledgeable about the car she's buying, she may get stuck with a painfully expensive deal. That's not to say that the same thing couldn't happen to you. Car dealers can turn normally assertive men into babbling idiots, and they're experts at making you think you've gotten a great price until you get home and run the numbers through a calculator.

The best way to deal with these characters is for you and your wife to go into a dealership as a unified team. Do your homework, research the kind of car you want, know what the dealer paid for the vehicle, then get in there and bargain. Rely on your wife's common sense during the test drive (for some reason, we men tend to get a bit emotional behind the wheel of a brand-new automobile), and rely on your intimidation skills when you get back to the dealer's desk. The dealer will probably try to talk mostly to your wife, reasoning that she's the weaker link of the couple and therefore the most vulnerable to persuasion.

One way to use this to your advantage is to have your wife play the bad guy. If she disagrees with everything the salesman says and peppers her conversation with comments like "That's really too much money" and "How much of a bonus are you making off of this deal?" he'll be forced to turn to you as the more reasonable customer.

It's important for both of you to remember to keep your emotions in check. Treat the negotiation exactly like the high-stakes business deal that it is. Sit down with your wife beforehand and discuss what you're going to say. Decide what the best deal on the car should be. Depending on the car, $400 to $1,000 over dealer's invoice is pretty reasonable, but don't be afraid to ask for a car at or below the invoice price. Don't worry about the dealer; these guys make money in ways you can't imagine.

Watch out for dealers who try to add costly features you don't want or need, like racing stripes or extra undercarriage rust protection. If the first dealer you talk to gives you the exact car you want at the price you're asking for, buy it from him. Otherwise, thank the dealer for his time and go on to another. Your chances of finding a good deal are much better if you shop around, and that first dealer will probably call you back in a day or two with the news that his boss miraculously agreed to knock another $500 off the price.

Another option to consider is leasing. With a three-year lease, you'll probably put down less money and maybe even have lower monthly payments than if you purchased the same car outright. Of course, you'll have to give the car back after three years, a period during which you've built no equity. But by then you may be ready for a new car, or you may be in a better financial position and able to afford a better vehicle. The choice is yours.

One last item. There are those of us who, even though we are married, fail to grasp the ideas of "our" money and "practical" purchases. Such a man may be found surprising his new wife with the keys to a slightly used '69 Pontiac GTO with a quadra-jet induction system. Since at the time she's probably sitting on the refrigerator box you've been using for a couch, surprise is typically not the only thing she'll feel. After a few victory laps around town, a vehicle purchased in this manner often winds up going back to the unfortunate fellow who sold it.

The moral of this story is clear. Now that you're married, your money is your wife's money, too, so she should be consulted in the making of any major purchase. And never try to pass off a toy that you've bought for yourself as a toy for her. This ploy has an extremely low success rate.

Buying a Car—Hers

Shopping for a car is probably the only scenario in married life in which your husband will be swept away by his emotions while you'll be ruled by your intellect. How sweet it is to stand in a car lot and hear, from the mouth of the man who doesn't understand one-day sales and the need to own more than one pair of black shoes, "I want it. Oh, I want it bad. Can we have it? Please? I'm going to die if I don't have it."

Men lose all rationality when faced with the opportunity to acquire a new vehicle. It's particularly important to keep this in mind on the test-drive, which is where the car-buying process starts. One test-drive, and your husband is a goner. It's the male shopping principle all over again: When your husband is trying on new clothes, he starts to feel like he owns something once it's on his body. When he's behind the wheel on a test-drive, he may look as though he's watching the road and testing the windshield wipers, but inside his head, it's July and he's in the driveway polishing that baby's hubcaps in front of all your envious neighbors. And he's fickle. Pry him out of the car, which he's already mentally purchased, and dump him behind the wheel of another new vehicle—and he'll want to buy that one, too.

Now let's say you manage to make it through a round of test-drives without your husband slipping his credit card to any of the salesmen. You drag him home, salivating, and sit down to calmly discuss the pros and cons of each car. You may have to make a final decision on your own. Your husband is in no state to evaluate the importance of things like dual-side airbags, four-wheel drive, and antilock brakes. He's drunk on the scent of new car, and he's thinking of nothing but horsepower.

Once you've made a decision, it's time to deal with that bastion of sexism, the car salesman. For some reason, almost all car salespeople in America are men, although Saturn does have a commercial that shows a woman on the showroom floor. (By the way, Saturn dealers also have a no-haggle policy, meaning the price on the car is the price you pay. Assuming the price is acceptable, this is a pleasantly stress-free way to buy a car. But needless to say, even Saturn dealers have to make money, so you may want to check out the invoice price of the car you're considering. If it's well below the sticker price, you may decide to work out a more satisfactory deal by going to a regular dealership and doing some bargaining.)

When you go to a typical car dealership, therefore, you will most likely be faced with a sales*man*. This individual will probably think your only interest in the car he wants to sell you is the color of the upholstery or how many cup-holders it has. Interestingly, because he assumes you know absolutely nothing about cars, he'll probably direct most of his attention toward you. He'll tell you how valuable extended rust-through protection is; he'll explain why you should purchase the company's exclusive roadside assistance service; and he'll tell you why you have to buy a hundred-dollar chrome tailpipe extender in a such a convincing way that you won't think to ask, "Why didn't they make the tailpipe the right length in the first place?"

Meanwhile, your husband is itching to make a deal. He's been in the presence of a state-of-the-art sound system, and he's hungry to get this part over with. However, the salesman isn't paying any attention to him because he assumes he'll be able to strike a more favorable deal with you and that you'll be able to persuade your husband to spend more money on useless optional features. Fortunately, you can use this to your advantage.

First, decide beforehand whether you or your husband is more financially savvy and more skilled at the art of negotiation. If it's you, surprise the salesman by doing everything right. Refuse all the costly extras. Ask questions about special sales, discounts, and cash-back incentives. And when you negotiate, start by asking the dealer to do better than the sticker price. Then, only after he throws out the first number, suggest a reasonable markup over the dealer invoice. Don't mention you want to trade in your current car until after you've agreed on a price for the new one.

When the dealer sees that you're the tough one in the family, he'll start treating your husband like the easy mark. He'll soon realize, however, that neither of you is a fool, and you'll end up with a deal you can live with. Don't worry if he seems angry at your tough tactics. You're not looking for his approval. You're there to buy a car, not make a friend.

It's fairly easy for two people to agree on what constitutes a good deal for a particular car. But when it comes to the car's color, your husband will be of no help whatsoever. In his mind, there's only one color a car should be. Red. Even if you're buying a station wagon, it should be flaming, screaming, fire-engine red. With a black interior. If you don't speak up loud and clear, you'll wind up with a car that looks like your husband's bachelor apartment.

After you pick a reasonable color for your new car, you may get to drive it home. But I wouldn't count on doing much driving after that, at least until the car stops being new. Now it's his baby. Even if he's a slob around the house, he'll keep his precious car pristine, inside and out. Thinking about putting a soda in that fancy cupholder? Don't count on it. You'll drip condensation all over the interior, and you know how harmful water is to—ah—interiors. Don't chew gum in the car. It might somehow fall out of your mouth and work its way unnoticed into the carpeting. No snack food, frozen yogurt, or sharp objects. And, especially, no pets! Did you know it takes one dog five minutes to coat the inside of a car with enough slobber and hair to decrease its resale value 40 percent?

But look on the bright side. You've purchased the car you wanted, and you got the deal you wanted. Relax and enjoy being a permanent passenger—just be sure to keep your muddy shoes off the dashboard.

Buying a House—His

When most couples get married, their debt experience is usually limited to credit cards and car loans. Well, welcome to the big time. The amount of cash involved in buying your first home is staggering. And when you learn that, over the course of a thirty-year loan (thirty years—yikes!) two-thirds of the money you'll pay is interest on the original cost of the home, you may begin to wonder why you should even bother.

Here's why: If you're paying rent right now, every month you kiss good-bye hundreds or even thousands of dollars with nothing more to show for it than the roof over your heads. And while it does keep the rain off your carpeting, this is hardly a satisfying financial experience. You don't have to worry about repairs when you rent, but you do have to deal with landlords who, depending on the luck of the draw, range from faceless corporations to kindly old ladies to heartless, money-grubbing misanthropes. While many of the people we polled have had good experiences with their landlords—one couple told us that theirs begged them to stay when their lease was up and even offered a rent reduction and free cable—almost everyone said they would buy their own place in a heartbeat if they could afford it.

The good news is that most couples *can* afford it, even if only one of you is employed. If you're thinking about buying a home, one of the best places to start is, believe it or not, the federal government. For a basic education, contact Fannie Mae, a private company chartered by Congress to provide information to regular people like us. Just call 1-800-688 HOME or write to The Fannie Mae Foundation, 4000 Wisconsin Avenue, N.W., Washington, DC 20016-2800, and ask for your free guides to mortgages and home ownership. In about sixty to ninety days (remember, this is the U.S. government), you'll get *Opening the Door to a Home of Your Own* and *Choosing the Mortgage That's Right For You,* two booklets that will help you figure out, among other things, exactly how much home you can afford. You'll also get a list of mortgage lenders in your area so you can compare rates.

While you're waiting for these guides to arrive, go to the bookstore and research the subject. Believe me, there's a book for every situation. Want to buy a condo or co-op? Want to buy with no down payment? Want

216

to live in a shack on the top of Mount McKinley? You'll find a book that shows you how. And the next time you're in the video store, look for useful videos in the how-to section. If there's a video on how to bathe your cat—and there is, we own it—then there's a video on how to buy a house.

Most couples say their biggest obstacle to buying now is that they don't have enough money for a down payment. Do yourself a favor. Call your bank, or ask around for a respectable mortgage broker, and see what you can purchase for the money you have. You're basically asking for an estimate, so there's no obligation. There are mortgages available that allow you to put down as little as five percent—or three percent in some special cases—of the cost of the home. That may just make it manageable for you.

One last bit of practical advice. Do all your research before you call a realtor. It's almost a given that your wife will want to jump to this part right away. She's ready to start thinking about what color curtains you'll need, whether the china you registered for will match the linoleum, and where the NordicTrak will go. But the last thing you want is to be standing in the kitchen of a home, which you have no idea if you can afford, surrounded by a salesman and pushy sellers. Even the smartest businessperson can't up and buy a home without knowing the right way to do it.

SEVEN SURVIVAL TIPS FOR AGREEING ON A HOME

1 Write a list of what you both want and agree on it *before* you begin to look at properties. There are too many variables for you to just walk into a realtor's office and say, "Show me what you got."

2 Don't ignore the major faults of a home in favor of one particularly attractive feature. A Jacuzzi hot tub does not cancel out the fact that a house needs a new roof or is in an undesirable neighborhood.

3 Before you put down a bid, both you and your wife should go through this exercise: Close your eyes and imagine coming home to this place. Imagine getting the mail, changing your clothes, preparing dinner, and relaxing for the evening. How does it feel? Could you call it home?

4 Don't ignore second thoughts. If you don't address doubts the minute they pop up, they can turn into serious regrets.

5 If you like a place the first time you see it, let it sink in for a bit. Then, if either of you has questions, go back and see it again. Don't worry about bothering the realtor or the owners. It's their job to make sure you're ready, willing, and able buyers.

6 You like it, your wife hates it. Or vice versa. Don't spend a lot of energy trying to convince each other; your home should feel great to you both from the beginning, and there's no reason you should settle for anything less.

7 Don't turn on each other. Buying a home is one of the most stressful things you'll ever do, and tempers can boil over very easily. Remember your wife is your partner, not your enemy, and you both want the same thing: a beautiful home you can grow in for years to come

Buying a House—Hers

The last time you made a decision this big, you ended up walking down the aisle shedding tears of joy all over your two-hundred-dollar bouquet. And now that you've decided who you're going to spend the rest of your life with, it's time to figure out *where*—a huge undertaking.

The first thing you need to do is talk about your goals as a couple. What kind of work do you see yourselves doing in the next ten years? Do you want to have kids soon? Do you prefer to live in the suburbs, or do you want to try life in the big city while you're young enough to keep up with it? Can you afford to invest in a large place right now, or do you want to start out small and trade up? These are big questions, but exploring the answers will put you in a strong position when it comes time to start circling listings in the real estate section of the paper.

The first decision you should make is where you want to live. If your jobs dictate that you reside in a specific area, then one of your toughest decisions has already been made. If this isn't the case, then muster all your communications skills to learn where you both stand on issues like country versus city versus suburbs; one hour from your family versus one hour from his family versus far away from everybody; terrific school district versus nearby tennis court and community swimming pool.

Thoroughly explore possible neighborhoods. Visit them at different times of the day—midafternoon, weekends, midnight, rush hour. Talk to each other about what you like. It's excellent practice for talking with realtors, because you need to be able to communicate to them exactly what you do and don't want in a property so they don't waste your time showing you inappropriate places. Draw upon the compromising skills you honed to razor-sharpness while organizing the wedding itself. Once you've decided on the geographical area in which you want to live, continue to exercise extreme patience as you explore issues like house versus apartment, old versus new, ranch versus Colonial versus Tudor versus trailer. Each decision you make leads to a new one, and they never get easier.

Before you start looking at actual properties, sit down with your husband and create a master list of what you both must have in a home. In a separate category, add those options that you would really *like* to have. Set an upper price limit, then give all these specifications to your realtor. Don't waste time looking at properties that don't fit your minimal requirements, and agree not to try to talk your spouse into living somewhere that too greatly compromises the list. On the other hand, try not to organize yourselves out of ever finding a place to live. Jill and Anthony drew up separate wish lists that when taken together narrowed their acceptable options to one particular size and style home on one particular block in one particular town. Their high expectations put them in the position of waiting for one of only five houses to go on the market. After two years, they've realized they're going to have to compromise somewhere.

Finally, decide which of you will be the contact person for your realtor. One of you probably hates talking on the phone and screening home listings. That person, left to his or her own devices, would set up an appointment to look at a six-bedroom mansion $300,000 over the price range you've set, just to get a realtor off the line.

As the two of you begin looking at homes together, you'll start to experience the "nesting" instinct. This phenomenon has the powerful effect of drawing you and your husband closer together. The process of finding and creating your first home emphasizes the matrimonial bond you've just created, and you'll start to feel "ourness" like never before.

In the midst of this coziness you may feel resentful if your husband tends toward big-picture rather than detail-oriented thinking when it comes to the creation of the new nest. He may not want to be included on decisions like "Do we need a formal dining room?" or "Can we live with only a bath and a half?" Instead, he finds it much more constructive to fret over the mind-blowing debt you're about to enter into, the physics of fitting a car plus all his junk into the garage, and the possibility that the musty smell in the basement means water damage. It's okay to have different concerns about the home you want to buy. Just make sure that you're both in total agreement when you sign on the dotted line.

The His & Hers Financial Pop Quiz

We trust you've learned quite a bit about each other's approach to money in this section. To make sure you were really paying attention, take this little His & Hers quiz. Both you and your spouse should fill in the appropriate blanks.

His 1. Your wife finds a fabulous Nicole Miller dress, regularly priced at $185, on sale for $120 and marked down another 15 percent. Plus, she's able to convince the salesperson that a missing button merits an additional $10 off. How much money did she make by purchasing the dress? _____

Hers 1. You go to the grocery store with your husband. At the checkout counter, you discover he's replaced the quilted toilet paper you picked out with one-ply; the toothpaste you like with a generic brand, and the tile cleaner you've always used with an 87-cent bottle of vinegar and a 45-cent S.O.S. pad. What fraction of a dollar has he saved? _____

His 2. You open the checkbook and notice that two checks are missing, but there's no record of who they were made out to or how much they were for. What are the odds your wife will remember writing them? _____

Hers 2. You open your husband's wallet and notice that the money is arranged neatly by denomination. Instead of taking a twenty and closing the wallet, you decide to have a little fun and mix up the bills. How long will it take for him to hit the roof? _____

His 3. It's time to balance the checkbook. You go to the refrigerator to gather the ATM receipts your wife has stuck there with a magnet. You see there are twelve withdrawal receipts, each for ten dollars. How many minutes has your wife spent in the last month going to and from the bank machine? _____

Hers 3. If your husband were a woman, how much would he earn per year doing the same job he's doing now? _____

His 4. You and your wife set out to buy a car. How many times over the course of the negotiation will the salesman describe to your wife the benefits of rust-proofing? _____

Hers 4. You send your husband out with $250 to buy a new motor for the refrigerator. How many snow tires does he return with? _____

His 5. Your wife has $200 to buy ten pairs of shoes. How many stores will she visit to achieve this goal? _____

Hers 5. Your husband has $50 to spend solely on underwear. How many pairs will he bring home from the store? _____

Answers:

His 1:	$93.00
Hers 1:	11/50 (22 percent)
His 2:	5 to 1
Hers 2:	2.8 seconds
His 3:	one hour
Hers 3:	28 percent less
His 4:	eight
Hers 4:	two (plus a free travel mug)
His 5:	fifty
Hers 5:	0

RECREATION

Going Out—His

There must be a million songs written about going out on Saturday night, and I'll bet not one of them was written by a married person. The symptoms of Saturday night fever often vanish once you tie the knot. Married folks who do still make the effort usually head out to a club, drink a few beers, meet some friends, and party all night, only to wake up the next morning asking themselves *"Why?"*

After a little while, probably during your first year with your wife, you may find that marriage changes your attitude toward Saturday night. You don't have to make big plans early in the week because it's pretty clear who you're going to wake up with on the weekend. By the time Saturday rolls around, you're sifting through the movie section and asking your wife if she's interested in catching the nine o'clock show. Soon even that will keep you out too late. Before you know it, every night's a Blockbuster night.

If you think this only happens once you have kids, ask your parents when they stopped going out. They'll give you some musty old story about how money was tight and they had to create their own entertainment. But what it really comes down to is, married people tend to go out less than their single counterparts.

Maybe that's not so bad. After all, marriage is also referred to as "settling down." Why not take it easy for a while? Let your single friends deal with the grind of getting in the car, turning it on, pushing the accelerator, parking, getting out, entering a bar, talking to people. With a little practice, this attitude will become second nature. If someone makes the mistake of asking you to go out once you're married, offer one of these all-purpose excuses:

❶ My wife won't let me.

❷ I have to go to work tomorrow.

❸ I'm saving money to put a new muffler in the Hyundai.

225

❹ Why should I pay to sit in a freezing-cold stadium when I've got a view from the fifty-yard line right on TV? (Dad's favorite)

❺ It's just too much damn effort.

Now you've got it! When you can use two or three of these excuses at once—for example, "My wife says we can't afford to miss work with the muffler thing and . . . oh, it's just too much damn effort"—you will have graduated to the ranks of a professional married person.

Of course, you may be one of those people who still loves the nightlife. Everyone knows at least one married party couple who never slows down. They're out there drinking, laughing, dancing, meeting people, and acting as though energy is not a limited resource. That's great. You'll find out soon enough whether you and your wife are like them. If you're not, there's no reason to try to be. Over time, every couple finds their own state of social equilibrium, and you shouldn't try to force yours. Don't fall into the trap of going out on Saturday night just because you don't want to be boring. After all, who's judging you? Is the world really going to look at you differently if you pass up the theater in favor of staying home?

If you think your wife is dull, or if she thinks you are, then you've got a different problem. One of you may be ready to settle down while the other hasn't partied it all out yet. So whatever you do, keep doing it together. If you still feel the need to go out every night, try to find an activity that your wife enjoys doing, too. If you're hanging out with friends, make sure she's accepted as a member of the gang. It's important to avoid the trap of constantly going out separately.

I'm not saying you can never go out *without* your wife. Just don't make it a nightly occurrence. Separation breeds anxiety, lack of communication, jealousy, and all the other mortal enemies of a successful marriage. Remember, the family that goes out together, stays together.

Going Out—Hers

You love each other truly, madly, and deeply. But let's face it, one more Friday night spent with a rented movie, take-out Chinese, and a bottle of cheap merlot, and you're going to go nuts. What happened to trying things like Rollerblading, or going out to long romantic dinners where you were too involved in conversation to look at the menu?

Well, you got married. And your husband got comfortable. Now he's got everything he needs at his fingertips: food; alcohol; the clicker; plus his beloved wife seated within his line of sight but at a noncrowding distance away. He's not budging until you peel him off the couch and tuck him into bed. Meanwhile, visions of having fun dance through your head.

Of all the things you thought would change once you get married, you may never have anticipated that matrimony would affect your social life. When you were single and dating, or engaged to your husband, the two of you went out as a couple; you went out as a couple with your single friends; you went out individually with your single friends; and you went out as a couple with your couple friends. You're still you, your friends are still your friends, and you and your new husband are the same couple you've always been. Now that you're married, your social patterns shouldn't change, right?

Wrong. Most of the newlyweds we interviewed experienced three distinct social phases in their first year of marriage. Phase 1: You start going out significantly less. You enter a sort of intense cocooning period that's part public withdrawal after twelve months of wedding hoopla, and part finding your togetherness sea-legs. You retire from society, doing solitary things like staying in bed for hours and cooking elaborate meals together.

After a few months of cloistered marital bliss, you look around at the outside world and realize, hey, there are a lot of interesting things going on. So you enter Phase 2: a flurry of social activity. Leslie and Andrew, a typical couple, started making elaborate plans to "spend quality time together out of the house." They organized big group dinners and tried out new nightclubs with their friends, both couples and singles. But they found after a while that the social dynamics had changed, and so their nights out ended much earlier in the evening.

Finally comes Phase 3: nesting. Nesting is a semipermanent marital state. Your husband becomes comfortable with intimacy, or with his idea of intimacy, which is similar to the Chinese food–and–video scenario we mentioned above, with the addition of a pair of shorts and his favorite ripped T-shirt. This is his natural state. He's sharing himself with you. Once you reach the nesting phase, you'd better reconcile yourself to being thrilled with that package seven nights a week. Women begin to nest in this phase as well, borrowing a T-shirt and their husband's boxers and whipping up batches of microwave popcorn.

But wait a minute, here! You don't have to settle for Phase 3. There are still things you can do to make your lives interesting without going overboard in classic Phase 2 style. Let's call it Phase 4. This Friday night, grab your husband by the scruff of his neck and tell him you're going out for dinner. Assure him that you know how to get there and there will be plenty of available parking spaces. Say you're meeting another couple, so he can't back out. Then, Saturday night, go out and play pool. Or go to an interesting bar and sit across from each other (when you go out with other couples, you spend a lot of time sitting side by side, but the face-to-face approach is a lot more conducive to conversation). If he refuses to get off the sofa, try going out alone with your friends. No doubt he'll react dramatically—heaven forbid someone, somewhere, should be having more fun than he is. The fact that you're having a good time will hopefully motivate your husband to ditch the couch potato act.

There's no standard for how often healthy couples go out. Most couples we know have evolved their own unique Phase 4, going out separately with friends, attending a reading group once a week, spending one night a week out together with another couple, and going out, just the two of them, a few times a month. The choice is yours: You can experiment to find what works for you, or accept the inevitable and suffer the couch potato consequences.

Hobbies—His

What are your hobbies? That sounds like a question you would find on a job or college application. But spelling it out on a marriage application wouldn't be such a bad idea, either. Your respective hobbies determine what you as a couple will do before and after work, where you'll go on vacation, the magazines you'll subscribe to, and the stuff you'll save up to buy. If your spouse isn't as gung ho about the World Wrestling Federation as you are, you may be headed for a hobby hammerlock.

To take a closer look at hobbies, let's divide them into two types: passive and active. Passive hobbies are things like listening to classical music, knitting, wine tasting, and test-driving cars you could never afford to buy. Active hobbies are skiing, tennis, scuba diving, jumping out of airplanes, and other things that might be labeled "sports" on desperate TV stations like ESPN 2. These hobbies require a certain amount of training, coordination, and skill.

Passive hobbies are typically less intimidating, but they do rely on individual taste. If you and your wife both enjoy fine French food, then you'll have no problem eating it together regularly (assuming you can afford it). But say your favorite pastime is watching football. You catch every game. You've got Cowboys' season tickets. In fact, you're the enthusiastic fellow we see on TV at half-time with his shirt off in thirty-degree weather, covered in blue paint, wearing a fake pig's nose, and barking at the camera. (Your wife must be very proud.) But chances are she's not up there barking with you. And it's entirely possible that she thinks football is nothing more than a bunch of fat guys getting paid millions to smack into each other. If so, you'll quickly find out whether she's willing to develop an appreciation for the sport, or if she's going to let you keep this particular hobby to yourself.

If she chooses the latter, you'll have to reach a compromise about your participation in it, and that may very well happen during your first year of marriage. Sooner or later, the annual showing of *Gone With the Wind* is going to conflict with that crucial Dallas versus San Francisco showdown, and the Civil War is going to break out all over again right in your living room.

Active hobbies require a different approach. Because they often involve expensive equipment, travel time, and usage fees, it's important to be sure both you and your wife share a particular interest. If you both ski, that's great. Both enjoy long-distance biking? Terrific. But watch out for the expert/novice syndrome. Al, for instance, is an expert skier, but he married a woman who had never set foot on the slopes. For their honeymoon, Al's wife, Angela, gamely agreed to spend two weeks in Vail learning to ski while he promised to spend the majority of his time patiently coaching her.

Anyone who has ever strapped skis to his feet has seen a couple like this progressing agonizingly down the mountain, one partner skiing and stopping, the other skiing and falling, over and over again, in a desperate attempt to reach flat land. It didn't take long for Angela to get frustrated at her lack of skill and for Al to start pining after Vail's incredible black diamond slopes. Angela was a trouper, and she eventually got pretty good at tackling the intermediate runs, but in retrospect she and Al decided that this probably hadn't been the best idea for their honeymoon. They spent less than half of each day together, and Al couldn't shake the feeling that Angela was just suffering in silence for his sake.

Dealing with different skill levels between married partners is never easy. And it can be especially tough on your partner's ego when you decide to learn a hobby together and one spouse progresses faster than the other. It's important to encourage each other in these situations, and to allow for individual needs. If your wife is better than you are at in-line skating, she may want to do it more often. Insisting that you always skate together is only going to make matters worse. And in hobbies where you have the upper hand, expect equal freedom from her.

In the end, it's not as important to find things you do *well* together as it is to find things you *like to do* together. Once you agree on both the hobbies you can share and the ones that are separate, you'll find that developing such interests is a huge part of what makes a successful marriage work.

Hobbies—Hers

A man can turn collecting garbage (beer cans that someone else drank out of, just imagine!) into a hobby. Together with the guy next door, he can turn weeding the garden into a competitive sport.

Your husband is by birth a creature of hobby. Hobbies are how he gets exercise, how he meets and communicates with other people, how he maintains relationships and networks. In general, he makes "hobby friends"— buddies who are an extension of his interests. (This is why he doesn't know his best friend's birthday, even though he's known the guy since grade school.)

Sure, we women have our activities, too. We collect things, we play games, we try things out. We're pretty self-sufficient at entertaining ourselves and developing our minds and bodies in new ways. In fact, in any given couple, when you think about it, the wife is usually the hobby bloodhound. We're constantly sniffing out different things to try or to learn together with our husbands—because we instinctively realize how important it is to develop interests as a couple. Otherwise, given the male mind, we know that our man will go find things to do without us. Usually they're the same four things: watch [fill in the sport here] on TV, play [fill in the sport here] with a bunch of pumped-up boneheads, play poker, or repair, paint, or plant something.

Before your wedding, your lives were consumed by constant planning and anticipation. Bridal showers, bachelor parties, rehearsal dinners, honeymoon planning, and the wedding itself kept you busy every hour of the day. Your postwedding life is slower. Sure, you're busy dealing with all the issues in this book, but let's face it, that's nothing compared to masterminding a plan to gather together upward of a hundred people on your wedding day without an international incident. This year, you're probably going to see less of your friends and family, and you'll probably have significantly less to do. What a perfect time to develop joint interests!

The creation of new hobbies is one of the strongest bonding techniques in your new marriage. The first wedded year holds an unbeatable combination of mutual inexhaustible energy plus a willingness on your husband's part to do whatever you want to do. (Warning: this will wear off.)

All the couples we surveyed for this book had similar advice: *Try every-thing.* You'll have the rest of your lives to get good at tennis if you discover early in married life that you have a mutual love for the sport. Identify as many things as possible that you both love doing or seeing or experienc-ing, and weed out interests that you don't share.

Here's are a few joint hobbies you might want to try. Brainstorm some of your own, and add them to the list.

- Take a wine-tasting class.
- Join a bicycling club.
- Learn a foreign language.
- Become garage sale junkies.
- Join a reading group.

In the case of hobbies that you and your husband don't pursue to-gether, there are two useful techniques that will allow you to follow sepa-rate interests in peace: Make a Deal and Fair Warning.

One husband explained to us that he enjoyed playing poker every Sun-day night at a friend's house. He tried to get his wife interested by teach-ing her how to play, but she thought it was boring, and so he stopped inviting her to the weekly games. That was fine at first, but after a while it started to bother her that he spent so much of their leisure time with his buddies. After some heated exchanges, they decided to Make a Deal. He got the guys to move poker night to Monday night when his wife had a book-club meeting anyway (the other guys were having conflicts at home, too), and she promised to sit down with him and plan something every Sunday night that they both enjoyed doing.

Fair Warning is typically used in matters of that all-important male hobby: television sports viewing. If your husband is planning to watch a ball game on Sunday, you deserve to know ahead of time so you can plan your day accordingly. If you're watching TV and he's been waiting half an hour for out-of-town sports scores, he should give you Fair Warning that he wants silence when they finally start announcing them. Otherwise, how are you supposed to know, amid five hours of unintelligible chatter, that this is the really important part?

Used properly, these techniques can be instrumental in preventing hobby problems—and in eliminating first-year-of-marriage difficulties of all sorts.

Traveling—His

The first real trip many couples take together is the honeymoon, and depending on how you work together as a team, it can be among the best or the worst two weeks of your marriage. The honeymoon poses a unique set of challenges, and though we're assuming this adventure is already behind you, it pays to examine the dynamics involved because they'll be present in every trip you take till death do you part.

It occurs to most couples on their honeymoon that, suddenly, you're more than just two people hopping in a car and setting off for a weekend of spontaneous adventure. Now you're married. In addition to the difficulties of postwedding duties, like writing thank-you notes and paying bills, and the rigors of arranging hotel bookings, traveler's checks, and plane tickets, you're now faced with the unexpectedly challenging prospect of being with your wife. Constantly.

Think of the last time you spent every minute of every day with somebody for two straight weeks. If you've ever experienced this, one of you probably came close to strangling the other. But your honeymoon should be different, right? You're spending two weeks with the woman you most want to be with. So why is it that after four or five days of making every single decision together you may be ready to hop the nearest boxcar to Albuquerque?

Simple. Many couples find that togetherness has its limits. This is perfectly all right. You and your wife promised to love and cherish each other forever, but nobody said anything about shadowing and crowding. If you're on a long trip and you start to get on each other's nerves, maybe it's time you went to the beach and she stayed by the pool, at least for an hour or so.

Once you've solved the crowding problem, there are literally hundreds of other things that can turn a great trip into a roller-coaster ride through hell. Fortunately, almost every one of those setbacks can be avoided with a little research. So before you go anywhere, read all you can about your destination. Find out what precautions you need to take before you land in a foreign country. Ask your friends, family, and co-workers about their experiences at your vacation destination. If their trip was bad, that's even better. You can learn from their mistakes without suffering through them yourself.

One couple told us about a horrible vacation they had in Mexico. They planned months ahead, got pictures of the beautiful resort where they were going to stay, and paid an all-inclusive fee in advance. But almost the minute they got there, the skies clouded over, the wind picked up, and every beach on the Caribbean coast was closed off. Apparently they had planned their trip at the height of hurricane season. After sitting inside for two weeks watching not one but two hurricanes batter their vacation to bits, they got on a plane and headed home with no tans, no pictures, and no memories of sipping margaritas at sunset. Their miserable experience could have been avoided with a little weather pattern research and the help of a decent travel agent. Find one who's recommended by friends or co-workers, and remember: Research, research, research.

It seems that in every vacation situation, one member of the couple plans everything, and the other complains. Let's say, for the sake of example, that you did the planning this time. Once you've taken every precaution, after you've booked the perfect hotel and secured the best deal on a rental car, now that you've charted out every minute of the vacation top to bottom, you arrive at your destination and your wife poses the excruciating question: "Are we having fun yet?"

Here's the answer that might come first to your mind: "We damn well better be. If I hadn't busted my butt planning every second of this trip to Kookaburra, we would both be sleeping under a rain gutter in a part of town even the roaches wouldn't visit."

Of course, that response is completely wrong. The correct reply is to ask your wife why she's not having fun, and to ask yourself if you're truly enjoying the trip, or if you're just following the plan you made because you made it. If the vacation's starting to look like a disaster, it can't hurt to do a little rearranging, even if it costs you a few dollars. Don't sacrifice safety, just sacrifice a little structure. Cancel the guided tour on Day 3 and do something spontaneous. Why can't a seven-day getaway turn into a ten-day excursion if you really love where you are? Stay up all night and watch the sunrise—it isn't like you have to work the next day. With a little ingenuity, you can turn even the most predictable trip into something memorable.

Most important, use vacations as an opportunity to get to know your spouse better. If you already know each other all too well, think of trips as a chance to get reacquainted. And whatever you do, don't skip vacations altogether. The major reason for working fifty weeks out of the year is to have enough money to enjoy the precious two you spend away.

Traveling—Hers

*E*ven if you and your husband lived together before you got married, you may not have done much traveling together. Sure, there was the weekend bed and breakfast here and there. But now that you're married, the world sees you as legitimate. No more signing in as Mr. and Mrs. Smith on prudish innkeepers' logbooks. Plus, as a committed couple, you now have the financial and logistical freedom to make bigger and better plans.

In short, you'll be going on trips.

From their very inception, trips demand mutual skill, tact, and understanding of your partner's travel speed, interests, and endurance. Look back on the first real trip you planned together, which was probably the honeymoon. You had to decide where to go, which was a journey in and of itself if your husband likes to flop on a beach for a week while you prefer to go rock climbing in Utah. You determined how you both like to travel—car or plane, book ahead or play it by ear, rough it or four-star-hotel it, take it easy or jam-pack every day—and you managed to find a travel destination that suited all your needs.

Then you made the travel reservations and packed. Packing. A task that seems so simple to your husband. A few pairs of shorts, a T-shirt or two, a snorkel, a toothbrush, and he's good to go. Meanwhile, you're struggling over whether to bring four suitcases or five. You need the black shoes that go with your jeans, the other black shoes that go with your dressy-occasion skirt that travels so well, the black shoes that go with the fun sundress, and the black shoes that are actually poolside sandals. Right there, you already need one suitcase for black shoes.

Now the big decision. Do you tell your husband that one of the suitcases he's lugging through the airport is filled entirely with black shoes, or do you wait for him to discover it and erupt like Mount Kilauea?

In the end, it's better not to bother justifying your packing job. He'll never understand that every pair of shoes you bring performs a specific function, but he will be enormously appreciative if you restrict your luggage to what you yourself can carry. He probably won't mind carrying one or two of your bags as you go, but he may be resentful if you pack for the trip with the assumption that he'll be your personal mule for its duration.

Traveling together involves a series of trade-offs. If your husband likes to wake up late, maybe he'll agree to start sight-seeing earlier if you schedule time each day for a nap. What if he insists on trying to speak the native language with every local you encounter? Fine—as long as he uses his linguistic skills to barter for the rug you've been coveting. One husband we spoke with is a stickler for eating three meals a day, every day, while his wife grazes throughout the day and barely stops sight-seeing long enough to eat one meal. Their solution? She gets to pick restaurants that fit in with the daily itinerary, and he travels with a supply of Snickers bars.

Whatever you do, encourage each other to make your expectations fit your trip, rather than the other way around. Take your honeymoon, for example. The first night of our honeymoon, the first thing Dave and I wanted to do was—eat. The second thing? Sleep. Guess what? It's the same for a lot of newlyweds. Think about it. For days before the wedding, you probably hadn't eaten or slept. Those couples who had the best time on their honeymoons accepted the fact that ordering room service and going to sleep were perfectly acceptable alternatives to the wild sex you're "supposed" to have on your first married night. Skipping the traditional wedding night consumma-

---

SEVEN SURVIVAL TIPS FOR TRAVELING WITH YOUR HUSBAND

1 Pack your extra stuff in his bag when he's not looking.

2 When driving, the minute you think you're lost, tell him you have to go to the bathroom. It's the only way you're going to get him to stop for directions.

3 Bring a little day pack wherever you go, and stock it with snacks. You won't always want to stop for lunch, so make do in a pinch with trail mix, Powerbars, and apples.

4 Play with your husband when he wants to play. Jet Skiing, parasailing, or snowboarding may not be your cup of tea, but he'll appreciate it if you join him in activities, and you may end up having fun despite yourself.

5 In foreign countries, your husband may be expected to take charge in situations like clearing customs and dealing with rental car offices, hotel front desks, and travel agents. But if it's clear that a woman's charms are needed to solve a problem, don't hesitate to offer your services.

6 If you're driving a long distance or renting a car, bring tapes or CDs. The countryside may be stunning, but a soundtrack never hurts. Local radio stations don't always play what you want to hear.

7 Think through the details. Protective cases for toothbrushes. Travel-size tubes of toothpaste. Feminine protection. Q-Tips. A travel iron. Birth control. Pepto-Bismol. For some reason your husband depends on you to remember these things and keep him civilized on the road.

tion has an added advantage: You'll wake up welcoming your first full day as a married couple, and what better way to ring in that day than by doing what you were too tired to do the night before? On any trip you take, remember to take it easy, enjoy the moment, and don't feel as though you've got to be together every second of every day.

One final tip: When you travel, try to get people in your snapshots as well as scenery. Have you ever had to listen to another couple describe their vacation while they show you sixteen pictures of a donkey's butt and blurry views of the Eiffel Tower? Pictures including people are not only more interesting to look at once you get home, but taking them can lead to fascinating conversations when you're traveling.

Driving—His

*I*f you're expecting this chapter to say the typical guy stuff about how women can't drive, forget it. There are women who drive for a living, and even women who have competed in the Indianapolis 500. There are plenty of women who can outdrive a man any day of the week, especially in terms of common sense.

Your wife, however, may not be one of them.

In humble deference to all of my wife's outstanding talents, and despite what you may read in her section on driving, my wife is a bad driver. Or, to be fair, she isn't as good a driver as me, which is to say she's not perfect. Actually, driving is something so few people do well that it's unfair to restrict the Bad Driver title to women. Therefore, even if your wife is as mobilely challenged as mine, you don't have to worry that the affliction will be genetically passed to your daughter by virtue of her gender.

There are fundamental differences in the way men and women drive, and that may be a source of tension when you and your spouse are doing 80 on the New Jersey Turnpike. Women tend to see driving as getting from point A to point B s-l-o-w-l-y, whereas men see it as a full contact sport. When some schmo blows past your wife, well then, he's an idiot, and she'll get her kicks when she sees a cop has pulled the guy over a half mile down the road. But in the same situation, you'll floor it in an attempt to preserve your reign as drag-racing champion of the world.

When your wife gets cut off, on the other hand, someone has broken an unspoken code of automotive courtesy. She might act aggressively, flashing the high beams, honking the horn, or retaliating by rushing ahead, cutting the same guy off, and slowing down in front of him. But you'll likely let it go and move on. Unless he can keep up with your pace, you've got bigger fish to fry.

Of course, not everyone acts in these predictable ways. That's the point—everybody acts differently. So you have to get used to the fact that few people drive as well as you do. When your wife is driving, let her do it her way, even if you're sure it's all wrong. And never grab the wheel, even if you think you're about to die.

Concentrate instead on your real responsibility as occupant of the passenger seat: navigation. Say what you want about men not stopping to ask directions, when it comes to reading a map, we clearly have the edge. Our big right brains know exactly how to solve spatial problems. A map to a man is like an old friend. But put that same piece of paper in your wife's hands, and you're liable to end up in China. Rarely is there so clearly a delineation in the tasks men and women were built to perform. When you're lost and your wife is the navigator, pull over and let her ask directions. When you're the navigator, follow the map. Problem solved.

Now suppose you're driving again.

> ### SEVEN SURVIVAL TIPS FOR DRIVING WITH YOUR WIFE
>
> 1 Pumping the invisible brake on the passenger side will get you elbowed.
> 2 The driver controls the radio, so if your wife is driving, bring a Walkman and headphones.
> 3 Grab the wheel—lose a hand. It's that simple.
> 4 That loud sound you keep hearing is just the sonic booms. Nothing to worry about.
> 5 Recline the seat and sleep if you can. It's much more comforting to look up than forward.
> 6 "That was a red light" is a pointless thing to say.
> 7 Dramamine is God.

Isn't it odd that, when your wife is safely buckled into the passenger seat, she magically becomes, in her mind, the best driver ever created? And this empowers her to tell you, at any and every moment, exactly what to do. She's got all the moves: fending off the dashboard with her outstretched arms, covering her eyes with her hands, and the ever-popular passenger-side braking action.

But that's nothing compared to the running soundtrack: "Can you please slow down?" "Do you see that truck?" "Watch out! There's a squirrel!" "I have to pee." "Are you *trying* to hit that guy?" And my personal favorite, "Do *I* drive like this?" Back-seat driving is a theatrical art, and if your wife doesn't get enough practice, she'll never win the Oscar.

Driving—Hers

Women are terrific drivers. I'm living proof: I've never been in an accident (which is more than my husband can say), and I've never received a speeding ticket (warnings don't count). Women in general have fewer automobile accidents and more commendable driving records than men. Just ask any insurance company which sex receives the lower rates.

Then ask them what demographic group carries the highest risk and the highest rates. The answer? Men, ages sixteen to twenty-five. Give or take a few years, and that's probably where your husband fits. Case closed. That being said, we female drivers have to stick together. When you see a woman determinedly merging into the fast lane and fending off the lascivious gestures of passing truckers while her husband is passed out with his face mashed against the passenger-side window, give her a wave. She deserves your support.

When you see a car ahead of you weaving in and out of traffic at twenty- five miles an hour and your husband snorts, "Huh, must be a woman," don't zap him with the cigarette lighter. Just remind him of his own driving history. When you pass the weaver and it turns out to be a guy, remind your husband that he shouldn't jump to conclusions. If it *is* a woman, give her the thumbs-up. She's doing the best she can on a man's highway.

Of course, male or female, all drivers are capable of getting lost. The difference is, women are also capable of admitting it, while men are missing the genetic coding that supplies the signal, "I am lost and I need help." They'll do anything to avoid turning around and will keep driving in the wrong direction for half an hour in the vain hope that the correct turn is just around the corner. They'll ask you repeatedly to scrutinize the map for roads that should, in their minds, logically exist: "Are you *positive* there's no Route 34A? Because if I'd laid out these roads, I would have made one to connect Route 14 with Old Mill Road exactly where we are."

If you get so sick of being lost that you simply can't stand it any longer, here's how to get your husband to ask for directions. First of all, avoid adding to his woes by using the pronoun *you* in connection with "are lost." Rather, say "*we're* lost" or "we seem to be slightly off course" so it's more a collaborative than a personal failure. That way he's allowed to think, heck, it's probably all your fault. Next, pretend you seriously have to go to the bathroom. Either your husband will sneak over to the attendant and ask for directions while you're using the facilities, or if he remains steadfast in his faith that he can find the way home, you can ask the attendant yourself while your spouse is off buying Twinkies. Of course the attendant probably hasn't bathed in a week, and you'll be stuck following the vague instructions he mumbled while staring at your boobs.

One more thing. The minute you make a plan to go somewhere, your husband starts suffering parking anxiety. While you're stepping out of the shower wondering what you should wear, he's thinking, "Where in God's name are we going to park?" Let him fret if he needs to. You know he'll eventually find someplace to put the car, and it can be curiously entertaining to watch a grown man reduced to tears as he tries to shoehorn the Blazer between two Porsches.

Long drives are especially eventful for married couples. There's something about being stuck together in a car that's conducive to deep conversation—and arguments. After you've listened to "Dark Side of the Moon" four times and played your eighth game of ghost, sheer boredom can drive you to start searching for the meaning of life. Beware, however, your deep discussions and mutual soul-searching may reach a point of vehement disagreement—over humanity's role in the cosmos, for example. You may find that your car has turned into a cauldron of conflict. "What do you mean, the universe is just a dust speck in the eye of some monstrous gnat?!?"

The situation gets worse if you happen to run into a traffic jam. To occupy themselves in gridlock, a recent survey reported that 75 percent of drivers sing along with the radio or a tape; 27 percent perfect their grooming; 5 percent take a quick snooze; and 5 percent change their clothes. Interestingly enough, among husbands who are driving, an informal personal study found that 61 percent lean on the horn as if it will make all the other drivers suddenly realize they're actually supposed to be moving; 27 percent pretend they're playing spy hunter and fantasize about blowing up the cars all around them; 75 percent will do absolutely anything to get ahead an inch; and 100 percent will pick a fight with their wives to provide a little entertainment.

So how do you, O dutiful wife in the passenger seat, avoid a fight? In yet another informal personal survey, we found that 50 percent of women pretend to nap; 28 percent crank up the radio to drown out the sound of their husbands' voices; 20 percent force-feed their husbands M&M's until their mouths are too full to argue; 10 percent can't speak at all because the g forces have pinned the words to the back of their throats; 2 percent flash their high beams at their husbands; and 100 percent resort to the time-honored technique described earlier in this book: "Yes, dear."

Gifts—His

Quick! What's your idea of a cool gift? It doesn't matter whether you're giving or receiving, what's the first thing that comes to mind when you imagine a great present? A set of stereo speakers? A Sega game? A nice baseball cap? A bottle of bourbon?

Now think of the gifts you received at your wedding. Towels. Dishes. Gravy ladles. Sure, you registered for that full surround-sound in-home theater system, but your wife let you do it only because she knew there was no way anybody was going to buy it for you.

My point? Married life changes everything, even the gifts you give and receive. On your birthday your buddies may still sneak you the odd bit of sports memorabilia, but you'll have to relegate it to the Hall of Fame closet your wife has rationed you. Your parents are through giving you guy stuff; from here on out, it's throw rugs and kitchen appliances for the happy newlyweds.

Worse still, remember when you were a little kid and your mother made you write a thank-you note to every relative who ever gave you a big, ugly, itchy sweater? Well, marriage is what you were practicing for. No matter how you try to get out of it, your wife will make you write a few of the gift acknowledgements after the wedding. And when you're done cranking those out, you'll have to write a thank-you note every time you eat dinner at another couple's house. No, calling your friend and saying "Thanks" is not good enough.

And you'd better not try visiting another couple's house empty-handed. You must bring them a gift. Something useful, like a deluxe universal remote control or perhaps a set of socket wrenches? Sorry, Charlie. You'll have to pick up a nice bottle of wine or some flowers for the table, or in a pinch you can make do with some precious little doily you purchased in the exotic locale of your honeymoon.

When your wife asks you to pick up a gift to bring to the Joneses' dinner party, your instincts will lead you to do one of two things: Ask the person at a shop what they would recommend, or pick a price range and grab the first bottle or botanical arrangement that fits into it. Mission accomplished, you'll arrive home, present your purchase to your wife, and promptly find out you made a mistake. "Everyone knows that Cabernet Sauvignon is not appropriate for fish," she'll say. "And who puts forsythia on a dinner table?" Your response will be, "Umm . . . I . . . well . . . duh . . . um," and she will fire back, "Oh, I knew I should have done it myself!" Which is, unfortunately, exactly what you wanted in the first place.

There are a few ways to spare yourself this frustrating scenario. One is to insist that your wife handle all gift buying for the family since she is apparently the only one who knows how to do it. The other is to educate yourself about wine and flowers. Read an etiquette book. Together with your wife, take a course in wine at your local college or learning center.

A creative way to solve the whole problem is to do what Sandy and Allen do every time they visit another couple's house. They bring something ridiculous that's guaranteed to be a conversation piece throughout the night, like a clock powered by fruit or a Jell-O mold that looks exactly like a human brain. Who cares if their hosts throw out these gifts the next day? Sandy and Allen have a reputation for being fun, interesting, and thoughtful party guests.

A word of caution about families and gifts. Your family wants to know what to give your wife for her birthday and for holidays. Do not get involved! Ask your wife to type up a list of acceptable presents, complete with make and model numbers, sizes, preferred colors, and catalog codes, and tell her to deliver it directly to your mother. The last place you want to be is in the line of fire when she and your wife start exchanging unwanted gifts. And finally, when thinking of gifts for your wife, here's a piece of advice about lingerie: This is really a gift for you, not her. Some wives want to receive lingerie, some don't. Get a read on your wife's nightie needs and preferences before you start waving your American Express around Victoria's Secret.

If you really want to score a big hit, go through her closet and drawers to check out her clothing sizes. Then give her something one size smaller and say, when pressed, "I described you to the saleslady, and this is what she said to buy."

Gifts—Hers

*T*he exchange of gifts among family members, friends, visitors and hosts, and husbands and wives has always been an important way to affirm and strengthen relationships. Receiving a heartfelt thank you is only a small part of what presents are all about. A proper gift says, "This is a representation of how I feel about you."

Because of this, you and your husband should choose every gift, regardless of cost, with care and consideration. Wrap gifts nicely, and present them graciously. And remember, though it may be difficult to convert your husband to this way of thinking, you don't necessarily need an occasion or a motive to give a gift to someone you love.

Men give their most thoughtful and romantic gifts when they're trying to get a little physical attention. Any of these sound familiar? A red rose on every stair step to the bedroom. A bottle of perfume he knows is your favorite because he's smelled it on you. Lingerie that accentuates your positives and hides your faults. These are just a few of the gifts you may have received before you first had sex with your husband. Now, you may be lucky to get some bubble bath for your birthday.

This occurs because there are two microchips in every man's brain through which thoughts must be processed. One microchip answers the question, "Will this make me rich?" The other provides the answer to, "Will this get me laid?" Unless you're talking about corporate gifts to customers and clients, gift giving is certainly no way to get rich. You actually have to *spend* money, and that idea strikes most males as counterproductive. Meanwhile, the other chip short-circuited the minute you got married, mainly because marriage is the ultimate answer to, "Will this get me laid?"

Now that the two of you are husband and wife, you'll start receiving the same presents he gives his family every year. To your spouse, buying in bulk is a fine idea. Anything that saves him money shoots right through the "Will this make me rich" microchip, so this Christmas you're likely to end up with the same blue sweater he gives his sisters. After all, they were priced at four for fifty dollars.

Largely deficient in whatever enzyme triggers tact and diplomacy, your husband will buy you whatever's on his mind. Has he noticed that you've gained a pound or two? You may be the lucky recipient of an exercise video—or, alternatively, a blouse a size or two too large. What else strikes your husband as a dandy gift? Housewares! Oh joy, a beautiful oven mitt in the shape of a cat, because you love cats so, and you live to bake him cookies. My, my, a Cuisinart! What with hauling the thing out from under the sink, locating the various attachments, and cleaning the whole mess when you're through, you may never have to leave the kitchen again.

So how can you convince your husband to rediscover his premarriage gift-giving thoughtfulness? Well, he either needs incentive (no sex) or a clue (no doubt). Withholding sex is not the healthiest way to strengthen a marriage, but if he's gone awhile without intimacy, your husband may surprise you with some nice little eighteen-karat knickknack. Aside from that, you'll have to tell him exactly what you want for your birthday; where to get it; what size and color it should be; and how much it will cost. Leave it up to him, and you'll get the *Best of the Three Stooges* video he's always wanted. Of course, all of your husband's gift-giving problems can be solved by reprogramming the circuits in his brain. A good place to start is the "Romance" chapter in this book. Once he gets used to thinking and acting in a more romantic way, more thoughtful gifts will follow. For you, anyway.

His family won't be so lucky. Unless they provide him with specific requests for birthdays and holidays, or unless you do all the gift buying for the both of you, you're going to hear a lot of "I love it . . . what is it?" from his family. Worst of all, they're going to assume that you did the shopping, and that's a real problem. A guy who gives bad gifts is just a guy. But a woman who gives bad gifts is a disaster. It helps to says things like "Yeah, honey, what is that?" Or "Jeez, where did you find that thing?" He might be a little insulted, but he's got to learn somehow that a bad gift is an insult all by itself.

Entertaining—His

You're married now, and things have changed. As a single man, your idea of entertaining may have involved waking up in your apartment on a Sunday morning—or rather, Sunday afternoon—and finding three guys passed out on the floor, pizza boxes everywhere, and your telephone receiver floating in the fish tank. As someone's husband, however, you're more likely to be winding down after a dinner for six couples at eleven o'clock on Saturday night, scrubbing the dishes and discussing china patterns with your wife's best friend.

Haven't experienced that yet? You will. And even scarier, you'll begin to prefer these quiet get-togethers with other couples to the raging, mind-blowing parties you used to throw.

That doesn't mean you have to stop *going* to those parties. That's what your single friends are for: to encourage the selfless and willing destruction of their own homes for the purpose of entertaining the free world. You and your wife will, no doubt, continue to go to these bashes for quite some time before the sheer weight of marriage conspires to keep you home on Saturday nights.

When it comes to hosting your own parties, however, the volume has definitely been turned down. You'll still have friends over to see the big game, or to maybe to play some cards, but postmarriage, all-night blowouts won't seem like much fun anymore. You have entered the era of your life when you host and attend dinner parties.

Although I do know quite a few men who are instinctive masters of the dinner party, many newly attached members of our gender have yet to encounter this marvelous activity. In a nutshell, here's your basic dinner party: Your wife spends two weeks planning a menu. She sends you to the supermarket with a list of things you've never heard of. The reason you can't find active dry baker's yeast, Kalamata olives, and individually wrapped caramel squares is because there's exactly one brand of each in existence, and they're all tucked away, as they have been for centuries, in the baking aisle behind the sacks of flour.

With assistance, you not only manage to locate these things but also to learn the difference between radicchio, arugula, endive, and iceberg lettuce and to buy everything else you need to create the magical dinner floating through your wife's mind. Or so you think. At the last minute, on dinner party day (or D-day), you will again be sent out for items you are ill equipped to buy, such as a single egg, color-coordinated paper napkins, and an "elegant but spring-like" flower arrangement.

Then throughout the party itself, your job is to act like Hugh Hefner. You're in charge of taking coats, serving drinks, and controlling the music. The women discuss work and clothes; the men discuss work and your stereo equipment; everybody says how wonderful dinner was; the guests go home; and then, because your wife planned the party and did all of the cooking, you clean up for the rest of the night.

Believe it or not, once you embrace this new method of entertainment, you

THE TRUTH ABOUT ENTERTAINING I

When she says:	She really means:
We're out of wine.	Stop what you're doing and go get some more.
I think the music's too loud.	Turn off that noisy crap and put on some Kenny G.
Would you like some coffee?	Last call, wino-boy.
Your friends from work are interesting.	Do you think they'll volunteer to replace our smoldering couch?
She has nice clothes, doesn't she?	Continue to stare at her cleavage, and I will clothesline you.

may even start to enjoy it. It's a great way to catch up with friends and network with business associates; you get a well-prepared home-cooked meal and the promise of more at other people's houses; and it's something to do on a Saturday night that you'll actually remember on Sunday morning.

Entertaining—Hers

The first few times you entertain as a married couple, it may feel as though you are playing house. You're surrounded by other couples who are chatting and sipping wine. You're serving dinner on the formal china you got for your wedding—the dishes you thought you'd use when you turned sixty or had the boss over for dinner, whichever came first. Suddenly, it's as though you've turned into your parents. The candles are lit; drinks have been served; there's elevator music playing on the stereo. And you're starting to feel as though it's past your bedtime.

Yes, when you're married, entertaining is a whole different kettle of fish. In fact, compared to single-girl entertaining, it's Dover sole sautéed in lemon butter. Which you have to make. Because "having people over" no longer means just having people over, it means a full-scale culinary production and weeks of angst.

The dinner party is a fixture of married life, and it evolves in a chain-letter fashion. You get invited to one lovely evening, then another, then another—until it becomes evident that the only way you're going to continue to receive these invitations is to throw a dinner party of your own. Your husband's response will likely be "But we just saw all these people!" Not much for getting the point, is he?

Your husband is good for one thing, though. Once he comes around to the idea of having a few friends over, he'll be a useful tool in pulling the event together. Since party planning does not number among his personal strengths, treat him as you would an indentured servant. Give instructions clearly, loudly, and repeatedly. If you're in desperate need of an onion, suddenly your husband is selectively deaf. Onion shopping may seem like an easy task, but he'll find complications you couldn't begin to imagine. Who knows what he'll come back with unless you make sure he knows the exact *kind* of onion you need? And don't take for granted he'll remember the word *red*. Write it on the back of his hand. He'll be so thrown by the produce section's array of white, yellow, and Spanish onions that he won't be able to remember the simplest oral instruction.

When he returns from the store, assign him bite-size tasks. Chopping said onion, for example. (He doesn't have to worry about his mascara running; you do.) Selecting music. Chilling wine. Washing pots and pans. Keeping the pets out of the way. When guests start to arrive, he should take coats, offer drinks, and introduce everyone.

There are several ways to make entertaining easier on you and your husband, and more fun for your guests. First, don't be overly ambitious with what you serve. It's much harder to make the aforementioned Dover sole for twelve taste good than it is to whip up a huge pot of chili that your guests can garnish to their own tastes. If your friends feel comfortable in your home and you feed them well, they'll have a much better time than if you served an elaborate gourmet meal that transformed you into a stressed-out harpy of a hostess.

Try to have a sense of humor when you throw a dinner party. If there's no particular occasion for your event, make one up. Celebrate the lesser holidays like Groundhog Day, Arbor Day, or National Sheep Shearing Week. Or develop a regular dinner party circle where, once every three weeks or so, a different couple hosts the meal and provides the main course, and the attendees bring wine and dessert or a salad.

Keep in mind that even the most casual event brings together potentially explosive elements: your friends and your husband's friends. We've attended affairs where the guest component echoed the right and left side of the church at a wedding ceremony. Again, making the event more casual seems to mix things up a bit. If your friends simply don't mesh with your husband's or vice versa, try having them over on separate nights or going out to dinner with them individually.

Once the party is over, don't let your husband forget the second half of

THE TRUTH ABOUT ENTERTAINING II

When he says:	He really means:
Well, *I'd* love another piece of lasagna!	Nobody likes the food, but I love you anyway.
Are you sure this is all you want from the store?	Because you will not get me up from this couch a second time.
These dishes aren't that dirty.	Please God, don't make me do them.
Oh good, the Robinsons are coming.	I hate them like black death.
You look wonderful, honey.	I'm not stupid—I want sex after the party tonight.

his duties: cleaning up. Just because you've finally relaxed, secure in the knowledge that everyone had a good time, it doesn't mean he can kick off his shoes and join you on the sofa. Well, maybe for a minute. Then it's off to the galley. And make sure he gets up the sauce spilled under the oven burners.

The Recreational Togetherness Quiz

Here's an easy and fun way to test how "together" you and your spouse are. Just list the recreational activities you enjoy—a partial list is provided below, but feel free to add or subtract as many as you like. Then give yourselves one point for every activity the two of you regularly do together and subtract one point for those you do separately.

Seeing movies	(Participating in any of the following sports—one point each:)
Renting movies	
Going to bars	Tennis
Going to friends' houses	Golf
Going to concerts	Bowling
Going to museums	Softball
Watching sports	Baseball
Singing	Football
Acting	In-line skating
Playing an instrument	Hockey
Writing	Basketball
Playing video games	Running
Playing cards	Boxing
Going out to restaurants	Skiing
Traveling	Swimming
Refinishing furniture	Snorkeling
House remodeling and repair	Scuba Diving
Collecting things	Water-skiing
Reading	Jet Skiing
Antiquing	Snowmobiling
Painting	Cycling
Shopping	Shooting
Sewing, crocheting, needlepoint	Darts

Going to the gym

Working out at home

Taking classes

Cooking

Dancing

Walking the dog

Rock climbing

Hang gliding

Playing pool

If your score is between +5 and −5, you've reached a reasonable balance. Like most couples, you've discovered that there are things you like to do together and things you prefer to do alone. As long as you agree on what those things are, you're not likely to have many problems in this area.

If your score is below −5, you may want to examine the items on your list. Is your spouse okay with the amount of time you spend apart? Are there some things on your list that you could do together? Maybe your spouse is afraid to play golf with you out of a fear that he or she will be terrible at it. Could you overcome this fear by taking lessons together? Doing only a few activities or sports with your spouse doesn't mean you're headed for divorce. It's simply something to think about the next time you make a plan that isn't for two.

If your score is above +5, you must be one heck of a team. It's great that you do so many things together as long as they're things that you both want to do. But if one of you is just following along with whatever the other dictates, maybe it's time you thought of hobbies that you can each do on your own. A successful marriage is more than two people with a lot in common; it's a couple made of distinct individuals who feel together even when they're apart.

Afterword:
Your First Anniversary—
His and Hers

And so you've arrived at the end of your first year together. If you've read this far, you've hopefully learned a great deal about your partner and gained tools essential to your future. Your ultimate goal for your first year, remember, is much more than mere survival—the word *survive* is simply our way of emphasizing how challenging it is to make a marriage thrive. We hope you have begun to build a strong foundation for your marriage and are growing stronger as a team than you ever could as individuals.

If every couple took the time before their first anniversary to lay the groundwork for a successful marriage, so many more would wake up on the morning of their fifty-first anniversary and reach for the hand of their true love, the one who has always been right there beside them. It's not just a romantic pipe dream. These aspirations can be realized. Your marriage can live happily forever if you work to make it stronger every day. We've suggested some ways to do that, but ensuring the success of your marriage isn't the responsibility of a book, or a therapist, or Oprah Winfrey, or your parents, or anybody else. Plain and simple, your marriage is in your hands. What you make of it is entirely up to you.

Your first anniversary is a day to celebrate, to look back, and to look ahead. It is far more important than its designation as "the paper anniversary" would suggest. In fact, while the required giving of paper gifts certainly makes economic sense, the symbolism of the tradition seems flawed. Even if the gifts you're exchanging on this first anniversary feel disposable, your marital bond should feel as durable and brilliant as a diamond. Do the legwork, build up the strength of your marriage in its first year, and you'll have the stamina and know-how to make every anniversary a gem.

As for gifts, if you have a strong imagination, you don't necessarily need a lot of money. Some of the most romantic and exciting anniversary gifts can be made of paper. A love letter or poem for example. A gift certificate for a night of wild passion. A special photograph of yourself or a professional photograph of the two of you to commemorate the occasion. An ad in the local newspaper professing your eternal love. Nice stationery for the purpose of writing to each other when you're traveling separately. Plane tickets back to your honeymoon destination.

Once you start thinking about it, you'll realize that many thoughtful things are made from paper. The point is to put some effort into it. Anybody can wander into a florist shop and point at the refrigerated case, but a gift that truly reflects how much you love and respect your spouse takes time and thought. Spend a moment rereading the "Gifts" chapter for more tips on making the right presentation on this special day.

Of course, giving gifts is only part of what makes your first anniversary memorable. Plan out exactly what you're going to do. Do we have any ideas to give you? Of course! Like a mother-in-law from hell, we're loaded with suggestions.

- Return to the place where you first kissed or made love and do it again. But do it right this time, without all that awkward uncertainty.

- Spend your anniversary at home, just the two of you. Make dinner; drink wine, indulge in a fattening dessert, play romantic music. Don't forget, you're also supposed to eat that chunk of your wedding cake you shoved in the back of the freezer twelve months ago.

- Take the day off from work, and have a picnic in the woods. Arrange it so you and the wildlife are the only ones around.

- Propose to each other again. Do the whole bit: Man gets down on his knees, takes woman's hand. If you do it in a public place, like a restaurant, you'll get a lot of applause and maybe even a free bottle of champagne.

- Buy something together to mark the occasion and your commitment, such as a crystal or candle, a pet, or a bottle of really good wine to be opened on your next anniversary.

- Do something a little crazy, such as jumping out of an airplane, swimming with dolphins, getting his & hers tattoos (just kidding).

- Do everything you can to let your partner know you love him or her—stare into your spouse's eyes, take a bath together, make out for hours—then say "I love you" at the stroke of midnight.

Whatever you do, be sure to spend your first anniversary happily together. We hope that this day, like so many more of your married days, is truly momentous and memorable.

Appendix

For couples seeking further guidance or counseling, the following workshops and programs come highly recommended:

Prevention and Relationship Enhancement Program (PREP®): a two-week version (one weekend day and two weekday evenings) and a two-day weekend version. Contact PREP, Inc., at (303) 759-9931.

Couple Communication: four two-hour classes that cost between $230 and $320. Contact Interpersonal Communications Programs at (303) 794-1764 or (800) 328-5099.

Relationship Enhancement: four four-hour Saturday afternoons, weekend courses, and full-day and half-day individual instruction. $285. Contact the National Institute for Relationship Enhancement at (800) 432-6454.

We Can Work It Out: Washington, D.C. area, a weekend ($1,100) or two hours a week for six weeks ($750). Contact the Center for Family Psychology at (202) 319-4474.

The Marriage Survival Kit: available from the Seattle Marital and Family Institute for $300. Call them at (206) 523-9042.

Practical Applications of Intimate Relationship Skills (PAIRS): a 120-hour course or an abbreviated weekend course; $2,000 per couple. Contact PAIRS at (888) 724-7748.

The First Year Anniversary Program: Contact Lynne Gold-Bikin at 516 DeKalb Street, Box 869, Norristown, PA 19404 or at (610) 272-5555.